For
Jon Stallworthy

CONTENTS

INTRODUCTION

'Do you know what would hold me together on a battlefield?', Wilfred Owen wrote to his mother in December 1914, before providing an unlikely answer: 'The sense that I was perpetuating the language in which Keats and the rest of them wrote!' Although few among Owen's contemporaries would have expressed their resolve quite like that, pride in their nation's literary achievements was a common ingredient in the patriotism of soldiers and civilians alike. Owen could think of no better reason to die for his country than that its language and poetry might live: 'I do not know in what else England is greatly superior, or dearer to me, than another land and people.'[1]

During the First World War, poetry became established as the barometer for the nation's values: the greater the civilization, the greater its poetic heritage. That choice was wisely made because, as Owen implied, poetry was the art in which Britain could confidently claim supremacy over its enemies. The composer–poet Ivor Gurney might freely confess his indebtedness to a German musical tradition, but he insisted—not *entirely* seriously—that Germany 'never had nor never would produce poets'.[2] That supposed flaw was considered by more unforgiving critics, such as the anthologist E. B. Osborn, to be a devastating exposure of ethical failings. Whereas British soldier poetry nobly demonstrated 'the complete absence of the note of hatred for a most hateful enemy', German poets betrayed their savagery, being moved 'more by hatred for other people's countries than by love of their own'.[3]

The close identification of war poetry with a British national character persists to the present day. Its origins can be found in the belief that the writing of verse was a patriotic act because it celebrated and (at least potentially) enhanced the nation's cultural ascendancy. This was, after all, the land of Shakespeare, the tercentenary of whose death in 1916 would become an occasion to find in his works

---

[1] Wilfred Owen to Susan Owen, 2 December 1914, *Collected Letters*, ed. Harold Owen and John Bell (London and Oxford: Oxford University Press, 1967), 300.

[2] Ivor Gurney, 'La Rime'. Unpublished for eighty years, Gurney's poem is collected in this anthology for the first time (pp. 125–6).

[3] E. B. Osborn, 'Introduction', *The Muse in Arms* (London: John Murray, 1917), p. xvii.

what has been described as 'a repository and guarantor of moral value'.[4] Poets were able to identify themselves as inheritors of a tradition expressing and embodying the very ideals that were threatened by foreign antagonists. Small wonder that the British government, understanding that poetry could be war by other means, set about marshalling their talents. Many of the most famous writers of the day, including Thomas Hardy, Henry Newbolt, and G. K. Chesterton, came together at Wellington House in London on 2 September 1914, as guests of the War Propaganda Bureau. There they were encouraged to dedicate their art to the war effort. Within a fortnight they appeared as signatories to a letter in *The Times* calling for the 'iron military bureaucracy of Prussia' to be resisted. Such ostentatious loyalty was well rewarded. Three establishment versifiers—Owen Seaman, Henry Newbolt, and William Watson—received knighthoods (in 1914, 1915, and 1917 respectively), the last after publishing a poetic eulogy in honour of the prime minister, David Lloyd George.

The grey eminences may not have noticed, but the War arrived at a time when English poetry was already being refashioned. A new generation of poets—the Georgians—had come to prominence in 1912, thanks to the first of a series of five highly popular anthologies edited by Winston Churchill's private secretary, Edward Marsh. Moderns but not Modernists, these young writers shared the desire to counteract florid late-Victorian rhetoric. They wanted intelligibility in art, they wrote with deceptive simplicity in celebration of the rural landscape, and their assumptions about poetic form tended to be traditional, even conservative. Their first anthology was a commercial triumph, selling 15,000 copies; its successor, published in 1915, shifted 19,000. (Contrast T. S. Eliot's *The Waste Land*, for which the UK print run of 443 copies took nearly eighteen months to sell out.) This was, in literary terms, a Georgian War. Rupert Brooke, Siegfried Sassoon, Robert Graves, and Isaac Rosenberg appeared in the Georgian anthologies, and Edward Thomas, Ivor Gurney, and Wilfred Owen were closely associated with the movement. Georgianism became the touchstone for poetic quality: Owen felt no greater literary honour than to be 'held peer by the Georgians',[5]

---

[4] John Lee, 'Shakespeare and the Great War', in Tim Kendall (ed.), *The Oxford Handbook of British and Irish War Poetry* (Oxford: Oxford University Press, 2007), 140.

[5] Wilfred Owen to Susan Owen, 31 December 1917, *Collected Letters*, 521.

while Gurney believed that 'The best way to learn to write is to read classics like Milton, Keats and Shakespeare, and the Georgian poets'.[6]

Despite (or because of) its popular appeal, Georgianism has not been treated kindly by subsequent generations of literary historians, who dismiss its style as ill equipped to face the trauma of mass technological warfare. In such accounts, the soldier–poets were *shell-shocked* Georgians, their aesthetic assumptions having rendered them particularly vulnerable to the front's unimagined brutalities; Modernists, meanwhile, were experimenters, responding with appropriate urgency to a broken world. This overlooks the Georgian origins of most surviving war poetry: the only Modernist soldier–poet of any note, David Jones, did not publish his masterpiece of the War, *In Parenthesis*, until nearly twenty years after the Armistice. It also overlooks the capacity for radicalism within Georgian poetry itself. Probably the first poet to describe trench life in its actualities was a civilian, Wilfrid Gibson, whose work would appear in all five of the Georgian anthologies. 'Breakfast', a short lyric written within two months of the War's outbreak, exemplifies the Georgian emphasis on tonal restraint and a deliberately narrow formal and linguistic range:

> We ate our breakfast lying on our backs,
> Because the shells were screeching overhead.
> I bet a rasher to a loaf of bread
> That Hull United would beat Halifax
> When Jimmy Stainthorp played full-back instead
> Of Billy Bradford. Ginger raised his head
> And cursed, and took the bet; and dropt back dead.
> We ate our breakfast lying on our backs,
> Because the shells were screeching overhead.

'Breakfast' could not be further from the loud rhetorical styles that dominated the early months of the War. The paucity of rhymes, the repetitions, the ordinariness of the diction—the poem derives its power from its understating of high drama. A soldier dies, but Gibson ends where he began as though nothing has changed. At its best, the spare style of Georgianism was perfectly suited to its new subject matter, which was why Gibson's example showed soldier–poets as otherwise diverse as Sassoon, Owen, and Gurney how to write about

[6] Ivor Gurney to Marion Scott, 9 September 1917, *Collected Letters*, ed. R. K. R. Thornton (Ashington and Manchester: Mid Northumberland Arts Group and Carcanet, 1991), 324.

battle. They would experiment linguistically (Sassoon was the first to
use the word 'syphilitic' in a poem), metrically (Rosenberg adopted
free verse for poetry 'as simple as ordinary talk'),[7] and even in their
rhymes (Owen's pararhymes, such as 'nervous' / 'knive us', deliber-
ately jarred the reader), but they did so from within a context of
Georgian beliefs and practices.

The Georgian poetry anthologies provided an influential model
for satisfying the needs of a reading public which, with so much verse
appearing at such speed, relied increasingly on editors to discern and
discriminate. The war years established the anthology as the age's
most representative literary medium. Dozens of anthologies appeared
before the Armistice. Some focused on poetry by civilians, others on
poetry by soldiers; some included foreign nationals from the Allied
powers; some concentrated on England at the expense of the rest of
Britain. Many continued to be filled with the kind of verse exempli-
fied by the poet laureate, Robert Bridges:

> Thou careless, awake!
> Thou peacemaker, fight!
> Stand, England, for honour,
> And God guard the Right![8]

Older poems on military subjects surged in popularity: Rudyard
Kipling's *Barrack-Room Ballads*, first published in the mid-1890s,
sold 29,000 copies in 1915 alone. But longevity was rare. In 1917,
E. B. Osborn boldly announced that wartime verse by civilians had
'nearly all been cast ere now into the waste-paper basket of oblivion'.[9]
His own soldier–poet anthologies have fared little better in the eyes of
posterity: Robert Graves later admitted that his fellow contributors
to Osborn's *The Muse in Arms* had been 'all very gallant and idealistic
but with hardly a poet among them'.[10] Gallantry and idealism among
soldier versifiers, and religious patriotism among their civilian coun-
terparts, were still commonly mistaken for poetic quality.

[7] Isaac Rosenberg to Edward Marsh, 4 August 1916, *Isaac Rosenberg*, ed. Vivien
Noakes (Oxford: Oxford University Press, 2008), 308.

[8] Robert Bridges, 'Wake up, England!', in Anon. (ed.), *Poems of the Great War
Published on Behalf of the Prince of Wales's National Relief Fund* (London: Chatto &
Windus, 1914), 7.

[9] Osborn (ed.), *The Muse in Arms*, p. xiv.

[10] Robert Graves, 'The Poets of World War II', *The Common Asphodel: Collected
Essays on Poetry, 1922–1949* (London: Hamish Hamilton, 1949), 308.

Apart from Rupert Brooke, whose early death occasioned an offi-
cially sanctioned martyrology, the best of the soldier–poets had no
significant wartime audience. Owen and Rosenberg went unread
until the 1920s; Graves and Edmund Blunden attracted only faint
praise; Sassoon, the most respected of them all, remained less known
for his poetry than for a courageous but ineffectual public protest in
1917 against the War's continuation. 'Did they look for a book of
wrought art's perfection, | Who promised no reading, nor praise, nor
publication?',[11] Gurney would angrily complain after the War. But
despite the noise generated by countless wartime versifiers, somehow
deep called to deep and was answered. Soldier–poets were linked by
complex networks, which ensured that they read, were influenced by,
and responded to one another's work. Sassoon, for example, had met
Brooke, read Gibson and Charles Sorley, dedicated a volume of
poetry to Thomas Hardy, and befriended Graves and Owen; Brooke
knew Edward Thomas, and was fond enough of Gibson to name
him as a legatee in his will; Patrick Shaw Stewart went to Eton with
Julian Grenfell, and led Brooke's burial party on Skyros, having been
part of the same battalion shipped to Gallipoli; Rosenberg, often
portrayed as an outsider, nevertheless corresponded with Laurence
Binyon as well as Edward Marsh. Many poets gravitated towards
Harold Monro's Poetry Bookshop in Bloomsbury, and several were
published by his imprint (as were the Georgian poetry anthologies).
New links were established by survivors after the War. Gurney set
poems by Thomas and Sassoon to music, and became acquainted
with Blunden, who in turn became a lifelong friend of Sassoon and
edited Owen and Gurney. New connections were still being forged as
late as 1964, when Sassoon and David Jones—those two veterans of
the Royal Welch Fusiliers—met for the first and only time, establish-
ing that, forty-eight years earlier in July 1916, Jones's company had
relieved Sassoon's near Mametz Wood.

The soldier–poets came from all backgrounds: Sassoon, Shaw
Stewart, and Grenfell were landed gentry, and therefore conformed
to what has since become the widespread (and inaccurate) percep-
tion that the officer classes were all educated at public schools
and Oxbridge. But officers such as Rickword and Owen were prod-
ucts of grammar schools, Private Gurney was the son of a tailor, and

[11] Ivor Gurney, 'War Books', *Collected Poems*, ed. P. J. Kavanagh (Manchester:
Carcanet, 2004), 258.

Private Rosenberg an East End Jew so desperately impoverished that his pacifist principles gave way to his need to earn money by enlisting. Their various circumstances point to one reason why the War produced so many fine writers: the conscripted army was far bigger, better educated, and more socially diverse than any that had preceded it. Unsurprisingly, attitudes to the War were just as various; Owen's desire to plead the sufferings of his men could hardly be shared by Rosenberg, who was the victim of anti-Semitic bullying within his battalion.

The well-worn argument that poets underwent a journey from idealism to bitterness as the War progressed is supported by Jones, who remembered a 'change' around the start of the Battle of the Somme (July 1916) as the War 'hardened into a more relentless, mechanical affair'.[12] Many poets experienced this fall, out of a world where gallantry and decency might still be possible and into an inferno of technological slaughter. Yet the complexity of individual cases reveals just as many exceptions. Elizabeth Vandiver has noted that the majority of soldiers, as well as civilians, 'continued to write in unironic terms about duty, glory, and honour throughout the war and afterwards'.[13] Neither Georgianism nor the Somme cured every soldier of grandiose sentiment. The poet Arthur Graeme West expressed his bewilderment at the mismatch between the sight and stench of the dead, 'hung in the rusting wire', and the ornate idiom with which even those 'young cheerful men' who had 'been to France' continued to describe their experiences.[14] Gilbert Frankau's 'The Other Side' made the point even more bluntly by attacking 'war-books, war-verse, all the eye-wash stuff | That seems to please the idiots at home'. 'Something's the matter,' Frankau's speaker tells one of these naïve versifiers: 'either you can't *see*, | Or else you see, and cannot write.'[15]

The soldier–poets who were capable of seeing *and* writing are

[12] David Jones, 'Preface', *In Parenthesis* (London: Faber, 1937), p. ix. (For extracts from *In Parenthesis* see pp. 200–6.)

[13] Elizabeth Vandiver, *Stand in the Trench, Achilles: Classical Receptions in British Poetry of the Great War* (Oxford: Oxford University Press, 2010), 3.

[14] Arthur Graeme West, 'God! How I Hate You, You Young Cheerful Men!', *The Diary of a Dead Officer: Being the Posthumous Papers of Arthur Graeme West*, ed. C. E. M. Joad (London: George Allen & Unwin, n.d. [1918]), 79–81. (See pp. 147–9.)

[15] Gilbert Frankau, 'The Other Side', *The Poetical Works of Gilbert Frankau*, ii: *1916–1920* (London: Chatto & Windus, 1923), 31–6.

often credited with having been 'anti-war', and their works are routinely recruited for propaganda by campaigners opposed to later conflicts. In accounts of the War and the art that it inspired, futility has defeated glory as the appropriate response, and Wilfred Owen has become the antidote to Rupert Brooke (who, it is often argued, would have come round to the right way of thinking if he had lived long enough). This risks damaging the achievements of the soldier–poets, because it neglects the extent to which their writings struggle with contradictory reactions to the War. Owen's description of himself as 'a conscientious objector with a very seared conscience' captures the internal divisions of the pacifist who fights, or the officer who (like Owen) acknowledges both the horrors of the War and the undeniable exhilaration and 'exultation' that battle occasionally inspires.[16] Even in his most anthologized poem, 'Dulce et Decorum Est', Owen does not subscribe to an anti-war manifesto. Like Frankau and West, he writes what can be more accurately labelled as anti-pro-war poetry, reminding civilians that the 'high zest' with which they convey their martial enthusiasms is based on ignorance of the terrible realities: 'dulce et decorum' it is certainly *not*, to die in a gas attack with blood 'gargling from the froth-corrupted lungs'. Most soldier–poets—like most soldiers—believed the War to be necessary, but wanted the costs acknowledged and the truths told.

How to tell truths to those in whose name they fought continued to be a vexed question. Having already disapproved of Sassoon's Declaration against the War, Graves advised Owen: 'For God's sake cheer up and write more optimistically—The war's not ended yet but a poet should have a spirit above wars.'[17] But on one issue, at least, the surviving veterans could agree: their experiences had set them apart from non-combatants. As Richard Aldington reported, 'there are two kinds of men, those who have been to the front and those who haven't'.[18] Whatever truths the soldier–poets brought back from the battle zone, they laid claim to a knowledge beyond the reach of civilians. A literate army drawn from all social classes was at last empowered to speak for itself with a fluency of which no previous

---

[16] Wilfred Owen to Colin Owen, 14 May 1917, *Collected Letters*, 458.

[17] Robert Graves to Wilfred Owen, *c.*22 December 1917, in Owen, *Collected Letters*, 596.

[18] Richard Aldington, *Life for Life's Sake: A Book of Reminiscences* (New York: Viking Press, 1941), 215.

army had been capable. Fortified with his new authority, the soldier–poet profoundly disrupted long debates about the nature and efficacy of poetry itself. Plato wanted to banish poets from his ideal republic because they were liars, lacking knowledge and deceiving with artful language. The figure of the soldier–poet reunited art and ethics, and undertook new obligations by speaking the truth to and about power. When Owen insisted, 'Above all, I am not concerned with Poetry', he artfully rebuked the artful language that Plato condemningly ascribed to poets. 'The true poet', Owen went on to explain, 'must be truthful',[19] not least because the official language of the state and its media had become untrustworthy.

Although Owen conceived the most politically radical account of the poet's role, one danger of his pre-eminence is that it has established exclusionary principles. Other soldier–poets have been measured (and inevitably found wanting) according to their ability to fulfil criteria that treat Owen as the exemplary case. Worse still, civilian poets of the War have been neglected and denigrated on account of an ideology that is overtly hostile to their contribution. Owen showed little patience even with admired precursors; compared with the extremities of combat, their emotions seemed like mere self-indulgence. Having read a biography of Tennyson, he failed to sympathize with that poet's unhappiness: 'But as for misery, was he ever frozen alive, with dead men for comforters?' Owen detected immaturities in the work as well as the man when he concluded that Tennyson 'was always a great child. So should I have been, but for Beaumont Hamel'.[20] (The village of Beaumont Hamel was virtually levelled during the Battle of the Somme.) The soldier–poet has been forced to grow up on the battlefield; the work of other poets amounts to child's play. If Tennyson could attract such resentment, what hope for Owen's civilian contemporaries, such as his cousin Leslie Gunston, whom he witheringly dismissed as rhyming 'with ease' but having 'no originality or power'?[21] Owen expressed this hard-won hauteur around the same time as Osborn's *The Muse in Arms* celebrated soldier–poetry at the expense of its

[19] Wilfred Owen, *The Complete Poems and Fragments*, ii: *The Manuscripts and Fragments*, ed. Jon Stallworthy (London: Chatto & Windus, Hogarth Press, and Oxford University Press, 1983), 535.

[20] Wilfred Owen to Susan Owen, 8 August 1917, *Collected Letters*, 482.

[21] Wilfred Owen to Susan Owen, 5 January 1918, ibid., 526.

civilian rival: 'The making of verse memorials', Osborn maintained, 'is perhaps the only task to which the non-combatant poet may address himself without fear of losing his sincerity, and with some hope of posterity's approval.'[22] Independently, Owen and Osborn made the case that civilians had no right to speak of war, because they knew nothing about it; all they were permitted to do was mourn.

These incipient signs of hostility towards civilian poetry in the latter years of the War seem especially conspicuous because they exist alongside a general animosity that Siegfried Sassoon directed towards civilians of many stripes (inter alia, Church of England bishops, the fathers of soldiers, women, politicians, journalists). In a representative poem like ' "Blighters" ', Sassoon could make a sadistic revenge fantasy sound unanswerably just:

> The House is crammed: tier beyond tier they grin
> And cackle at the Show, while prancing ranks
> Of harlots shrill the chorus, drunk with din;
> 'We're sure the Kaiser loves our dear old Tanks!'
>
> I'd like to see a Tank come down the stalls,
> Lurching to rag-time tunes, or 'Home, sweet Home',
> And there'd be no more jokes in Music-halls
> To mock the riddled corpses round Bapaume.

These brutal caricatures (the cackling crowd, the shrill and drunken harlots) command our assent; reader sides instinctively with poet, not wishing to risk becoming implicated along with that music-hall audience. The enemy is found not across no-man's-land but on the home front where 'tiers' have replaced tears. The 'corpses round Bapaume' are 'riddled' but also riddling, because the poem disguises their nationality: Bapaume was a site of mutual slaughter at the Battle of the Somme. Music-hall jokes, Sassoon claims, 'mock' all soldiers, who are united in opposition to this morally complacent civilian enemy.

These attacks on the civilian population by Sassoon and Owen exerted a disproportionate influence in the post-war years; similar prejudices among other soldier–poets were rare and fleeting. Yet after the Armistice a number of polemical anthologies appeared that marginalized civilian poetry by presenting it as homogenous and tainted with pro-war rhetoric. Poets like Gibson were overlooked, or

[22] Osborn (ed.), *The Muse in Arms*, p. xiv.

their biographies were conveniently distorted to suggest that they had, in fact, seen active service. The term 'war poetry' itself shifted meaning to reflect new preferences, and became increasingly synonymous with 'soldier poetry'. Bertram Lloyd's anthology *The Paths of Glory* (1919) developed the trend in its pioneering promotion of an explicit anti-war agenda: war was simply 'an execrable blot upon civilization'. Chief among the guilty, in Lloyd's account, were 'the silver-haired swashbucklers, journalists, and poetical armchair-warriors',[23] the implication being that civilians—poets explicitly listed among them—had been uninformed warmongers. Sassoon, the most generously represented poet in the anthology, seems to have dictated the terms of Lloyd's attack: his short lyric 'The Fathers' depicts two men rather like Lloyd's 'armchair-warriors' as they sit 'Snug at the club' and discuss their sons' good fortune in having the opportunity to fight.

Not all civilian poets spent the War writing stirring verse about God and England and the glorious justice of the cause. Rudyard Kipling was never one to shirk that particular challenge, and his reputation suffered for it after the War; but with a major poem like 'Epitaphs' he stood virtually alone in reminding readers that this was a *world* war, fought by sea and air as well as on land: Kipling gave equal honour to the Hindu sepoy, the VAD nurse, the RAF pilot, the drowned sailor, the civilian bombed in London, and the victim of conflict in Cairo or Halfa. Other poets, notwithstanding Lloyd's criticism, remained sharply aware of ethical dangers in pontificating from the safety of their armchairs. Gibson worried that he might be a kind of war profiteer, 'just making copy of the bloody business';[24] tactfully, he stopped writing about trench life in mid-1915, having influenced the generation of soldier–poets that was just starting to make itself heard. For Thomas Hardy, who privately opposed the War but felt obliged to perform a public role as an encourager of the nation's morale, profound anxieties over transforming other people's sufferings into his own artistic product shaped his poetry and, on occasion, became its subject. In 'I Looked Up from My Writing', the Moon addresses the poet directly, having paused in her search for the

---

[23] Bertram Lloyd, 'Preface', *The Paths of Glory: A Collection of Poems written during the War, 1914–1919* (London: George Allen & Unwin, 1919), 10, 8.

[24] Wilfrid Gibson to Edward Marsh, 4 December 1915, quoted by Dominic Hibberd, *Harold Monro and Wilfrid Gibson: The Pioneers* (London: Cecil Woolf, 2006), 19.

drowned body of a father driven to suicide by his son's death 'in brut-
ish battle':

> 'And now I am curious to look
>   Into the blinkered mind
> Of one who wants to write a book
>   In a world of such a kind.'
>
> Her temper overwrought me,
>   And I edged to shun her view,
> For I felt assured she thought me
>   One who should drown him too.

This encapsulates the civilian poet's dilemma. A 'blinkered mind' will
not be distracted from its work, and makes no effort to alleviate the
pain; it either exploits wars and suicides as its subject, or callously
and inhumanely ignores them. Self-incrimination merely creates the
opportunity for another poem.

This question of entitlement, occasionally broached during the
War, dominated its aftermath as returning veterans laid claim to a
privileged understanding of the conflict. Women's war poetry, twice
removed from the work of the male combatant, therefore became
doubly vulnerable to disparagement and neglect. Women had been
well represented in wartime anthologies; Claire Buck has estimated
that, while 'soldiers on active service wrote less than a fifth of the total
output',[25] women comprised a quarter of the published poets. Their
subsequent exclusion from the canon by a series of male editors and
commentators took no account of the fact that several of the more
prominent among them—May Wedderburn Cannan, Mary Borden,
May Sinclair, Vera Brittain—had served in France or Belgium in
different capacities. Borden's experiences as a nurse at the Somme,
sometimes under bombardment, proved that exposure to extremes of
suffering were not unique to the soldier: 'All day and often all night
I am at work over dying and mutilated men',[26] she wrote in 1916.

Yet the best-known of the women poets continues to be Jessie
Pope, whose notoriety relies not on the literary merits of her jingling

[25] Claire Buck, 'British Women's Writing of the Great War', in Vincent Sherry (ed.),
The Cambridge Companion to the Literature of the First World War (Cambridge: Cambridge
University Press, 2005), 87.
[26] Quoted by Jane Conway, *A Woman of Two Wars: The Life of Mary Borden* (London:
Munday Books, 2010), 52.

recruitment verse, but on the knowledge that Owen angrily dedicated an early draft of 'Dulce et Decorum Est' to her. Although he eventually dropped the dedication altogether, scholars encouraged by that initial judgement have taken the opportunity to present Pope as the epitome of civilians' ignorance. This disapproval often conceals a gender bias capable of accepting without question the frank misogyny of a poem like Sassoon's 'Glory of Women' (with its vicious pun: 'You make us shells'). Anthologies like *Up the Line to Death* (1964), which finds room for male civilians among its seventy-two poets but not a single woman, have led Judith Kazantzis to wonder whether there is a silent assumption at work, 'that war is man's concern . . . and that women quite simply cannot speak on the matter'.[27] The strongest women poets wrote powerfully throughout the War about life at home, guilt and loneliness and anxiety, and the private grief endured by wives, sisters, and mothers. Charlotte Mew's 'May, 1915' makes a drama of old poetic tropes, testing their ability to deal with the unprecedented destruction:

> Let us remember Spring will come again
> To the scorched, blackened woods, where all the wounded trees
> Wait, with their old wise patience for the heavenly rain,
> Sure of the sky: sure of the sea to send its healing breeze,
> Sure of the sun. And even as to these
> Surely the Spring, when God shall please
> Will come again like a divine surprise
> To those who sit to-day with their great Dead, hands in their
> hands, eyes in their eyes,
> At one with Love, at one with Grief: blind to the scattered
> things and changing skies.

This is no mere verse memorial of the sort approved by Osborn as suitable for civilian poets. Mew may evoke the processes of mourning by which winter leads inevitably to spring, and analogically, pain leads to 'healing', but in her switch from 'Sure' to 'Surely', she lapses from confidence into doubt. For those who 'sit to-day with their great Dead', Love and Grief have become synonymous: they are 'blind' to the blandishments of hope.

Mew's poem was remarkably prescient in its awareness that traditional assumptions about recovery and remembrance would no

longer suffice. These concerns became pervasive in later war poetry—
which, except in the most pedantic sense, did not stop with the
Armistice of November 1918. Poems like Mew's 'The Cenotaph' and
Sassoon's 'On Passing the New Menin Gate' addressed the inade-
quacies of commemoration and the many ways in which the living
continued to betray the dead. For other poets, such as Ivor Gurney,
whose asylum writings from 1922 to 1926 included some of the most
powerful lyric poetry about the War, the victims of betrayal were the
surviving soldiers who came back to a destitute existence 'on State-
doles'.[28] Edmund Blunden—another poet who wrote his best work
after 1918—admitted in the 1960s that he continued to be haunted
by the War, and his final poem described a return, half a century
later, to the site of the Battle of Ancre. David Jones, writing in 1937,
expressed the earnest wish that his 'War Book' (*In Parenthesis*) might
instead have been about 'a good kind of peace', but quoted from the
medieval travel writer Sir John Mandeville to convey the impossibil-
ity: 'Of Paradys ne can I not speken propurly I was not there.'[29] War
is what these poets knew, and it did not let them escape. In turn, they
have determined the ways in which the War has been remembered
and mythologized. Not since the Siege of Troy has a conflict been so
closely defined by the poetry that it inspired.

[28] Ivor Gurney, 'Strange Hells', *Collected Poems*, 141. (See p. 124.)
[29] Jones, 'Preface', *In Parenthesis*, p. xiii.

NOTE ON THE ANTHOLOGY

THIS anthology concerns itself with poetry related to the War by poets from Britain and Ireland who lived through part or all of it. The poems selected were written over a period of more than fifty years, between autumn 1914 and autumn 1966. Publication dates range more widely still: Rudyard Kipling's ' "For All We Have and Are" ' first appeared on 2 September 1914, whereas two of Ivor Gurney's poems are here published for the first time.

Donald Davie has defined an anthology poem as one that, 'whether by luck or design, and whatever its other virtues, cannot give offence'.[1] This would prove a fatal problem for many war poems, which would lose their force if they could not continue to disconcert, even offend and outrage, parts of their audience. Familiarity with the best-known poems, via anthologies and school curricula, risks sapping their power: because of its reception history, the consensus that a poem like 'Dulce et Decorum Est' inspires about the horrors of war can sometimes feel too comfortable. My introduction to each poet is intended as a means of returning to the immediate biographical and historical circumstances of the poems' composition, just as my explanatory notes track the complex literary traditions and debates with which the poems often engage. Information can help to make the familiar strange once more, and unsettle received opinion.

I have interpreted my editorial role as being to arrange the best poems in the best order. No matter how many pages their publishers allow them, anthologists will always fret over writers who have been excluded. With more space, I would have added work by Herbert Read, Vera Brittain, W. N. Hodgson, F. W. Harvey, Gilbert Frankau, and Francis Ledwidge, leaving a new group of near misses to make their silent complaint. However, brutal economics dictate that space awarded to any one of these figures would have entailed a corresponding reduction elsewhere. For an anthology that roams more widely but explores less deeply, I recommend Vivien Noakes's *Voices of Silence: The Alternative Book of First World War Poetry* (2006). Noakes is frank in her acknowledgement that she focuses on 'the

---

[1] Donald Davie, *Thomas Hardy and British Poetry* (London: Routledge and Kegan Paul, 1973), 38.

work of less gifted writers', but she performs a valuable service in bringing to attention a body of verse that, 'precisely because it does not have to answer to high literary demands[,] is often a more immediate, less poetically self-conscious, response to war'.[2]

I have preferred to seem unkind to minor writers, believing that by generously representing the War's most important poets I could best illustrate the extent and variety of their achievements and the ways in which individual voices developed over time. I have followed the simple rule of giving the largest allowance of space to those poets who seem to me the most important: Wilfred Owen, Ivor Gurney, and Siegfried Sassoon among the soldier–poets, Rudyard Kipling and Thomas Hardy among the civilians. I have also included a modest selection of music-hall and trench songs, the best of which are more verbally ingenious than all but the strongest war poetry. For reasons of convenience, any anthologist's favoured form is the lyric, but I have found room for longer poems (Gibson's 'Between the Lines', Borden's 'Unidentified', Gurney's 'The Retreat') where I judge that they successfully extend the possibilities of the War's poetry. I have not used excerpts except in a single unavoidable case. David Jones's book-length hybrid, *In Parenthesis*, does not lend itself to anthologizing, but I have decided that exclusion is still less appropriate than unsatisfactory inclusion. I share T. S. Eliot's opinion that *In Parenthesis* is 'a work of genius', so I hope that the selections published here will encourage readers to read it in its astonishing entirety.

Selecting the copy text for each poet's work, I have sought reliability above all else; I have followed the copy text in every respect (including the formulation of titles and, of course, the texts of the poems), unless otherwise indicated in an explanatory note. Often there are complex challenges in editing texts by soldier–poets who did not live to see their work published. It comes as no surprise, then, that war poetry should have attracted some of the most brilliant and innovative textual scholars of our time. Not all the poets in this anthology have been so well served, but I am grateful to be able to draw on the editorial work of Jon Stallworthy, Vivien Noakes, and Edna Longley for definitive texts by Wilfred Owen, Isaac Rosenberg, and Edward Thomas respectively.

[2] Vivien Noakes (ed.), *Voices of Silence: The Alternative Book of First World War Poetry* (Stroud: Sutton Publishing, 2006), p. xi.

In making my decision about how to arrange the poets' work, I have chosen a chronological structure by author's date of birth. War poetry anthologies arranged by theme have not always resisted the temptation to disguise or muddle composition dates in order to fit works into a convenient narrative. The editorial trajectory of Ian Parsons's *Men Who March Away*, for example, is semaphored by section titles, according to which 'Visions of Glory' are soon corrected by 'The Bitter Truth', 'No More Jokes', 'The Pity of War', 'The Wounded', 'The Dead', and 'Aftermath'. Yet in order to force this argument, Parsons's book opens with Edward Thomas's 'The Trumpet', written in 1916, and ends with Hardy's 'In Time of "The Breaking of Nations"' from 1915.

Parsons partially pre-empted criticism by arguing that '[T]o ascertain the precise date of composition of more than a hundred poems, many of which were written in the trenches and not published until long afterwards, was clearly impossible.' Thanks to detailed scholarship undertaken since the 1960s, modern editors have no such excuses. Dominic Hibberd and John Onions, in their fine anthology *The Winter of the World* (2007), arrange their selection purely by date of composition: the drawback of breaking up and scattering each poet's work is weighed against the considerable advantage of allowing poems written in the same period of the War to be read alongside each other. Wanting to keep each poet's work together, I have provided detailed notes that give the composition dates and publication history. (A degree sign (°) at the end of a line of verse indicates that a note will be found at the back of the book.) Poets themselves often added dates in titles or as footnotes, ostentatiously inserting their works into particular moments in history. If they broached universal truths, they did so by drawing attention to specific times and places. Practice varied widely: there are fewer place names in the complete war poetry of Sassoon and Owen than in two lines by Ivor Gurney.

Reviewing Ian Parsons's *Men Who March Away* in 1965, Ted Hughes noted that 'The First World War goes on getting stronger—our number one national ghost.'[3] Since Hughes wrote those words, the War has passed out of living memory. Yet its haunting of our language and culture—our deepest sense of ourselves as a nation—shows no sign of being exorcised.

[3] Ted Hughes, 'National Ghost', *Winter Pollen: Occasional Prose*, ed. William Scammell (London: Faber, 1994), 70.

SELECT BIBLIOGRAPHY

LAURENCE BINYON

The Winnowing Fan: Poems on the Great War (London: Elkin Mathews, 1914).

Laurence Binyon, *Collected Poems*, 2 vols. (London: Macmillan, 1931).
John Hatcher, *Laurence Binyon: Poet, Scholar of East and West* (Oxford: Clarendon Press, 1995).

EDMUND BLUNDEN

The Poems of Edmund Blunden, 1914–30 (London: Cobden-Sanderson, 1930).
An Elegy and Other Poems (London: Cobden-Sanderson, 1937).
The Deceitful Calm: A New Selection of Poems by Edmund Blunden, ed. Rennie Parker and Margi Blunden (Holt: Laurel Books, 2006).

Edmund Blunden, *Undertones of War* (London: Cobden-Sanderson, 1928); repr. (London: Penguin Classics, 2000).
Barry Webb, *Edmund Blunden: A Biography* (New Haven: Yale University Press, 1990).

MARY BORDEN

'At the Somme', in *English Review* (August 1917).
'Unidentified', in *English Review* (December 1917).

Mary Borden, *The Forbidden Zone* (London: Heinemann, 1929); repr. with introduction by Hazel Hutchison (London: Hesperus, 2008).
Jane Conway, *A Woman of Two Wars: The Life of Mary Borden* (London: Munday Books, 2010).

RUPERT BROOKE

1914 and Other Poems (London: Sidgwick & Jackson, 1915).
The Collected Poems of Rupert Brooke (New York: Dodd, Mead & Co., 1931).

Rupert Brooke, *The Letters of Rupert Brooke*, ed. Geoffrey Keynes (London: Faber, 1968).
Nigel Jones, *Rupert Brooke: Life, Death & Myth* (London: Richard Cohen, 1999).

MAY WEDDERBURN CANNAN

In War Time: Poems (Oxford: B. H. Blackwell, 1917).

The Splendid Days: Poems (Oxford: B. H. Blackwell, 1919).
'Perfect Epilogue', in *The Tears of War: The Love Story of a Young Poet and a War Hero*, ed. Charlotte Fyfe (Upavon: Cavalier Books, 2000).

May Wedderburn Cannan, *Grey Ghosts and Voices* (Kineton: Roundwood Press, 1976).
Jane Potter, 'Cannan, May Wedderburn (1893–1973)', in *Oxford Dictionary of National Biography* (Oxford: Oxford University Press, Oct. 2008; online edn., May 2012 <http://www.oxforddnb.com/view/article/98106>).

MARGARET POSTGATE COLE

Margaret Postgate's Poems (London: George Allen & Unwin, 1918).

Margaret Cole, *Growing up into Revolution* (London: Longmans, Green, 1949).
Marc Stears, 'Cole, Dame Margaret Isabel (1893–1980)', in *Oxford Dictionary of National Biography* (Oxford: Oxford University Press, 2004 <http://www.oxforddnb.com/view/article/30953>).
Betty D. Vernon, *Margaret Cole, 1893–1980* (London: Croom Helm, 1986).

WILFRID GIBSON

Battle (London: Elkin Mathews, 1915).
Livelihood: Dramatic Reveries (London: Macmillan, 1917).
Whin (London: Macmillan, 1918).
Neighbours (London: Macmillan, 1920).

Dominic Hibberd, *Harold Monro and Wilfrid Gibson: The Pioneers* (London: Cecil Woolf, 2006).
Sean Street, *The Dymock Poets* (Bridgend: Seren, 1994).

ROBERT GRAVES

Complete Poems, ed. Beryl Graves and Dunstan Ward, 3 vols. (Manchester: Carcanet, 1995, 1997, 1999).

Richard Perceval Graves, *Robert Graves: The Assault Heroic, 1895–1926* (London: George Weidenfeld and Nicolson, 1986).
Robert Graves, *Good-bye to All That: An Autobiography* (London: Jonathan Cape, 1929); rev. edn. as *Goodbye to All That* (London: Cassell, 1957).
——*In Broken Images: Selected Letters of Robert Graves, 1914–1946*, ed. Paul O'Prey (London: Hutchinson, 1982).

JULIAN GRENFELL

'Prayer for Those on the Staff', Grenfell Family Papers, 1860–1947, Hertfordshire Archives and Local Studies, DE/X789.

'Into Battle', in Elizabeth Vandiver, *Stand in the Trench, Achilles: Classical Receptions in British Poetry of the Great War* (Oxford: Oxford University Press, 2010).

Nicholas Mosley, *Julian Grenfell: His Life and the Times of His Death, 1888–1915*, rev. edn. (London: Persephone Books, 1999).

E. B. Osborn, *The New Elizabethans: A First Selection of the Lives of Young Men who have Fallen in the Great War* (London: John Lane, 1919).

IVOR GURNEY

Severn & Somme (London: Sidgwick & Jackson, 1917).

War's Embers (London: Sidgwick & Jackson, 1919).

Collected Letters, ed. R. K. R. Thornton (Ashington and Manchester: Mid Northumberland Arts Group and Carcanet, 1991).

Manuscripts and typescripts in the Gurney Papers, Gloucestershire Archives.

Pamela Blevins, *Ivor Gurney and Marion Scott: Song of Pain and Beauty* (Woodbridge: Boydell, 2008).

Ivor Gurney, *Collected Poems*, ed. P. J. Kavanagh, rev. edn. (Manchester: Carcanet, 2004).

Michael Hurd, *The Ordeal of Ivor Gurney* (Oxford: Oxford University Press, 1978).

THOMAS HARDY

The Complete Poems, ed. James Gibson (London: Macmillan, 1976).

Florence Hardy, *The Later Years of Thomas Hardy, 1892–1928* (London: Macmillan, 1930).

Thomas Hardy, *Collected Letters*, v: *1914–1919*, ed. Richard Little Purdy and Michael Millgate (Oxford: Oxford University Press, 1985).

——*Selected Poetry*, ed. Tim Armstrong (London: Longman, 1993).

Ralph Pite, *Thomas Hardy: The Guarded Life* (London: Picador, 2006).

Claire Tomalin, *Thomas Hardy: The Time-Torn Man* (London: Viking, 2006).

A. E. HOUSMAN

The Poems of A. E. Housman, ed. Archie Burnett (Oxford: Oxford University Press, 1997).

Richard Perceval Graves, *A. E. Housman: The Scholar Poet* (London: Faber, 2009).

A. E. Housman, *Collected Poems and Selected Prose*, ed. Christopher Ricks (London: Penguin, 1988).

——*The Letters of A. E. Housman*, ed. Archie Burnett (Oxford: Clarendon Press, 2007).

DAVID JONES

In Parenthesis (London: Faber, 1937); rev. edn. (London: Faber, 1963).

David Jones, *The Dying Gaul and Other Writings*, ed. Herman Grisewood (London: Faber, 1978).
——*Dai Greatcoat: A Self-Portrait of David Jones in His Letters*, ed. René Hague (London: Faber, 1980).
Jonathan Miles and Derek Shiel, *David Jones: The Maker Unmade* (Bridgend: Seren, 1995).

RUDYARD KIPLING

Sea Warfare (London: Macmillan, 1916).
A Diversity of Creatures (London: Macmillan, 1917).
The Years Between (London: Methuen, 1919).
Debits and Credits (London: Macmillan, 1926).
The Cambridge Edition of the Poems of Rudyard Kipling, ed. Thomas Pinney, 3 vols. (Cambridge: Cambridge University Press, 2013).

Charles Carrington, *Rudyard Kipling: His Life and Work* (London: Macmillan, 1955).
Rudyard Kipling, *The Letters of Rudyard Kipling*, iv: *1911–19*, ed. Thomas Pinney (Basingstoke: Palgrave, 2004).
——*Something of Myself* (London: Macmillan, 1937).
Andrew Lycett, *Rudyard Kipling* (London: Weidenfeld & Nicolson, 1999).

CHARLOTTE MEW

'The Cenotaph', in *Westminster Gazette* (7 September 1919).
The Rambling Sailor (London: Poetry Bookshop, 1929).

Penelope Fitzgerald, *Charlotte Mew and Her Friends* (London: William Collins Sons & Co., 1984).
Charlotte Mew, *Collected Poems & Prose*, ed. Val Warner (London: Virago, 1982).

MUSIC-HALL AND TRENCH SONGS

Max Arthur (ed.), *When this Bloody War Is Over: Soldiers' Songs of the First World War* (London: Judy Piatkus, 2001).
George Asaf and Felix Powell, *Pack up your troubles in your old kit-bag* (London: Francis, Day & Hunter, 1915).
John Brophy and Eric Partridge (eds.), *The Long Trail: What the British Soldier Sang and Said in the Great War of 1914–1918*, rev. edn. (London: André Deutsch, 1965).
J. P. Long and Maurice Scott, *Oh! It's a Lovely War* (London: Star Music, 1917).

F. T. Nettleingham (ed.), *Tommy's Tunes: A Comprehensive Collection of Soldiers' Songs, Marching Melodies, Rude Rhymes, and Popular Parodies* (London: Erskine Macdonald, 1917).

——*More Tommy's Tunes: An Additional Collection of Soldiers' Songs, Marching Melodies, Rude Rhymes and Popular Parodies, Composed, Collected, and Arranged on Active Service with the B.E.F.* (London: Erskine Macdonald, 1918).

Roy Palmer (ed.), *'What a Lovely War!' British Soldiers' Songs from the Boer War to the Present Day* (London: Michael Joseph, 1990).

John Press (ed.), *Trench Songs of the First World War* (London: Cecil Woolf, 2008).

R. P. Weston and Bert Lee, *Good-bye-ee!* (London: Francis, Day & Hunter, 1917).

WILFRED OWEN

The Complete Poems and Fragments, ed. Jon Stallworthy, 2 vols. (London: Chatto & Windus, Hogarth Press, and Oxford University Press, 1983).

Dominic Hibberd, *Wilfred Owen: A New Biography* (London: Weidenfeld & Nicolson, 2002).

Harold Owen, *Journey from Obscurity: Wilfred Owen, 1893–1918*, 3 vols. (Oxford: Oxford University Press, 1963, 1964, 1965).

Wilfred Owen, *Collected Letters*, ed. Harold Owen and John Bell (London and Oxford: Oxford University Press, 1967).

——*The Poems of Wilfred Owen*, ed. Jon Stallworthy (London: Chatto & Windus, 1990).

Jon Stallworthy, *Wilfred Owen* (London: Chatto & Windus, 1974).

EDGELL RICKWORD

Collected Poems, ed. Charles Hobday (Manchester: Carcanet, 1991).

Michael Copp, *Edgell Rickword: No Illusions* (London: Cecil Woolf, 2008).

Charles Hobday, *Edgell Rickword: A Poet at War* (Manchester: Carcanet, 1989).

ISAAC ROSENBERG

The Poems and Plays of Isaac Rosenberg, ed. Vivien Noakes (Oxford: Oxford University Press, 2004).

Jean Liddiard, *Isaac Rosenberg: The Half-Used Life* (London: Victor Gollancz, 1975).

Isaac Rosenberg, *The Collected Works of Isaac Rosenberg: Poetry, Prose, Letters, Paintings, and Drawings*, ed. Ian Parsons (London: Chatto & Windus and Hogarth Press, 1984).

——*Poetry Out of My Head and Heart: Unpublished Letters & Poem Versions*, ed. Jean Liddiard (London: Enitharmon, 2008).

——*Isaac Rosenberg*, ed. Vivien Noakes (Oxford: Oxford University Press, 2008).

Jean Moorcroft Wilson, *Isaac Rosenberg: Poet and Painter* (London: Cecil Woolf, 1975).

SIEGFRIED SASSOON

Collected Poems, 1908–1956 (London: Faber, 1961).

The War Poems, ed. Rupert Hart-Davis (London: Faber, 1983).

Max Egremont, *Siegfried Sassoon: A Biography* (London: Picador, 2005).

Siegfried Sassoon, *Memoirs of an Infantry Officer* (London: Faber, 1930).

——*Sherston's Progress* (London: Faber, 1936).

——*Diaries, 1915–1918*, ed. Rupert Hart-Davis (London: Faber, 1983).

ROBERT SERVICE

Rhymes of a Red Cross Man (New York: Barse & Hopkins, 1916).

James Mackay, *Robert Service: Vagabond of Verse. A Biography* (Edinburgh: Mainstream Publishing, 1995).

Enid Mallory, *Robert Service: Under the Spell of the Yukon* (Surrey, British Columbia: Heritage House, 2006).

Robert Service, 'Records of a Red Cross Man', in *Toronto Daily Star* and *Ottawa Journal* (11 December 1915–29 January 1916).

——*The Complete Poems of Robert Service* (New York: Dodd, Mead & Co., 1940).

——*Harper of Heaven: A Record of Radiant Living* (New York: Dodd, Mead & Co., 1948).

MAY SINCLAIR

'Field Ambulance in Retreat', in Hall Caine (ed.), *King Albert's Book: A Tribute to the Belgian King and People from Representative Men and Women throughout the World* (London: The Daily Telegraph in conjunction with The Daily Sketch, The Glasgow Herald, and Hodder & Stoughton, 1914).

'After the Retreat', in *The Egoist* 5.2 (1 May 1915).

A Journal of Impressions in Belgium (London: Macmillan, 1915).

Suzanne Raitt, *May Sinclair: A Modern Victorian* (Oxford: Oxford University Press, 2000).

CHARLES SORLEY

Marlborough and Other Poems (Cambridge: Cambridge University Press, 1916).

Charles Sorley, *The Letters of Charles Sorley, with a Chapter of Biography*, ed. W. R. Sorley (Cambridge: Cambridge University Press, 1919).

Jean Moorcroft Wilson, *Charles Hamilton Sorley: A Biography* (London: Cecil Woolf, 1985).

John Press, *Charles Hamilton Sorley* (London: Cecil Woolf, 2006).

PATRICK SHAW STEWART

'[I saw a man this morning]', in Patrick Shaw Stewart's copy of A. E. Housman's *A Shropshire Lad*. Eton College Library, lcc5.2.33.

Miles Jebb, *Patrick Shaw Stewart: An Edwardian Meteor* (Wimborne Minster: Dovecote Press, 2010).

EDWARD THOMAS

The Annotated Collected Poems, ed. Edna Longley (Tarset: Bloodaxe, 2008).

Matthew Hollis, *Now All Roads Lead to France: The Last Years of Edward Thomas* (London: Faber, 2011).

Matthew Spencer (ed.), *Elected Friends: Robert Frost and Edward Thomas to One Another* (New York: Handsel, 2003).

Edward Thomas, *Selected Letters*, ed. R. George Thomas (Oxford: Oxford University Press, 1995).

——*Collected Poems*, ed. R. George Thomas (London: Faber, 2004).

ARTHUR GRAEME WEST

The Diary of a Dead Officer: Being the Posthumous Papers of Arthur Graeme West (London: George Allen & Unwin, n.d. [1919]).

Dominic Hibberd, 'West, (Arthur) Graeme (1891–1917)', in *Oxford Dictionary of National Biography* (Oxford: Oxford University Press, Oct. 2008; online edn., Jan. 2011 <http://www.oxforddnb.com/view/article/98098>).

T. P. CAMERON WILSON

Waste Paper Philosophy, to which has been added Magpies in Picardy and Other Poems (New York: George H. Doran Company, 1920).

Laurence Housman (ed.), *War Letters of Fallen Englishmen* (London: Victor Gollancz, 1930).

Merryn Williams, *T. P. Cameron Wilson* (London: Cecil Woolf, 2006).

W. B. YEATS

The Wild Swans at Coole (London: Macmillan, 1919).

R. F. Foster, *W. B. Yeats: A Life*, 2 vols. (Oxford: Oxford University Press, 1997, 2003).

W. B. Yeats (ed.), *The Oxford Book of Modern Verse, 1892–1935* (Oxford: Oxford University Press, 1936).

—— *The Letters of W. B. Yeats*, ed. Allan Wade (London: Rupert Hart-Davis, 1954).

—— *The Variorum Edition of the Poems of W. B. Yeats*, ed. Peter Allt and Russell K. Alspach (London: Macmillan, 1956).

ANTHOLOGIES OF FIRST WORLD WAR POETRY

Anon. (ed.), *Poems of the Great War Published on Behalf of the Prince of Wales's National Relief Fund* (London: Chatto & Windus, 1914).

Brereton, Frederick (ed.), *An Anthology of War Poems* (London: Collins Sons & Co., 1930).

Clarke, George Herbert (ed.), *A Treasury of War Poetry: British and American Poems of the World War, 1914–1919* (London: Hodder & Stoughton, 1919).

Cross, Tim (ed.), *The Lost Voices of World War I* (London: Bloomsbury, 1988).

Gardner, Brian (ed.), *Up the Line to Death: the War Poets, 1914–1918* (London: Methuen, 1964).

Hibberd, Dominic, and John Onions (eds.), *The Winter of the World: Poems of the Great War* (London: Constable, 2007).

Kyle, Galloway (ed.), *Soldier Poets: Songs of the Fighting Men* (London: Erskine Macdonald, 1916).

—— *More Songs by the Fighting Men* (London: Erskine Macdonald, 1917).

Lloyd, Bertram (ed.), *The Paths of Glory: A Collection of Poems written during the War, 1914–1919* (London: George Allen & Unwin, 1919).

Motion, Andrew (ed.), *First World War Poems* (London: Faber, 2003).

Nichols, Robert (ed.), *Anthology of War Poetry, 1914–1918* (London: Nicholson & Watson, 1943).

Noakes, Vivien (ed.), *Voices of Silence: The Alternative Book of First World War Poetry* (Stroud: Sutton, 2006).

Osborn, E. B. (ed.), *The Muse in Arms: A Collection of War Poems, for the Most Part Written in the Field of Action, by Seamen, Soldiers, and Flying Men who are Serving, or have Served, in the Great War* (London: John Murray, 1917).

Parsons, I. M. (ed.), *Men Who March Away: Poems of the First World War* (London: Chatto & Windus, 1965).

Reilly, Catherine (ed.), *Scars Upon My Heart: Women's Poetry & Verse of the First World War* (London: Virago, 1981).

Roberts, David (ed.), *Minds at War: Poetry and Experience of the First World War* (Burgess Hill: Saxon Books, 1996).

Silkin, Jon (ed.), *The Penguin Book of First World War Poetry* (London: Penguin, 1979).

Stallworthy, Jon, and Jane Potter (eds.), *Three Poets of the First World War: Ivor Gurney, Isaac Rosenberg, Wilfred Owen* (London: Penguin, 2011).

Taylor, Martin (ed.), *Lads: Love Poetry of the Trenches* (London: Constable, 1989).

Trotter, Jacqueline T. (ed.), *Valour and Vision: Poems of the War, 1914–1918* (London: Longmans & Co., 1920).

Walter, George (ed.), *In Flanders Fields: Poetry of the First World War* (London: Penguin, 2004).

CRITICAL STUDIES

Bergonzi, Bernard, *Heroes' Twilight: A Study of the Literature of the Great War* (London: Macmillan, 1965).

Brearton, Fran, *The Great War in Irish Poetry: W. B. Yeats to Michael Longley* (Oxford: Oxford University Press, 2003).

Campbell, James, 'Combat Gnosticism: The Ideology of First World War Poetry Criticism', in *New Literary History* 30.1 (1999), 203–15.

Das, Santanu, *Touch and Intimacy in First World War Literature* (Cambridge: Cambridge University Press, 2005).

Fussell, Paul, *The Great War and Modern Memory* (Oxford: Oxford University Press, 1975).

Graham, Desmond, *The Truth of War: Owen, Rosenberg and Blunden* (Manchester: Carcanet, 1984).

Hibberd, Dominic, *Poetry of the First World War: A Casebook* (London: Macmillan, 1981).

Hynes, Samuel, *The War Imagined: The First World War and English Culture* (London: Bodley Head, 1990).

Johnston, John H., *English Poetry of the First World War: A Study in the Evolution of Lyric and Narrative Form* (Princeton, NJ: Princeton University Press, 1964).

Kendall, Tim, *Modern English War Poetry* (Oxford: Oxford University Press, 2006).

——(ed.), *The Oxford Handbook of British and Irish War Poetry* (Oxford: Oxford University Press, 2007).

Khan, Nosheen, *Women's Poetry of the First World War* (Harlow: Harvester Wheatsheaf, 1988).

Lyon, Philippa, *Twentieth-Century War Poetry: A Reader's Guide to Essential Criticism* (Basingstoke: Palgrave, 2005).

Murray, Nicholas, *The Red Sweet Wine of Youth: British Poets of the First World War* (London: Little, Brown, 2010).

Reilly, Catherine W., *English Poetry of the First World War: A Bibliography* (London: G. Prior, 1978).

Ricketts, Harry, *Strange Meetings: The Poets of the Great War* (London: Chatto & Windus, 2010).

Sherry, Vincent (ed.), *The Cambridge Companion to the Literature of the First World War* (Cambridge: Cambridge University Press, 2005).

Silkin, Jon, *Out of Battle: The Poetry of the Great War* (Oxford: Oxford University Press, 1972).

Stallworthy, Jon, *Anthem for Doomed Youth: Twelve Soldier Poets of the First World War* (London: Constable, 2002).

——*Survivors' Songs: From Maldon to the Somme* (Cambridge: Cambridge University Press, 2008).

Todman, Dan, *The Great War: Myth and Memory* (London: Hambledon, 2005).

Vandiver, Elizabeth, *Stand in the Trench, Achilles: Classical Receptions in British Poetry of the Great War* (Oxford: Oxford University Press, 2010).

Winter, Jay, *Sites of Memory, Sites of Mourning: The Great War in European Cultural History* (Cambridge: Cambridge University Press, 1995).

WEBSITES

The First World War Poetry Digital Archive: <http://www.oucs.ox.ac.uk/ww1lit/>.

Great War Fiction (George Simmers): <http://greatwarfiction.wordpress.com/>.

War Poetry (Tim Kendall): <http://war-poets.blogspot.com/>.

The War Poetry Website (David Roberts): <http://www.warpoetry.co.uk/>.

LITERARY SOCIETIES

The Rupert Brooke Society: <http://www.rupertbrooke.com/>.

Friends of the Dymock Poets: <http://www.dymockpoets.co.uk/>.

Robert Graves Society: <http://www.robertgraves.org/>.

The Ivor Gurney Society: <http://www.ivorgurney.org.uk/>.

The Thomas Hardy Society: <http://www.hardysociety.org/>.

The Kipling Society: <http://www.kipling.org.uk/>.

The Wilfred Owen Association: <http://www.wilfredowen.org.uk/>.

The Siegfried Sassoon Fellowship: <http://www.sassoonfellowship.org/>.

The Edward Thomas Fellowship: <http://www.edward-thomas-fellowship.org.uk/>.

War Poets Association: <http://www.warpoets.org/>.

A CHRONOLOGY OF THE WAR YEARS

Year *Historical Event*   *The Poets*

1914 (28 June) Archduke Franz Ferdinand
      assassinated in Sarajevo.
      (28 July) Austria–Hungary declares war
      on Serbia.
      (3 August) Germany declares war on
      France and Belgium.
      (4 August) Germany invades Belgium.
      Britain (and the British Empire)
      declares war on Germany.
      (9 August) Embarcation of the British
      Expeditionary Force to France under
      way.
      (12 August) Britain declares war on
      Austria–Hungary.
      (23 August) Battle of Mons, and the
      beginning of the Great Retreat.
      (5–12 September) First Battle of the   (2 September) Prominent
      Marne halts the German advance.   writers meet at Wellington
                                                 House, London; encouraged by
                                                 the War Propaganda Bureau to
                                                 support the war effort.

      (19 October–22 November) First Battle
      of Ypres, and the establishment of
      entrenched positions.

                                                 (December) Laurence Binyon,
                                                 The Winnowing Fan.

1915 (19–20 January) First Zeppelin raids on
      Britain.
      (4 February) Germany announces a
      blockade of British ports after U-boat
      attacks on shipping.
      (19 February) Naval attack by British
      and French forces on the Darda-
      nelles.
      (22 April) First day of the Second Battle
      of Ypres sees the first use of poison gas
      by Germany against French and
      Algerian soldiers.

                                                 (23 April) Rupert Brooke dies
                                                 of septicaemia on the way to
                                                 Gallipoli.

      (25 April) Battle of Gallipoli begins.

Year	Historical Event	The Poets

Year Historical Event

The Poets

1915

(May) Rupert Brooke, *1914 and Other Poems*.

(7 May) U-boat sinks the British liner *Lusitania* off Kinsale, with the loss of 1,198 lives.
(22 May) Quintinshill rail disaster near Gretna Green kills 226, mostly soldiers.
(25 May) Prime Minister Asquith creates a new coalition government.

(26 May) Julian Grenfell dies of wounds at Boulogne.

(31 May) First Zeppelin raid on London.

(September) Wilfrid Gibson, *Battle*; May Sinclair, *A Journal of Impressions in Belgium*.

(25 September–14 October) Battle of Loos sees the first Allied use of poison gas.

(27 September) Rudyard Kipling's son John killed at Loos.
(13 October) Charles Sorley killed by a sniper at Loos.
(November) *Georgian Poetry, 1913–1915*.
(December) Rudyard Kipling, *The Fringes of the Fleet*.

(7 December) British evacuation from Gallipoli begins.
(19 December) Sir Douglas Haig takes command of the British Expeditionary Force from Sir John French.

1916

(January) Charles Sorley, *Marlborough and Other Poems*.

(27 January) Conscription introduced in Britain.

(April) Wilfrid Gibson, *Friends*.

(24–29 April) Easter Rising in Dublin against British rule.

(May) Robert Graves, *Over the Brazier*; Charlotte Mew, *The Farmer's Bride*; Edmund Blunden, *The Harbingers*.

(31 May–1 June) Battle of Jutland, the biggest naval battle in history, in the North Sea near Denmark.

(June) Edmund Blunden, *Pastorals*.

Year	Historical Event	The Poets

(1 July) First day of the Battle of the Somme; over 19,000 British soldiers killed.

(11 July) David Jones wounded in the leg during the assault on Mametz Wood.
(20 July) Robert Graves severely wounded by a shell near High Wood; mistakenly reported dead.

(15 September) Tanks used by British forces for the first time in battle.
(18 November) Battle of the Somme ends without a clear victor.

(December) Rudyard Kipling, *Sea Warfare*; Robert Service, *Rhymes of a Red Cross Man*.

(7 December) Lloyd George succeeds Asquith as prime minister.

1917

(January) Wilfrid Gibson, *Livelihood*.

(23 February) German forces begin a retreat to fortified positions at the Hindenburg Line.

(March) Laurence Binyon, *The Cause*.

(11 March) Baghdad falls to British Indian army.
(15 March) Tsar Nicholas II of Russia abdicates.

(April) Rudyard Kipling, *A Diversity of Creatures*.
(3 April) Arthur Graeme West killed by a sniper near Bapaume.
(6 April) USA declares war on Germany.
(6 April) Ivor Gurney shot through the right arm at Vermand.
(9 April) Edward Thomas killed by a shell at Vimy Ridge.
(16 April) Siegfried Sassoon shot in the back by a sniper.
(2 May) Wilfred Owen evacuated from Savy Wood suffering from shell shock.
(May) Mutinies in French divisions.
(May) Siegfried Sassoon, *The Old Huntsman*.

Year	Historical Event	The Poets

1917

(June) May Wedderburn Cannan, *In War Time*.

(25 June) First US troops arrive in France.

(6 July) Siegfried Sassoon sends his 'Declaration' against the War to his commanding officer, refusing to perform further military duties.

(16 July) Third Battle of Ypres begins.

(12 September) Ivor Gurney gassed at Saint-Julien.
(October) Edward Thomas, *Poems*.
(November) Thomas Hardy, *Moments of Vision*; Ivor Gurney, *Severn & Somme*; Robert Graves, *Fairies and Fusiliers*; W. B. Yeats, *The Wild Swans at Coole*; *Georgian Poetry, 1916–1917*.

(7 November) Lenin comes to power in Russia after the Bolshevik Revolution.
(10 November) Third Battle of Ypres ends without a clear victor.
(5 December) Armistice signed between Germany and Russia.

(30 December) Patrick Shaw Stewart killed by a shell at Cambrai.

1918

(January) Wilfrid Gibson, *Whin*.

(21 March) First of the German Spring Offensives begins, pushing back Allied forces.
(21 March–August) Long-range bombardment of French capital by the German 'Paris Gun'.

(23 March) T. P. Cameron Wilson killed at Hermies.
(1 April) Isaac Rosenberg killed near Fampoux.
(12 May) Edgell Rickword wounded at Beaumont Hamel.
(June) Siegfried Sassoon, *Counter-Attack*.
(13 July) Siegfried Sassoon shot in the head by friendly fire near Saint-Floris.

Year Historical Event	The Poets
(15 July) Second Battle of the Marne sees the final German offensive of the War.	
(8–12 August) Allies' Hundred Days Offensive begins with victory at Battle of Amiens.	
(29 September–10 October) Battle of Saint-Quentin Canal; Allied victory creates the first breach in the Hindenburg Line.	
	(October) Laurence Binyon, *The New World*.
(3 October) Germany asks for armistice. (30 October) Turkey signs armistice with Allies.	
	(4 November) Wilfred Owen killed on the bank of the Sambre and Oise Canal near Ors.
(9 November) Abdication of Kaiser Wilhelm II of Germany. (11 November) Germany signs the Armistice with the Allies. Ceasefire at 11 a.m.	
	(December) Margaret Postgate Cole, *Margaret Postgate's Poems*.

POETRY
OF THE
FIRST WORLD WAR

THOMAS HARDY
(1840–1928)

━━━

ONE of the great novelists of the nineteenth century, in his fifties
Thomas Hardy transformed himself into one of the great poets of
the twentieth. Keen to justify his new direction, he later denied that
any major break had occurred. Poetry, he claimed, had come first:
approximately one-third of *Wessex Poems* (1898) dated from the
1860s, before his earliest published novel. Yet Hardy's retrospective
remakings ignore an extraordinary shift of emphasis. During the first
five decades of his life he wrote around sixty poems; over the next
four, almost one thousand.

In the autobiography published posthumously under his second
wife's name, Hardy recounted that, lacking any ambition, he wrote
poetry purely for personal pleasure. This does not accord with the
facts, which reveal a poet acutely sensitive to criticism and eager to
pen occasional verse in response to public events such as the death of
Queen Victoria or the sinking of the *Titanic*. War seemed particularly
inspiring: the outbreak of the Boer War in 1899 prompted Hardy
to write a group of eleven 'War Poems', later collected in *Poems of
the Past and the Present* (1901), including the most famous poem of
that war, 'Drummer Hodge'. Hardy had witnessed the departure of a
battery of artillery from his home town of Dorchester, and had cycled
to Southampton to see the fleet embark for South Africa. But he was
profoundly opposed to the War, and did not share the widespread
sense of patriotic adventure. As he told his friend Florence Henniker,
herself the wife of a distinguished officer, none of his Boer War poems
had been 'Jingo or Imperial—a fatal defect according to the judgment
of the British majority at present, I dare say'.[1] Yet he also admitted
that he loved to 'write of war in prose & rhyme'. Proving the point, he
published *The Dynasts*, his epic verse 'diorama' of the Napoleonic
campaigns, in three volumes between 1904 and 1908.

Hardy came to believe that 'common sense had taken the place

[1] Thomas Hardy, *Collected Letters*, ii: 1893–1901, ed. Richard Little Purdy and
Michael Millgate (Oxford: Oxford University Press, 1980), 277.

of bluster in men's minds'; war had grown 'too coldly scientific' to promise anything in the way of 'ardent romance'. He was therefore left shocked and devastated by the outbreak of hostilities in 1914, and obliged to discard his faith in 'the gradual ennoblement of man'. His own contribution to the war effort followed his attendance at a private conference of men of letters organized by the British government on 2 September 1914. Writers were urged to place 'the strength of the British case and the principles for which the British troops and their allies are fighting before the populations of neutral countries'.[2] The diligence with which Hardy fulfilled that brief is suggested by the unwieldy title of a poem he published later that year: 'An Appeal to America on Behalf of the Belgian Destitute'.

'Poems of War and Patriotism', a section of seventeen poems in *Moments of Vision* (1917), includes these dutiful and often awkward public performances, even though Hardy conceded that he could not 'do patriotic poems very well—seeing the other side too much'.[3] Such poems appear amid more profound meditations on the pity, the tragedy, the guilt, and the grief of war. Hardy returned frequently to the kinship between the English and the Germans, and reserved his wrath for the German political classes who, 'The Pity of It' implied, had 'flung this flame | Between kin folk'. Having visited a large prisoner-of-war camp at Dorchester, and a nearby hospital filled with English wounded, he concluded that the afflicted soldiers were reflections of each other: 'Men lie helpless here [in the POW camp] from wounds: in the hospital a hundred yards off other men, English, lie helpless from wounds—each scene of suffering caused by the other!'[4] His experiences led him to advocate a benign internationalism in which sovereign interests would be overridden by a greater brotherhood. Yet after the War, he was not hopeful that humankind would survive—or deserved to—so bent it seemed on its own destruction. As he wrote in the bitter epigram 'Christmas: 1924', the Christian vision of 'Peace upon earth!' seemed further away than ever: 'After two thousand years of mass | We've got as far as poison-gas.'

[2] Hardy, *The Later Years of Thomas Hardy*, 162, 164, 163.
[3] Hardy, *Collected Letters*, v: *1914–1919*, 276.
[4] Hardy, *The Later Years of Thomas Hardy*, 173.

Men Who March Away

(Song of the Soldiers)

What of the faith and fire within us
    Men who march away
    Ere the barn-cocks say
    Night is growing gray,
Leaving all that here can win us;
What of the faith and fire within us
    Men who march away?

Is it a purblind prank, O think you,°
    Friend with the musing eye,
    Who watch us stepping by   10
    With doubt and dolorous sigh?
Can much pondering so hoodwink you!
Is it a purblind prank, O think you,
    Friend with the musing eye?

Nay. We well see what we are doing,
    Though some may not see—
    Dalliers as they be—
    England's need are we;
Her distress would leave us rueing:
Nay. We well see what we are doing,   20
    Though some may not see!

In our heart of hearts believing
    Victory crowns the just,
    And that braggards must
    Surely bite the dust,
Press we to the field ungrieving,
In our heart of hearts believing
    Victory crowns the just.

Hence the faith and fire within us
    Men who march away   30
    Ere the barn-cocks say
    Night is growing gray,

Leaving all that here can win us;
Hence the faith and fire within us
Men who march away.

5 September 1914

England to Germany in 1914

'O England, may God punish thee!'
—Is it that Teuton genius flowers°
Only to breathe malignity
Upon its friend of earlier hours?
—We have eaten your bread, you have eaten ours,
We have loved your burgs, your pines' green moan,°
Fair Rhine-stream, and its storied towers;°
Your shining souls of deathless dowers°
Have won us as they were our own:

We have nursed no dreams to shed your blood,   10
We have matched your might not rancorously
Save a flushed few whose blatant mood°
You heard and marked as well as we
To tongue not in their country's key;
But yet you cry with face aflame,
'O England, may God punish thee!'
And foul in outward history,
And present sight, your ancient name.

Autumn 1914

On the Belgian Expatriation

I dreamt that people from the Land of Chimes°
Arrived one autumn morning with their bells,
To hoist them on the towers and citadels
Of my own country, that the musical rhymes

Rung by them into space at meted times°
Amid the market's daily stir and stress,
And the night's empty star-lit silentness,
Might solace souls of this and kindred climes.

Then I awoke; and lo, before me stood
The visioned ones, but pale and full of fear;   10
From Bruges they came, and Antwerp, and Ostend,°

No carillons in their train. Foes of mad mood°
Had shattered these to shards amid the gear°
Of ravaged roof, and smouldering gable-end.

                                        18 October 1914

The Pity of It

I walked in loamy Wessex lanes, afar
From rail-track and from highway, and I heard
In field and farmstead many an ancient word
Of local lineage like 'Thu bist', 'Er war',

'Ich woll', 'Er sholl', and by-talk similar,°
Nigh as they speak who in this month's moon gird
At England's very loins, thereunto spurred
By gangs whose glory threats and slaughters are.

Then seemed a Heart crying: 'Whosoever they be
At root and bottom of this, who flung this flame   10
Between kin folk kin tongued even as we are,

'Sinister, ugly, lurid, be their fame;
May their familiars grow to shun their name,
And their brood perish everlastingly.'
                                        April 1915

In Time of 'The Breaking of Nations'[1]

I

Only a man harrowing clods
  In a slow silent walk
With an old horse that stumbles and nods
  Half asleep as they stalk.

II

Only thin smoke without flame
  From the heaps of couch-grass;°
Yet this will go onward the same
  Though Dynasties pass.°

III

Yonder a maid and her wight°
  Come whispering by: 10
War's annals will cloud into night
  Ere their story die.

[1] Jer., LI 20. [Hardy's note]

Before Marching and After

(In Memoriam F.W.G.)

Orion swung southward aslant
Where the starved Egdon pine-trees had thinned,°
The Pleiads aloft seemed to pant°
With the heather that twitched in the wind;
But he looked on indifferent to sights such as these,
Unswayed by love, friendship, home joy or home sorrow,
And wondered to what he would march on the morrow.

The crazed household-clock with its whirr
Rang midnight within as he stood,
He heard the low sighing of her   10
Who had striven from his birth for his good;

But he still only asked the spring starlight, the breeze,
What great thing or small thing his history would borrow
From that Game with Death he would play on the morrow.

When the heath wore the robe of late summer,
And the fuchsia-bells, hot in the sun,
Hung red by the door, a quick comer
Brought tidings that marching was done
For him who had joined in that game overseas
Where Death stood to win, though his name was to borrow   20
A brightness therefrom not to fade on the morrow.

September 1915

A New Year's Eve in War Time

I

Phantasmal fears,
And the flap of the flame,
And the throb of the clock,
And a loosened slate,
And the blind night's drone,
Which tiredly the spectral pines intone!

II

And the blood in my ears
Strumming always the same,
And the gable-cock°
With its fitful grate,   10
And myself, alone.

III

The twelfth hour nears
Hand-hid, as in shame;°
I undo the lock,
And listen, and wait
For the Young Unknown.°

IV

In the dark there careers—
As if Death astride came
To numb all with his knock—
A horse at mad rate   20
Over rut and stone.°

V

No figure appears,
No call of my name,
No sound but 'Tic-toc'
Without check. Past the gate
It clatters—is gone.

VI

What rider it bears
There is none to proclaim;
And the Old Year has struck,
And, scarce animate,   30
The New makes moan.

VII

Maybe that 'More Tears!—
More Famine and Flame—
More Severance and Shock!'
Is the order from Fate
That the Rider speeds on
To pale Europe; and tiredly the pines intone.

                                    1915–1916

I Looked Up from My Writing

I looked up from my writing,
   And gave a start to see,
As if rapt in my inditing,°
   The moon's full gaze on me.

Her meditative misty head
   Was spectral in its air,
And I involuntarily said,
   'What are you doing there?'

'Oh, I've been scanning pond and hole
   And waterway hereabout   10
Or the body of one with a sunken soul
   Who has put his life-light out.

'Did you hear his frenzied tattle?°
   It was sorrow for his son
Who is slain in brutish battle,
   Though he has injured none.

'And now I am curious to look
   Into the blinkered mind
Of one who wants to write a book
   In a world of such a kind.'   20

Her temper overwrought me,
   And I edged to shun her view,
For I felt assured she thought me
   One who should drown him too.

'According to the Mighty Working'

I

When moiling seems at cease°
   In the vague void of night-time,
   And heaven's wide roomage stormless
   Between the dusk and light-time,
   And fear at last is formless,
We call the allurement Peace.

II

Peace, this hid riot, Change,
   This revel of quick-cued mumming,°

> This never truly being,
> This evermore becoming,   10
> This spinner's wheel onfleeing
> Outside perception's range.

1917

'And There Was a Great Calm'
(On the Signing of the Armistice, 11 Nov. 1918)

I

There had been years of Passion—scorching, cold,
And much Despair, and Anger heaving high,
Care whitely watching, Sorrows manifold,
Among the young, among the weak and old,
And the pensive Spirit of Pity whispered, 'Why?'°

II

Men had not paused to answer. Foes distraught
Pierced the thinned peoples in a brute-like blindness,
Philosophies that sages long had taught,
And Selflessness, were as an unknown thought,
And 'Hell!' and 'Shell!' were yapped at Lovingkindness.   10

III

The feeble folk at home had grown full-used
To 'dug-outs', 'snipers', 'Huns', from the war-adept
In the mornings heard, and at evetimes perused;
To day-dreamt men in millions, when they mused—
To nightmare-men in millions when they slept.

IV

Waking to wish existence timeless, null,
Sirius they watched above where armies fell;°
He seemed to check his flapping when, in the lull
Of night a boom came thencewise, like the dull
Plunge of a stone dropped in some deep well.   20

V

So, when old hopes that earth was bettering slowly
Were dead and damned, there sounded 'War is done!'
One morrow. Said the bereft, and meek, and lowly,
'Will men some day be given to grace? yea, wholly,
And in good sooth, as our dreams used to run?'

VI

Breathless they paused. Out there men raised their glance
To where had stood those poplars lank and lopped,
As they had raised it through the four years' dance
Of Death in the now familiar flats of France;°
And murmured, 'Strange, this! How? All firing stopped?'   30

VII

Aye; all was hushed. The about-to-fire fired not,
The aimed-at moved away in trance-lipped song.
One checkless regiment slung a clinching shot
And turned. The Spirit of Irony smirked out, 'What?°
Spoil peradventures woven of Rage and Wrong?'°

VIII

Thenceforth no flying fires inflamed the gray,
No hurtlings shook the dewdrop from the thorn,
No moan perplexed the mute bird on the spray;
Worn horses mused: 'We are not whipped to-day;'
No weft-winged engines blurred the moon's thin horn.°   40

IX

Calm fell. From Heaven distilled a clemency;
There was peace on earth, and silence in the sky;
Some could, some could not, shake off misery:
The Sinister Spirit sneered: 'It had to be!'°
And again the Spirit of Pity whispered, 'Why?'

A. E. HOUSMAN
(1859–1936)

———

HOUSMAN published only two books of poetry during his lifetime: *A Shropshire Lad* (1896) and *Last Poems* (1922). He died aged 77 in 1936, having spent the latter half of his career as Professor of Latin at Cambridge. His will instructed his brother Laurence to print any remaining poems which seemed to him 'not inferior in quality to the average' of his published work and to destroy all others.[1] *More Poems* appeared posthumously in 1936, and *Additional Poems* the following year.

Housman made his reputation with *A Shropshire Lad*, a collection of sixty-three lyrics initially published at his own expense. Its nostalgia for rural England, its melancholic poems of enlistment and early death, its apparent simplicity, and its clear quality would help make the volume one of the most popular books among soldiers in the trenches.

Uncertainty over composition dates and a lack of identifying detail in the poems themselves ensure that the task of assigning any of Housman's poems to particular wars remains precarious. Rudyard Kipling reportedly admired 'Epitaph on an Army of Mercenaries' as the finest poem of the First World War; it is the only war poem by Housman that can be classified with certainty as having been written during the conflict.

[1] Quoted by Laurence Housman, 'Preface', in A. E. Housman, *More Poems* (London: Jonathan Cape, 1936), 7.

———

Epitaph on an Army of Mercenaries

These, in the day when heaven was falling,
   The hour when earth's foundations fled,
Followed their mercenary calling°
   And took their wages and are dead.°

Their shoulders held the sky suspended;°
   They stood, and earth's foundations stay;
What God abandoned, these defended,
   And saved the sum of things for pay.

MAY SINCLAIR
(1863–1946)

MAY SINCLAIR, novelist, feminist, and poet, was born in Cheshire and schooled in Cheltenham. Her third novel, *The Divine Fire* (1904), established her reputation on both sides of the Atlantic. Settled in London, she became part of an impressive literary circle, counting among her friends Thomas Hardy, W. B. Yeats, and (slightly later) Charlotte Mew. She was deeply involved in campaigns for women's suffrage, and became a founder member of London's first clinic to offer psychoanalytical therapies.

Sinclair greeted the War as an opportunity to experience a new and more intense life, freed from stultifying conventions. Having joined a voluntary ambulance corps, she arrived in Flanders towards the end of September 1914. The three weeks she spent there—insisting that she be allowed into the battle zones, nursing the wounded, leaving Ghent at no more than a few hours' notice as the Germans advanced—provided the inspiration for two wartime novels. They also became the subject of her *Journal of Impressions in Belgium* (1915), in which she wrote frankly of her increasing excitement as danger approached: 'But the thrill, mounting steadily, overtakes the regret. It is only a little thrill, so far (for you don't really believe that there is any danger), but you can imagine the thing growing, growing steadily, till it becomes ecstasy. Not that you imagine anything at the moment. At the moment you are no longer an observing, reflecting being; you have ceased to be aware of yourself; you exist only in that quiet, steady thrill that is so unlike any excitement that you have ever known.'[1]

Believing that arrangements would be made for her return to Belgium, Sinclair travelled back to England to raise funds in the second half of October 1914. She felt a profound sense of betrayal when it became clear that she was no longer wanted by her ambulance corps. Her verse 'Dedication', first published as the preface to the

---

[1] Sinclair, *A Journal of Impressions in Belgium*, 12–13.

Journal, barely kept at bay her anger at those erstwhile colleagues who had 'taken [her] dream'.

======

Field Ambulance in Retreat

Via Dolorosa, Via Sacra

I

A straight flagged road, laid on the rough earth,
A causeway of stone from beautiful city to city,
Between the tall trees, the slender, delicate trees,
Through the flat green land, by plots of flowers, by black canals
    thick with heat.

II

The road-makers made it well
Of fine stone, strong for the feet of the oxen and of the great
    Flemish horses,°
And for the high waggons piled with corn from the harvest.
But the labourers are few;
They and their quiet oxen stand aside and wait
By the long road loud with the passing of the guns, the rush of
    armoured cars and the tramp of an army on the march
    forward to battle;   10
And, where the piled corn-wagons went, our dripping
    Ambulance carries home
Its red and white harvest from the fields.

III

The straight flagged road breaks into dust, into a thin white cloud,
About the feet of a regiment driven back league by league,
Rifles at trail, and standards wrapped in black funeral cloths.
    Unhasting, proud in retreat,
They smile as the Red Cross Ambulance rushes by.°
(You know nothing of beauty and of desolation who have not seen
That smile of an army in retreat.)
They go: and our shining, beckoning danger goes with them,

And our joy in the harvests that we gathered in at nightfall in the
    fields;   20
And like an unloved hand laid on a beating heart
Our safety weighs us down.
Safety hard and strange; stranger and yet more hard
As, league after dying league, the beautiful, desolate Land,
Falls back from the intolerable speed of an Ambulance in retreat°
On the sacred, dolorous Way.

After the Retreat

If I could only see again
The house we passed on the long Flemish road°
That day
When the Army went from Antwerp, through Bruges, to the sea;
The house with the slender door,
And the one thin row of shutters, grey as dust on the white wall.
It stood low and alone in the flat Flemish land,
And behind it the high slender trees were small under the sky.

It looked
Through windows blurred like women's eyes that have cried
    too long.   10

There is not anyone there whom I know,
I have never sat by its hearth, I have never crossed its threshold,
    I have never opened its door,
I have never sat by its windows looking in;
Yet its eyes said: 'You have seen four cities of Flanders:
Ostend, and Bruges, and Antwerp under her doom,
And the dear city of Ghent;°
And there is none of them that you shall remember
As you remember me.'

I remember so well,
That at night, at night I cannot sleep in England here;   20
But I get up, and I go:
Not to the cities of Flanders,

Not to Ostend and the sea,
Not to the city of Bruges, or the city of Antwerp, or the city of
   Ghent,
But somewhere
In the fields,
Where the high slender trees are small under the sky—

If I could only see again
The house we passed that day.

Dedication

(To a Field Ambulance in Flanders)

I do not call you comrades,
You,
Who did what I only dreamed.
Though you have taken my dream,
And dressed yourselves in its beauty and its glory,
Your faces are turned aside as you pass by.
I am nothing to you,
For I have done no more than dream.

Your faces are like the face of her whom you follow,
Danger,   10
The Beloved who looks backward as she runs, calling to her lovers,
The Huntress who flies before her quarry, trailing her lure.°
She called to me from her battle-places,
She flung before me the curved lightning of her shells for a lure;
And when I came within sight of her,
She turned aside,
And hid her face from me.

But you she loved;
You she touched with her hand;
For you the white flames of her feet stayed in their running;   20
She kept you with her in her fields of Flanders,
Where you go,

Gathering your wounded from among her dead.
Grey night falls on your going and black night on your returning.
You go
Under the thunder of the guns, the shrapnel's rain and the curved
   lightning of the shells,
And where the high towers are broken,
And houses crack like the staves of a thin crate filled with fire;
Into the mixing smoke and dust of roof and walls torn asunder
You go;   30
And only my dream follows you.

That is why I do not speak of you,
Calling you by your names.°
Your names are strung with the names of ruined and immortal
   cities,
Termonde and Antwerp, Dixmude and Ypres and Furnes,°
Like jewels on one chain—

Thus,
In the high places of Heaven,
They shall tell all your names.

March 8th, 1915.

W. B. YEATS

(1865–1939)

'I SHALL keep the neighbourhood of the seven sleepers of Ephesus, hoping to catch their comfortable snores till bloody frivolity is over.'[1] Keen though he was to see Germany defeated, W. B. Yeats hesitated over the prospect of giving full-throated support to an imperialist nation that had still not delivered Home Rule in his native Ireland. The War, in Yeats's estimation, was neither his own nor his country's quarrel; and whereas the 1916 Easter Rising in Dublin against British rule profoundly affected him, the tens of thousands of Irish losses in France and Belgium went unmentioned.

Yeats was possibly the most famous—certainly the most respected—poet of his day. His ostentatious refusal to put his work to the service of the war effort drew sharp criticism: 'A Reason for Keeping Silent' (later revised to 'On Being Asked For a War Poem') prompted his patron John Quinn to complain that the poem was 'quite unworthy of [him] and the occasion'.[2] At those rare times when Yeats did directly address the War in his verse, it was from an Irish and a personal perspective, as when he mourned the death of his friend Lady Gregory's son, Robert, who had been shot down over Italy.

The War's shadow falls across Yeats's later work. Towards the end of his life, he caused controversy by excluding Wilfred Owen, and many other soldier–poets, from his edition of *The Oxford Book of Modern Verse* (1936), admitting to 'a distaste for certain poems written in the midst of the great war'. 'Passive suffering', he declared, quoting Matthew Arnold, 'is not a theme for poetry.'[3] Privately, he wrote to Dorothy Wellesley on Boxing Day 1936 in still more forthright tones. Owen 'is all blood, dirt and sucked sugar stick,' he told her. 'There is every excuse for him but none for those who like him.'

[1] Yeats, *The Letters of W. B. Yeats*, 600.

[2] Alan Himber and George Mills Harper (eds), *The Letters of John Quinn to William Butler Yeats* (Ann Arbor: UMI Research Press, 1983), 192.

[3] Yeats, 'Introduction', *The Oxford Book of Modern Verse*, p. xxxiv.

On Being Asked for a War Poem

I think it better that in times like these
A poet keep his mouth shut, for in truth°
We have no gift to set a statesman right;
He has had enough of meddling who can please
A young girl in the indolence of her youth,
Or an old man upon a winter's night.

An Irish Airman Foresees His Death

I know that I shall meet my fate
Somewhere among the clouds above;
Those that I fight I do not hate,
Those that I guard I do not love;
My country is Kiltartan Cross,°
My countrymen Kiltartan's poor,
No likely end could bring them loss
Or leave them happier than before.
Nor law, nor duty bade me fight,
Nor public man, nor angry crowds,°   10
A lonely impulse of delight
Drove to this tumult in the clouds;
I balanced all, brought all to mind,
The years to come seemed waste of breath,
A waste of breath the years behind
In balance with this life, this death.

RUDYARD KIPLING
(1865–1936)

RUDYARD KIPLING'S relationship with the military began as a schoolboy in the United Services College at Westward Ho!, and deepened during his seven years as a journalist in the army-controlled Punjab. His early poetry and prose returned often to stories heard around 'a Mess-table at midnight'.[1] Kipling soon became an advocate for the common soldier, his two volumes of *Barrack-Room Ballads* (1892 and 1896) giving voice to Tommy Atkins and deploring a culture that treated its military so hypocritically: 'For it's Tommy this, an' Tommy that, an' "Chuck him out, the brute!" | But it's "Saviour of 'is country" when the guns begin to shoot.'[2] By the mid-1890s, Kipling had anatomized a national complacency that might prove fatal if not addressed. The British, he believed, had forgotten their duties and their debts. In subsequent decades, he urged the case for military reform and a revolution in public opinion.

Already famous by the time of the Boer War, Kipling went to South Africa in early 1900 as a correspondent, at one point briefly coming under fire as he watched a British attack. What he heard and witnessed during his three months near the war zone confirmed him in his opinion that soldiers were being betrayed by an incompetent political and military hierarchy. Kipling's despised generals, in his bitter poem 'Stellenbosh', receive their 'decorations thick' while leaving the rank and file with 'the work to do again'; they are the immediate forefathers of Siegfried Sassoon's 'scarlet Majors' who run the War from the safety of their base. But even those portrayals seem mild compared with Kipling's later poem, 'Mesopotamia' (1917), an evisceration of the 'idle-minded overlings' whom he held responsible for the catastrophic failures of that ill-fated campaign.

A character in one of Kipling's stories describes the Boer War as

---

[1] Rudyard Kipling, 'The Drums of the Fore and Aft', *Wee Willie Winkie and Other Stories* (London: Macmillan, 1895), 315.

[2] Kipling, 'Tommy', in *The Cambridge Edition of the Poems of Rudyard Kipling*, i. 178–9.

'a first-class dress-parade for Armageddon'.[3] Kipling had foreseen
a greater war with Germany, and campaigned for the failings of
leadership exposed by the South African conflict to be urgently
corrected in preparation for this European war. He also supported
compulsory military service, and played a part in the founding of the
Scout Movement by his friend Robert Baden-Powell. But Kipling
was already a divisive figure, attacked by liberals as a warmonger
and a jingoist. When Armageddon did break out in August 1914,
the young soldier–poet Charles Sorley detected a silver lining: 'I'm
thankful to see that Kipling hasn't written a poem yet.'[4] (Sorley
would have been disappointed to learn that ' "For All We Have
and Are" ' would be published within a month.) Although Kipling
remained immensely popular with a broad reading public—as the
thousands of copies of *Barrack-Room Ballads* sold for each year of the
War demonstrate—from certain political perspectives he had been
reduced to a caricature.

Kipling worked tirelessly for the Allied cause. A rumour in
September 1914 that he might be sent to the United States as a
goodwill ambassador provoked threats of resignation from Sir
Edward Grey, the Liberal foreign secretary, but Kipling did carry
out a variety of literary commissions on behalf of the War Propaganda
Bureau and the navy. He also spoke passionately at recruitment
drives, travelled to France (1915) and Italy (1917) as a war reporter,
encouraged correspondents such as Theodore Roosevelt to bring an
end to American neutrality, and railed against the 'Hun' (an appel-
lation that Kipling himself had popularized) with ever more rabid
intensity. The death of his only son at the Battle of Loos in September
1915 no doubt crystallized his animosity. Whereas 'Piet', the
Boer rebel, had won Kipling's grudging admiration, the Hun were
'outside any humanity we have had any experience of', and were to
be treated like 'the germs of any malignant disease'.[5] 'Justice', written
in the closing days of the War, calls for a punitive settlement against
'Evil Incarnate', so that the Allied war dead might be allowed to
'sleep | In honour, unbetrayed'.

Kipling's imaginative writings about the War are extraordinarily
rich and varied. The stories in *A Diversity of Creatures* (1917) and

[3] Rudyard Kipling, 'The Captive', *Traffics and Discoveries* (London: Macmillan, 1904), 27.
[4] Charles Sorley, *The Letters of Charles Sorley*, 222.
[5] Kipling, *The Letters of Rudyard Kipling*, iv: *1911–1919*, 405.

Debits and Credits (1926) remain unsurpassed in their descriptions of sudden violent death, shell shock, trauma, and grief. And his detailed accounts of sea warfare in *The Years Between* (1919), the volume which collected much of his wartime poetry, go some way towards compensating for the absence of a significant *sailor*–poet.

During the War, Kipling accepted a commission to write the recent history of his son's regiment: *The Irish Guards in the Great War* appeared in two volumes in 1923. He also served on the Commonwealth War Graves Commission until his death in 1936. It was Kipling who suggested the phrase from Ecclesiasticus—'Their name liveth for evermore'—as a suitable inscription on war memorials, and the epigraph 'Known Unto God' on the graves of unknown casualties. He lived long enough to foresee the next world war. In 'The Storm Cone' (1932) he warned, as he had warned so often in previous decades, that until the danger had passed no man should 'deem that he is free'.

━━

'For All We Have and Are'

1914

For all we have and are,
For all our children's fate,
Stand up and take the war,
The Hun is at the gate!°
Our world has passed away,
In wantonness o'erthrown.
There is nothing left to-day
But steel and fire and stone!
    Though all we knew depart,
    The old Commandments stand:—   10
    'In courage keep your heart,
    In strength lift up your hand.'

Once more we hear the word
That sickened earth of old:—
'No law except the Sword
Unsheathed and uncontrolled.'

Once more it knits mankind,
Once more the nations go
To meet and break and bind
A crazed and driven foe.   20

Comfort, content, delight,
The ages' slow-bought gain,
They shrivelled in a night.
Only ourselves remain
To face the naked days
In silent fortitude,
Through perils and dismays
Renewed and re-renewed.
    Though all we made depart,
    The old Commandments stand:—   30
    'In patience keep your heart,
    In strength lift up your hand.'

No easy hope or lies
Shall bring us to our goal,
But iron sacrifice
Of body, will, and soul.
There is but one task for all—
One life for each to give.
Who stands if Freedom fall?
Who dies if England live?   40

'Tin Fish'

The ships destroy us above
    And ensnare us beneath.
We arise, we lie down, and we move
    In the belly of Death.

The ships have a thousand eyes
    To mark where we come . . .
And the mirth of a seaport dies
    When our blow gets home.

The Children

These were our children who died for our lands: they were dear
    in our sight.
  We have only the memory left of their home-treasured sayings
    and laughter.
  The price of our loss shall be paid to our hands, not another's
    hereafter.
Neither the Alien nor Priest shall decide on it. That is our right.°
  But who shall return us the children?

At the hour the Barbarian chose to disclose his pretences,
  And raged against Man, they engaged, on the breasts that they
    bared for us,
  The first felon-stroke of the sword he had long-time prepared
    for us—
Their bodies were all our defence while we wrought our defences.

They bought us anew with their blood, forbearing to blame us,   10
Those hours which we had not made good when the Judgment
    o'ercame us.
They believed us and perished for it. Our statecraft, our learning
Delivered them bound to the Pit and alive to the burning
Whither they mirthfully hastened as jostling for honour.
Not since her birth has our Earth seen such worth loosed
    upon her.

Nor was their agony brief, or once only imposed on them.
  The wounded, the war-spent, the sick received no exemption:
  Being cured they returned and endured and achieved our
    redemption,
Hopeless themselves of relief, till Death, marvelling, closed on
    them.

That flesh we had nursed from the first in all cleanness was given   20
To corruption unveiled and assailed by the malice of Heaven—
By the heart-shaking jests of Decay where it lolled on the wires—
To be blanched or gay-painted by fumes—to be cindered by
    fires—°

To be senselessly tossed and retossed in stale mutilation
From crater to crater. For this we shall take expiation.°
    But who shall return us our children?

'The Trade'

They bear, in place of classic names,
    Letters and numbers on their skin.°
They plan their grisly blindfold games
    In little boxes made of tin.
    Sometimes they stalk the Zeppelin,°
Sometimes they learn where mines are laid,
    Or where the Baltic ice is thin.°
That is the custom of 'The Trade.'

Few prize-courts sit upon their claims.°
    They seldom tow their targets in.   10
They follow certain secret aims
    Down under, far from strife or din.
    When they are ready to begin
No flag is flown, no fuss is made
    More than the shearing of a pin.°
That is the custom of 'The Trade.'

The Scout's quadruple funnel flames°
    A mark from Sweden to the Swin,°
The Cruiser's thunderous screw proclaims°
    Her comings out and goings in: 20
    But only whiffs of paraffin
Or creamy rings that fizz and fade
    Show where the one-eyed Death has been.°
That is the custom of 'The Trade.'

Their feats, their fortunes and their fames
    Are hidden from their nearest kin;
No eager public backs or blames,
    No journal prints the yarn they spin

(The Censor would not let it in!)°
When they return from run or raid.   30
   Unheard they work, unseen they win.
That is the custom of 'The Trade.'

My Boy Jack

'Have you news of my boy Jack?'
   Not this tide.
'When d'you think that he'll come back?'
   Not with this wind blowing, and this tide.

'Has any one else had word of him?'
   Not this tide.
For what is sunk will hardly swim,
   Not with this wind blowing, and this tide.

'Oh, dear, what comfort can I find?'
   None this tide,   10
   Nor any tide,
Except he did not shame his kind—
   Not even with that wind blowing, and that tide.

Then hold your head up all the more,
   This tide,
   And every tide;
Because he was the son you bore,
   And gave to that wind blowing and that tide!

The Verdicts

(Jutland)

Not in the thick of the fight,
   Not in the press of the odds,
Do the heroes come to their height,
   Or we know the demi-gods.

That stands over till peace.
    We can only perceive
Men returned from the seas,
    Very grateful for leave.

They grant us sudden days
    Snatched from their business of war;   10
But we are too close to appraise
    What manner of men they are.

And, whether their names go down
    With age-kept victories,
Or whether they battle and drown
    Unreckoned, is hid from our eyes.

They are too near to be great,
    But our children shall understand
When and how our fate
    Was changed, and by whose hand.   20

Our children shall measure their worth.
    We are content to be blind . . .
But we know that we walk on a new-born earth
    With the saviours of mankind.

Mesopotamia

1917

They shall not return to us, the resolute, the young,
    The eager and whole-hearted whom we gave:
But the men who left them thriftily to die in their own dung,
    Shall they come with years and honour to the grave?

They shall not return to us, the strong men coldly slain
    In sight of help denied from day to day:
But the men who edged their agonies and chid them in their pain,
    Are they too strong and wise to put away?

Our dead shall not return to us while Day and Night divide—
   Never while the bars of sunset hold:
But the idle-minded overlings who quibbled while they died,
   Shall they thrust for high employments as of old?

Shall we only threaten and be angry for an hour?
   When the storm is ended shall we find
How softly but how swiftly they have sidled back to power
   By the favour and contrivance of their kind?°

Even while they soothe us, while they promise large amends,
   Even while they make a show of fear,
Do they call upon their debtors, and take counsel with their
    friends,
   To confirm and re-establish each career?

Their lives cannot repay us—their death could not undo—
   The shame that they have laid upon our race:
But the slothfulness that wasted and the arrogance that slew,
   Shall we leave it unabated in its place?

Gethsemane

   The Garden called Gethsemane
     In Picardy it was,°
   And there the people came to see
     The English soldiers pass.
   We used to pass—we used to pass
     Or halt, as it might be,
   And ship our masks in case of gas
     Beyond Gethsemane.

   The Garden called Gethsemane,
     It held a pretty lass,
   But all the time she talked to me
     I prayed my cup might pass.°

The officer sat on the chair,
   The men lay on the grass,
And all the time we halted there
   I prayed my cup might pass—

It didn't pass—it didn't pass—
   It didn't pass from me.
I drank it when we met the gas
   Beyond Gethsemane.   20

Epitaphs

'EQUALITY OF SACRIFICE'

A. 'I was a "have."' *B*. 'I was a "have-not."'
(*Together*). 'What hast thou given which I gave not?'

A SERVANT

We were together since the War began.
He was my servant—and the better man.

A SON

My son was killed while laughing at some jest. I would I knew
What it was, and it might serve me in a time when jests are few.

AN ONLY SON

I have slain none except my Mother. She
(Blessing her slayer) died of grief for me.

EX-CLERK

Pity not! The Army gave
Freedom to a timid slave:
In which Freedom did he find
Strength of body, will, and mind:
By which strength he came to prove
Mirth, Companionship, and Love:
For which Love to Death he went:
In which Death he lies content.

THE WONDER

Body and Spirit I surrendered whole
To harsh Instructors—and received a soul . . .
If mortal man could change me through and through
From all I was—what may The God not do?

HINDU SEPOY IN FRANCE°

This man in his own country prayed we know not to what Powers.
We pray Them to reward him for his bravery in ours.

THE COWARD

I could not look on Death, which being known,
Men led me to him, blindfold and alone.

SHOCK

My name, my speech, my self I had forgot.
My wife and children came—I knew them not.
I died. My Mother followed. At her call
And on her bosom I remembered all.

A GRAVE NEAR CAIRO°

Gods of the Nile, should this stout fellow here°
Get out—get out! He knows not shame nor fear.

PELICANS IN THE WILDERNESS
(A GRAVE NEAR HALFA)°

The blown sand heaps on me, that none may learn
  Where I am laid for whom my children grieve . . .
O wings that beat at dawning, ye return
  Out of the desert to your young at eve!

THE FAVOUR

Death favoured me from the first, well knowing I could not
    endure
  To wait on him day by day. He quitted my betters and came
Whistling over the fields, and, when he had made all sure,
  'Thy line is at end,' he said, 'but at least I have saved its name.'

THE BEGINNER

On the first hour of my first day
  In the front trench I fell.
(Children in boxes at a play
  Stand up to watch it well.)

R. A. F. (AGED EIGHTEEN)

Laughing through clouds, his milk-teeth still unshed,
Cities and men he smote from overhead.
His deaths delivered, he returned to play
Childlike, with childish things now put away.

THE REFINED MAN

I was of delicate mind. I went aside for my needs,
  Disdaining the common office. I was seen from afar and killed . . .
How is this matter for mirth? Let each man be judged by his deeds.
  I have paid my price to live with myself on the terms that I willed.

NATIVE WATER-CARRIER (M. E. F.)°

Prometheus brought down fire to men.°
  This brought up water.
The Gods are jealous—now, as then,
  They gave no quarter.

BOMBED IN LONDON°

On land and sea I strove with anxious care
To escape conscription. It was in the air!

THE SLEEPY SENTINEL°

Faithless the watch that I kept: now I have none to keep.
I was slain because I slept: now I am slain I sleep.
Let no man reproach me again, whatever watch is unkept—
I sleep because I am slain. They slew me because I slept.

BATTERIES OUT OF AMMUNITION

If any mourn us in the workshop, say
We died because the shift kept holiday.

COMMON FORM

If any question why we died,
Tell them, because our fathers lied.

A DEAD STATESMAN

I could not dig: I dared not rob:
Therefore I lied to please the mob.
Now all my lies are proved untrue,
And I must face the men I slew.
What tale shall save me here among
Mine angry and defrauded young?

THE REBEL

If I had clamoured at Thy Gate
  For gift of Life on Earth,
And, thrusting through the souls that wait,
  Flung headlong into birth—
Even then, even then, for gin and snare
  About my pathway spread,
Lord, I had mocked Thy thoughtful care
  Before I joined the Dead!
But now? . . . I was beneath Thy Hand
  Ere yet the Planets came.
And now—though Planets pass, I stand
  The witness to Thy Shame.

THE OBEDIENT

Daily, though no ears attended,
  Did my prayers arise.
Daily, though no fire descended
  Did I sacrifice . . .
Though my darkness did not lift,
  Though I faced no lighter odds,
Though the Gods bestowed no gift,
                None the less,
None the less, I served the Gods!

A DRIFTER OFF TARENTUM°

He from the wind-bitten north with ship and companions
    descended,
  Searching for eggs of death spawned by invisible hulls.°
Many he found and drew forth. Of a sudden the fishery ended
  In flame and a clamorous breath not new to the eye-pecking gulls.

DESTROYERS IN COLLISION

For Fog and Fate no charm is found
  To lighten or amend.
I, hurrying to my bride, was drowned—
  Cut down by my best friend.

CONVOY ESCORT

I was a shepherd to fools
  Causelessly bold or afraid.
They would not abide by my rules.
  Yet they escaped. For I stayed.

UNKNOWN FEMALE CORPSE

Headless, lacking foot and hand,
Horrible I come to land.
I beseech all women's sons
Know I was a mother once.

RAPED AND REVENGED

One used and butchered me: another spied
Me broken—for which thing a hundred died.
So it was learned among the heathen hosts
How much a freeborn woman's favour costs.

SALONIKAN GRAVE°

I have watched a thousand days
Push out and crawl into night
Slowly as tortoises.
Now I, too, follow these.
It is fever, and not fight—
Time, not battle—that slays.

THE BRIDEGROOM

Call me not false, beloved,
    If, from thy scarce-known breast
So little time removed,
    In other arms I rest.

For this more ancient bride
    Whom coldly I embrace
Was constant at my side
    Before I saw thy face.

Our marriage, often set—
    By miracle delayed—   10
At last is consummate,
    And cannot be unmade.

Live, then, whom Life shall cure,
    Almost, of Memory,
And leave us to endure
    Its immortality.

V. A. D. (MEDITERRANEAN)°

Ah, would swift ships had never been, for then we ne'er had found,
These harsh Ægean rocks between, this little virgin drowned,°
Whom neither spouse nor child shall mourn, but men she nursed through pain
And—certain keels for whose return the heathen look in vain.

A Death-Bed

'This is the State above the Law.
    The State exists for the State alone.'°
[*This is a gland at the back of the jaw,*
    And an answering lump by the collar-bone.]

Some die shouting in gas or fire;
 Some die silent, by shell and shot.
Some die desperate, caught on the wire;
 Some die suddenly. This will not.

'Regis suprema Voluntas lex'°
 [*It will follow the regular course of—throats.*] 10
Some die pinned by the broken decks,
 Some die sobbing between the boats.

Some die eloquent, pressed to death
 By the sliding trench, as their friends can hear.
Some die wholly in half a breath.
 Some—give trouble for half a year.

'There is neither Evil nor Good in life
 Except as the needs of the State ordain.'
[*Since it is rather too late for the knife,
 All we can do is to mask the pain.*] 20

Some die saintly in faith and hope—
 One died thus in a prison-yard—
Some die broken by rape or the rope;
 Some die easily. This dies hard.

'I will dash to pieces who bar my way.
 Woe to the traitor! Woe to the weak!'
[*Let him write what he wishes to say.
 It tires him out if he tries to speak.*]

Some die quietly. Some abound
 In loud self-pity. Others spread 30
Bad morale through the cots around . . . °
 This is a type that is better dead.

'The war was forced on me by my foes.
 All that I sought was the right to live.'
[*Don't be afraid of a triple dose;
 The pain will neutralize half we give.*

Here are the needles. See that he dies
While the effects of the drug endure . . .
What is the question he asks with his eyes?—
Yes, All–Highest, to God, be sure.]
40

Justice
October 1918

Across a world where all men grieve
And grieving strive the more,
The great days range like tides and leave
Our dead on every shore.
Heavy the load we undergo,
And our own hands prepare,
If we have parley with the foe,
The load our sons must bear.

Before we loose the word
That bids new worlds to birth,
10
Needs must we loosen first the sword
Of Justice upon earth;
Or else all else is vain
Since life on earth began,
And the spent world sinks back again
Hopeless of God and Man.

A people and their King
Through ancient sin grown strong,
Because they feared no reckoning
Would set no bound to wrong;
20
But now their hour is past,
And we who bore it find
Evil Incarnate held at last
To answer to mankind.

For agony and spoil
Of nations beat to dust,
For poisoned air and tortured soil
And cold, commanded lust,

And every secret woe
  The shuddering waters saw—   30
Willed and fulfilled by high and low—
  Let them relearn the Law.

That when the dooms are read,
  Not high nor low shall say:—
'My haughty or my humble head
  Has saved me in this day.'
That, till the end of time,
  Their remnant shall recall
Their fathers' old, confederate crime
  Availed them not at all.   40

That neither schools nor priests,
  Nor Kings may build again
A people with the heart of beasts
  Made wise concerning men.°
Whereby our dead shall sleep
  In honour, unbetrayed,
And we in faith and honour keep
  That peace for which they paid.

The Changelings

Or ever the battered liners sank
  With their passengers to the dark,
I was head of a Walworth Bank,°
  And you were a grocer's clerk.°

I was a dealer in stocks and shares,°
  And you in butters and teas,
And we both abandoned our own affairs
  And took to the dreadful seas.

Wet and worry about our ways—
  Panic, onset, and flight—   10
Had us in charge for a thousand days
  And a thousand-year-long night.

We saw more than the nights could hide—
   More than the waves could keep—
And—certain faces over the side
   Which do not go from our sleep.

We were more tired than words can tell
   While the pied craft fled by,°
And the swinging mounds of the Western swell
   Hoisted us Heavens-high . . .   20

Now there is nothing—not even our rank—
   To witness what we have been;
And I am returned to my Walworth Bank,
   And you to your margarine!

The Vineyard

At the eleventh hour he came,
But his wages were the same
As ours who all day long had trod
The wine-press of the Wrath of God.

When he shouldered through the lines
Of our cropped and mangled vines,
His unjaded eye could scan
How each hour had marked its man.

(Children of the morning-tide
With the hosts of noon had died;   10
And our noon contingents lay
Dead with twilight's spent array.)

Since his back had felt no load,
Virtue still in him abode;
So he swiftly made his own
Those last spoils we had not won.

We went home, delivered thence,
Grudging him no recompense
Till he portioned praise or blame
To our works before he came.

20

Till he showed us for our good—
   Deaf to mirth, and blind to scorn—
How we might have best withstood
   Burdens that he had not borne!

LAURENCE BINYON
(1869–1943)

━━

LAURENCE BINYON was Keeper of Prints and Drawings at the British Museum; scholar of British, Japanese, and Persian art; a Red Cross volunteer in a military hospital at the Western Front; champion of Isaac Rosenberg's poetry during the 1920s; Norton Professor at Harvard in the early 1930s; author of more than a dozen volumes of poetry; translator of *The Divine Comedy*; and friend of Ezra Pound, Walter Sickert, Lucien Pissarro, Edmund Dulac, and countless other literary and artistic figures of the day. He wrote many poems of the War, as well as a prose account of wartime Red Cross activity, titled *For Dauntless France* (1918). Yet despite these accomplishments, he is now best known as the author of a single poem quoted round the world each year on Remembrance Day: 'For the Fallen'. The fourth stanza is read and memorized, chiselled on tombstones, and recited as the 'Ode of Remembrance' across much of the English-speaking world.

━━

For the Fallen

With proud thanksgiving, a mother for her children,
England mourns for her dead across the sea.
Flesh of her flesh they were, spirit of her spirit,
Fallen in the cause of the free.

Solemn the drums thrill: Death august and royal
Sings sorrow up into immortal spheres.
There is music in the midst of desolation
And a glory that shines upon our tears.

They went with songs to the battle, they were young,
Straight of limb, true of eye, steady and aglow.   10
They were staunch to the end against odds uncounted,
They fell with their faces to the foe.

They shall grow not old, as we that are left grow old:
Age shall not weary them, nor the years condemn.°
At the going down of the sun and in the morning
We will remember them.

They mingle not with their laughing comrades again;
They sit no more at familiar tables of home;
They have no lot in our labour of the day-time;
They sleep beyond England's foam.   20

But where our desires are and our hopes profound,
Felt as a well-spring that is hidden from sight,
To the innermost heart of their own land they are known
As the stars are known to the Night;

As the stars that shall be bright when we are dust
Moving in marches upon the heavenly plain,
As the stars that are starry in the time of our darkness,
To the end, to the end, they remain.

CHARLOTTE MEW
(1869–1928)

━━

BORN in Bloomsbury, London, in 1869, Mew was the third child of an architect, Frederick Mew, and his wife, Anna Maria. Her childhood was devastated by losses of various kinds: the early deaths of three siblings were followed by the institutionalization of two others suffering from mental illness. For the first half of her writing career, Mew focused almost exclusively on prose, her greatest success having been to place a short story in *The Yellow Book* alongside works by Henry James, John Davidson, and Aubrey Beardsley. Most of her surviving poetry dates from 1912 and later. She published only one poetry collection, *The Farmer's Bride* (1916, expanded 1921), although further poems appeared posthumously in *The Rambling Sailor* (1929). Despite this meagre output, Mew won the admiration of Virginia Woolf, May Sinclair, Siegfried Sassoon, and Thomas Hardy (who called her 'far and away the best living woman poet').[1] Despairing after the death from cancer of her beloved sister Anne, Mew committed suicide in 1928.

Mew's poetry has proven hard to place. Neither Georgian nor Modernist, it has been described by Angela Leighton as 'practically the end of the road of Victorian women's poetry' because of its indebtedness to predecessors such as Emily Brontë and Christina Rossetti.[2] But Mew's prosody is uniquely her own, and the line lengths of 'The Cenotaph'—ranging between four syllables and twenty-three—demonstrate her radical experimentation with accentual-syllabic metre.

Mew wrote three poems overtly about the War. Unmarried, and having by then lost all her brothers, she had 'no men to give'; her poems dwell on the innocent children and the suffering wives and mothers. Mew invokes, but can no longer place absolute faith in, the healing powers of seasonal renewal.

[1] Quoted by Penelope Fitzgerald, *Charlotte Mew and Her Friends*, 181.
[2] Angela Leighton, 'Charlotte Mew (1869–1928)', in *Victorian Women Poets: An Anthology*, ed. Angela Leighton and Margaret Reynolds (Oxford: Blackwell, 1995), 646.

━━

May, 1915

Let us remember Spring will come again
To the scorched, blackened woods, where all the wounded trees
Wait, with their old wise patience for the heavenly rain,
Sure of the sky: sure of the sea to send its healing breeze,
    Sure of the sun. And even as to these
      Surely the Spring, when God shall please
    Will come again like a divine surprise
To those who sit to-day with their great Dead, hands in their
      hands, eyes in their eyes,
At one with Love, at one with Grief: blind to the scattered things
      and changing skies.

June, 1915

Who thinks of June's first rose to-day?°
    Only some child, perhaps, with shining eyes and rough bright
      hair will reach it down
In a green sunny lane, to us almost as far away
    As are the fearless stars from these veiled lamps of town.°
What's little June to a great broken world with eyes gone dim
From too much looking on the face of grief, the face of dread?
    Or what's the broken world to June and him
Of the small eager hand, the shining eyes, the rough bright head?

The Cenotaph

Not yet will those measureless fields be green again
Where only yesterday the wild sweet blood of wonderful youth
    was shed;
There is a grave whose earth must hold too long, too deep a stain,
Though for ever over it we may speak as proudly as we may tread.
But here, where the watchers by lonely hearths from the thrust of
    an inward sword have more slowly bled,

We shall build the Cenotaph: Victory, winged, with Peace, winged
  too, at the column's head.°
And over the stairway, at the foot—oh! here, leave desolate,
  passionate hands to spread
Violets, roses, and laurel, with the small sweet twinkling country
  things
Speaking so wistfully of other Springs
From the little gardens of little places where son or sweetheart
  was born and bred.   10
In splendid sleep, with a thousand brothers
          To lovers—to mothers
          Here, too, lies he:
Under the purple, the green, the red,
It is all young life: it must break some women's hearts to see
Such a brave, gay coverlet to such a bed!
Only, when all is done and said,
God is not mocked and neither are the dead.°
For this will stand in our Market-place—
          Who'll sell, who'll buy   20
          (Will you or I
Lie each to each with the better grace)?
While looking into every busy whore's and huckster's face°
As they drive their bargains, is the Face
Of God: and some young, piteous, murdered face.

ROBERT SERVICE
(1874–1958)

━━

ROBERT SERVICE was born in Preston to Scottish parents. Although he kept his British passport throughout his life, in 1895 he emigrated to Canada, and became famous as 'the Bard of the Yukon' because of the extraordinary popularity of verse like 'The Shooting of Dan McGrew' and 'The Cremation of Sam McGee'. *Songs of a Sourdough* (1907), his first volume, is estimated to have sold more than three million copies.

In 1913 Service married a Frenchwoman, and he was living in Paris when war broke out. After an unsuccessful attempt to enlist, he became a war reporter for Canadian newspapers and joined the American Red Cross as an ambulance driver and stretcher bearer. He described events with unflinching honesty: 'The skin of [the burned soldier] is a bluish colour and cracked open in ridges. I am sorry I saw him. After this, when they put the things that once were men into my car I will turn away my head.' The editor of the *Toronto Daily Star* chose not to print that passage; the *Ottawa Journal* went ahead, and incurred the Canadian censor's wrath.

While convalescing from these traumatic experiences, Service wrote *Rhymes of a Red Cross Man* (1916). The volume was dedicated to his brother Albert, who had been killed in August 1916 while fighting in the Canadian infantry.

━━

Tipperary Days

Oh, weren't they the fine boys! You never saw the beat of them,
Singing all together with their throats bronze-bare;
Fighting-fit and mirth-mad, music in the feet of them,
Swinging on to glory and the wrath out there.
Laughing by and chaffing by, frolic in the smiles of them,°
On the road, the white road, all the afternoon;

Strangers in a strange land, miles and miles and miles of them,°
Battle-bound and heart-high, and singing this tune:

> *It's a long way to Tipperary,*
> *It's a long way to go;*   10
> *It's a long way to Tipperary,*
> *And the sweetest girl I know.*
> *Good-bye to Piccadilly,*
> *Farewell, Lester Square:*
> *It's a long, long way to Tipperary,*
> *But my heart's right there.°*

Come, Yvonne and Juliette! Come, Mimi, and cheer for them!
Throw them flowers and kisses as they pass you by.
Aren't they the lovely lads! Haven't you a tear for them
Going out so gallantly to dare and die?   20
What is it they're singing so? Some high hymn of Motherland?
Some immortal chanson of their Faith and King?
Marseillaise or Brabançon, anthem of that other land,°
Dears, let us remember it, that song they sing:—

> *'C'est un chemin long "to Tepararee,"*
> *C'est un chemin long, c'est vrai;*
> *C'est un chemin long "to Tepararee,"*
> *Et la belle fille qu'je connais.*
> *Bonjour, Peekadeely!*
> *Au revoir, Lestaire Square!*   30
> *C'est un chemin long "to Tepararee,"*
> *Mais mon coeur "ees zaire."'°*

The gallant old 'Contemptibles!' There isn't much remains of them,°
So full of fun and fitness, and a-singing in their pride;
For some are cold as clabber and the corby picks the brains of them,°
And some are back in Blighty, and a-wishing they had died.°
And yet it seems but yesterday, that great, glad sight of them,
Swinging on to battle as the sky grew black and black;
But oh their glee and glory, and the great, grim fight of them!—
Just whistle Tipperary and it all comes back: 40

> *It's a long way to Tipperary*
> *(Which means "'ome' anywhere);*

It's a long way to Tipperary
(And the things wot make you care).
Good-bye, Piccadilly
('Ow I 'opes my folks is well);
It's a long, long way to Tipperary—
('R! Ain't War just 'ell?)

Only a Boche

We brought him in from between the lines: we'd better have let
     him lie;
For what's the use of risking one's skin for a *tyke* that's going
     to die?°
What's the use of tearing him loose under a gruelling fire,
When he's shot in the head, and worse than dead, and all messed
     up on the wire?

However, I say, we brought him in. *Diable!* The mud was bad;°
The trench was crooked and greasy and high, and oh, what a time
     we had!
And often we slipped, and often we tripped, but never he made
     a moan;
And how we were wet with blood and with sweat! but we carried
     him in like our own.

Now there he lies in the dug-out dim, awaiting the ambulance,
And the doctor shrugs his shoulders at him, and remarks 'he
     hasn't a chance.'   10
And we squat and smoke at our game of bridge on the glistening,
     straw-packed floor,
And above our oaths we can hear his breath deep-drawn in a kind
     of snore.

For the dressing station is long and low, and the candles gutter dim,
And the mean light falls on the cold clay walls and our faces bristly
     and grim;
And we flap our cards on the lousy straw, and we laugh and jibe as
     we play,

And you'd never know that the cursed foe was less than a mile away.
As we con our cards in the rancid gloom, oppressed by that snoring
    breath,°
You'd never dream that our broad roof-beam was swept by the
    broom of death.

Heigh-ho! My turn for the dummy hand; I rise and I stretch a bit;°
The fetid air is making me yawn, and my cigarette's unlit,   20
So I go to the nearest candle flame, and the man we brought
    is there,
And his face is white in the shabby light, and I stand at his feet and
    stare.
Stand for awhile, and quietly stare, for strange though it seems
    to be,
The dying Boche on the stretcher there has a queer resemblance
    to me.

It gives one a kind of a turn, you know, to come on a thing like that.
It's just as if I were lying there, with a turban of blood for a hat,
Lying there in a coat grey-green instead of a coat grey-blue,°
With one of my eyes all shot away, and my brain half tumbling
    through;
Lying there with a chest that heaves like a bellows up and down,
And a cheek as white as snow on a grave, and lips that are coffee
    brown.   30

And confound him, too! He wears like me on his finger a wedding
    ring,
And around his neck, as around my own, by a greasy bit of string,
A locket hangs with a woman's face, and I turn it about to see:
Just as I thought . . . on the other side the faces of children three;
Clustered together cherub-like three little laughing girls,
With the usual tiny rosebud mouths and the usual silken curls.
'Zut!' I say. 'He has beaten me; for me, I have only two,'°
And I push the locket beneath his shirt, feeling a little blue.

Oh, it isn't cheerful to see a man, the marvellous work of God,
Crushed in the mutilation mill, crushed to a smeary clod;   40
Oh, it isn't cheerful to hear him moan; but it isn't that I mind,

It isn't the anguish that goes with him, it's the anguish he leaves
   behind.
For his going opens a tragic door that gives on a world of pain,
And the death he dies, those who live and love, will die again and
   again.

So here I am at my cards once more, but it's kind of spoiling my play,
Thinking of those three brats of his so many a mile away.
War is war, and he's only a Boche, and we all of us take our chance;
But all the same I'll be mighty glad when I'm hearing the
   ambulance.
One foe the less, but all the same I'm heartily glad I'm not
The man who gave him his broken head, the sniper who fired the
   shot.   50

No trumps you make it, I think you said? You'll pardon me if I err;
For a moment I thought of other things . . . *Mon Dieu! Quelle vache
de guerre.*°

Tri-colour

Poppies, you try to tell me, glowing there in the wheat;
Poppies! Ah no! You mock me: It's blood, I tell you, it's blood.
It's gleaming wet in the grasses; it's glist'ning warm in the wheat;
It dabbles the ferns and the clover; it brims in an angry flood;°
It leaps to the startled heavens; it smothers the sun; it cries
With scarlet voices of triumph from blossom and bough and blade.
See, the bright horror of it! It's roaring out of the skies,
And the whole red world is a-welter . . . Oh God! I'm afraid!
   I'm afraid!°

Cornflowers, you say, just cornflowers, gemming the golden grain;
Ah no! You can't deceive me. Can't I believe my eyes?   10
Look! It's the dead, my comrades, stark on the dreadful plain,
All in their dark-blue blouses, staring up at the skies.°
Comrades of canteen laughter, dumb in the yellow wheat.
See how they sprawl and huddle! See how their brows are white!
Goaded on to the shambles, there in death and defeat . . .
Father of Pity, hide them! Hasten, O God, Thy night!

Lilies (the light is waning), only lilies you say,
Nestling and softly shining there where the spear-grass waves.
No, my friend, I know better; brighter I see than day:
It's the poor little wooden crosses over their quiet graves.   20
Oh, how they're gleaming, gleaming! See! Each cross has a crown.
Yes, it's true I am dying; little will be the loss . . .
Darkness . . . but look! In Heaven a light, and it's shining down . . .
God's accolade! Lift me up, friends. I'm going to win—*my Cross*.

EDWARD THOMAS

(1878–1917)

EDWARD THOMAS wrote all his significant poetry between December 1914 and his death at the Battle of Arras on Easter Monday, 9 April 1917. Until that late transformation he had considered himself a 'doomed hack', driven by financial pressures that sometimes sank him into suicidal depression. He had married while still a student at Oxford, and after graduation he struggled to earn a precarious living to support his family by feverishly producing books and reviews on any subject that paid—from Swinburne's poetry to biographies of historical figures to the beauties of the English or Welsh landscape. His reviews alone total more than one million words.

Recent critics have preferred to downplay the distinction between Thomas's prose writings and his breakthrough into poetry. There is an obvious continuity of preoccupations, centred on the natural world, country life, seasonal cycles, and ideas of nationhood. However, after such a long gestation it required extraordinary circumstances to bring about their birth. Chief among them was Thomas's friendship with the American poet Robert Frost, beginning when they first met in October 1913 and strengthened the following April by Thomas's three celebratory reviews of Frost's second volume, *North of Boston*. A month later, Thomas asked if Frost could imagine him writing poetry. 'I referred him to paragraphs in his travel book, *In Pursuit of Spring*,' Frost later recalled, 'and told him to write it in verse form in exactly the same cadence.'[1] Finally, on 3 December 1914, Thomas wrote 'Up in the Wind', to be followed by a poem a day for the next four days, another five poems that same month, and seventeen poems during January. His *Collected* contains 144 poems.

Despite being over age and in mediocre health, Thomas enlisted with the Artists' Rifles in July 1915. Ten months previously, he had described the sudden revelation that would lead him to France: 'it seemed to me that either I had never loved England, or I had loved it

---

[1] Quoted by Elizabeth Sergeant, *Robert Frost: The Trial by Existence* (New York: Holt, Rinehart and Winston, 1960), 136.

foolishly, aesthetically, like a slave, not having realised that it was not mine unless I were willing and prepared to die rather than leave it as Belgian women and old men and children had left their country'.[2] Even so, Thomas was given the opportunity to serve without fighting: he spent many months at a training camp in Essex, teaching map-reading skills to officer recruits, among whom may have been Wilfred Owen. Having declined an invitation to join the permanent staff, Thomas took a commission with the Royal Artillery and was sent to France in late January 1917. Little more than two months later, at Vimy Ridge, he was killed instantly by a shell blast.

Thomas wrote no poetry from or about the trenches. His work prefers to show the effects of war on the home front among familiar landscapes: the fallen tree unmoved, the flowers unpicked. In doing so, it sets itself in opposition to the kind of war poetry that Thomas deplored, the worst of which was written 'for an audience: there is more in it of the shouting of rhetorician, reciter, or politician, than of the talk of friends and lovers'.[3] His reaction to the 'rage of gladness' which war provoked was horror: as he confessed in 'This is no case of petty right or wrong', 'I hate not Germans, nor grow hot | With love of Englishmen, to please newspapers.' Love of England—a form of self-love—was the only justification for fighting: 'She is all we know and live by'. 'Do you know what you are fighting for?', Thomas's friend Eleanor Farjeon had asked him during a countryside walk. 'He stopped, and picked up a pinch of earth. "Literally, for this". He crumbled it between finger and thumb, and let it fall.'[4]

[2] Edward Thomas, 'This England', *The Last Sheaf* (London: Jonathan Cape, 1928), 221.
[3] 'Anthologies and Reprints', in *Poetry and Drama*, 2 (1914), 384.
[4] Eleanor Farjeon, *Edward Thomas: The Last Four Years* (London: Oxford University Press, 1958), 154.

A Private

This ploughman dead in battle slept out of doors
Many a frosty night, and merrily
Answered staid drinkers, good bedmen, and all bores:
'At Mrs Greenland's Hawthorn Bush,' said he,°
'I slept.' None knew which bush. Above the town,
Beyond 'The Drover', a hundred spot the down°
In Wiltshire. And where now at last he sleeps°
More sound in France—that, too, he secret keeps.

The Owl

Downhill I came, hungry, and yet not starved;
Cold, yet had heat within me that was proof
Against the North wind; tired, yet so that rest
Had seemed the sweetest thing under a roof.

Then at the inn I had food, fire, and rest,
Knowing how hungry, cold, and tired was I.
All of the night was quite barred out except
An owl's cry, a most melancholy cry

Shaken out long and clear upon the hill,
No merry note, nor cause of merriment,   10
But one telling me plain what I escaped
And others could not, that night, as in I went.

And salted was my food, and my repose,
Salted and sobered, too, by the bird's voice°
Speaking for all who lay under the stars,
Soldiers and poor, unable to rejoice.

In Memoriam (Easter, 1915)

The flowers left thick at nightfall in the wood
This Eastertide call into mind the men,
Now far from home, who, with their sweethearts, should
Have gathered them and will do never again.

This is no case of petty right or wrong

This is no case of petty right or wrong
That politicians or philosophers
Can judge. I hate not Germans, nor grow hot
With love of Englishmen, to please newspapers.
Beside my hate for one fat patriot
My hatred of the Kaiser is love true:—°
A kind of god he is, banging a gong.
But I have not to choose between the two,
Or between justice and injustice. Dinned
With war and argument I read no more   10
Than in the storm smoking along the wind
Athwart the wood. Two witches' cauldrons roar.°
From one the weather shall rise clear and gay;
Out of the other an England beautiful
And like her mother that died yesterday.
Little I know or care if, being dull,
I shall miss something that historians
Can rake out of the ashes when perchance
The phoenix broods serene above their ken.°
But with the best and meanest Englishmen   20
I am one in crying, God save England, lest
We lose what never slaves and cattle blessed.°
The ages made her that made us from the dust:
She is all we know and live by, and we trust
She is good and must endure, loving her so:
And as we love ourselves we hate her foe.

Rain

Rain, midnight rain, nothing but the wild rain
On this bleak hut, and solitude, and me°
Remembering again that I shall die
And neither hear the rain nor give it thanks
For washing me cleaner than I have been
Since I was born into this solitude.
Blessed are the dead that the rain rains upon:
But here I pray that none whom once I loved
Is dying tonight or lying still awake
Solitary, listening to the rain,   10
Either in pain or thus in sympathy
Helpless among the living and the dead,
Like a cold water among broken reeds,
Myriads of broken reeds all still and stiff,
Like me who have no love which this wild rain
Has not dissolved except the love of death,°
If love it be towards what is perfect and
Cannot, the tempest tells me, disappoint.

Roads

I love roads:
The goddesses that dwell
Far along invisible
Are my favourite gods.

Roads go on
While we forget, and are
Forgotten like a star
That shoots and is gone.

On this earth 'tis sure
We men have not made   10
Anything that doth fade
So soon, so long endure:

The hill road wet with rain
In the sun would not gleam
Like a winding stream
If we trod it not again.

They are lonely
While we sleep, lonelier
For lack of the traveller
Who is now a dream only.   20

From dawn's twilight
And all the clouds like sheep
On the mountains of sleep
They wind into the night.

The next turn may reveal
Heaven: upon the crest
The close pine clump, at rest
And black, may Hell conceal.

Often footsore, never
Yet of the road I weary,   30
Though long and steep and dreary
As it winds on for ever.

Helen of the roads,
The mountain ways of Wales
And the Mabinogion tales,
Is one of the true gods,°

Abiding in the trees,
The threes and fours so wise,
The larger companies,
That by the roadside be,   40

And beneath the rafter
Else uninhabited
Excepting by the dead:
And it is her laughter

At morn and night I hear
When the thrush cock sings
Bright irrelevant things,
And when the chanticleer°

Calls back to their own night
Troops that make loneliness   50
With their light footsteps' press,
As Helen's own are light.

Now all roads lead to France
And heavy is the tread
Of the living; but the dead
Returning lightly dance:

Whatever the road bring
To me or take from me,
They keep me company
With their pattering,   60

Crowding the solitude
Of the loops over the downs,
Hushing the roar of towns
And their brief multitude.

The Cherry Trees

The cherry trees bend over and are shedding
On the old road where all that passed are dead,
Their petals, strewing the grass as for a wedding
This early May morn when there is none to wed.

No one cares less than I

'No one cares less than I,
Nobody knows but God,
Whether I am destined to lie
Under a foreign clod,'
Were the words I made to the bugle call in the morning.

But laughing, storming, scorning,
Only the bugles know
What the bugles say in the morning,
And they do not care, when they blow
The call that I heard and made words to early this morning.   10

As the team's head-brass

As the team's head-brass flashed out on the turn°
The lovers disappeared into the wood.
I sat among the boughs of the fallen elm
That strewed an angle of the fallow, and°
Watched the plough narrowing a yellow square
Of charlock. Every time the horses turned°
Instead of treading me down, the ploughman leaned
Upon the handles to say or ask a word,
About the weather, next about the war.
Scraping the share he faced towards the wood,°   10
And screwed along the furrow till the brass flashed
Once more.
              The blizzard felled the elm whose crest
I sat in, by a woodpecker's round hole,
The ploughman said. 'When will they take it away?'
'When the war's over.' So the talk began—
One minute and an interval of ten,
A minute more and the same interval.
'Have you been out?' 'No.' 'And don't want to, perhaps?'
'If I could only come back again, I should.
I could spare an arm. I shouldn't want to lose   20
A leg. If I should lose my head, why, so,
I should want nothing more . . . Have many gone°
From here?' 'Yes.' 'Many lost?' 'Yes: a good few.
Only two teams work on the farm this year.
One of my mates is dead. The second day
In France they killed him. It was back in March,
The very night of the blizzard, too. Now if
He had stayed here we should have moved the tree.'
'And I should not have sat here. Everything

Would have been different. For it would have been   30
Another world.' 'Ay, and a better, though
If we could see all all might seem good.' Then
The lovers came out of the wood again:
The horses started and for the last time
I watched the clods crumble and topple over
After the ploughshare and the stumbling team.

The Trumpet

Rise up, rise up,
And, as the trumpet blowing
Chases the dreams of men,
As the dawn glowing
The stars that left unlit
The land and water,
Rise up and scatter
The dew that covers
The print of last night's lovers—
Scatter it, scatter it!   10

While you are listening
To the clear horn,
Forget, men, everything
On this earth newborn,
Except that it is lovelier
Than any mysteries.
Open your eyes to the air
That has washed the eyes of the stars
Through all the dewy night:
Up with the light,   20
To the old wars;
Arise, arise!

WILFRID GIBSON

(1878–1962)

━━━

ALTHOUGH largely forgotten today, Wilfrid Gibson was admired by many of the important soldier–poets of the War. Gurney, Sassoon, Owen, Graves, and Rosenberg praised his work, and several of them learned how to write in an unheroic style about war from his early example. Gibson's *Battle* (1915) was among the first volumes of poetry to convey the actualities of the War as experienced by common soldiers. This required a profound act of imagination: because of ill health, he never saw active service.

Gibson was born in Hexham, and started writing verse under the tutelage of an elder sister. He was nothing if not prolific, publishing more than thirty volumes of poems and verse-plays during his career. The war years inspired his best work, but the origins of his achievement can be traced to aesthetic decisions taken in the previous decade. Gibson had a 'horror of ultra-poetic words', and in volumes like *The Stonefolds* (1907) he sought to expose social injustice by writing plainly for and about the 'inarticulate poor'.

Gibson moved to London in 1912, and was instrumental in establishing the popular and influential *Georgian Poetry* anthologies, which were published under Edward Marsh's editorship between 1912 and 1922. As one of only five poets to be represented in all five anthologies, he found that his reputation became entwined with the status of Georgian poetry (to his great cost after the War, when the triumph of Modernism seemed complete). In 1913 he went to Dymock in north Gloucestershire, and there helped to form a community of poets that briefly included Robert Frost, Edward Thomas, Lascelles Abercrombie, and Rupert Brooke. That community was scattered by the War, but Gibson kept writing, and his first *Battle* poems started to appear as early as October 1914. Many were short, unembellished lyrics based on newspaper accounts (see 'Breakfast'), or stories he had heard from returning soldiers. Gibson worried that he might be 'just making copy of the bloody business', but he told Edward Marsh that he wanted the poems 'to get at

people' by highlighting the War's personal tragedies in a language
freed from patriotic afflatus.[1]

   Myopic, almost over age, and suffering from underlying health prob-
lems, Gibson tried to enlist at least four times from the end of 1915
to August 1916, but was turned down repeatedly. He spent the first
half of the following year on a successful reading tour of the United
States; after his return, he was considered fit enough to join the Army
Service Corps Motor Transport, and he passed the rest of the War in
London carrying out packing and clerical work. His war poetry con-
tinued to appear, in *Friends* (1916), *Livelihood* (1917), *Whin* (1918),
and *Neighbours* (1920). The best of these demonstrated Gibson's
ability to convey psychological states beyond his own experience:
'Strawberries', for example, is a character study that captures a wife's
anxiety for her soldier husband, while 'Between the Lines', a late
addition to the manuscript of *Battle*, situates its disorientated
protagonist in no-man's-land. Rarely would Gibson's poetry reach
these heights after the War. As he wrote to Frost in 1934, 'I am one
of those unlucky writers whose books have predeceased him.'[2]

   [1] Quoted by Dominic Hibberd, *Harold Monro and Wilfrid Gibson*, 19.
   [2] Quoted by Lesley Lee Francis, *Robert Frost: An Adventure in Poetry*, rev. edn. (New
Brunswick: Transaction Publishers, 2004), 190.

━━━━

The Messages

'I cannot quite remember . . . There were five
Dropt dead beside me in the trench—and three
Whispered their dying messages to me . . .'

Back from the trenches, more dead than alive,
Stone-deaf and dazed, and with a broken knee,
He hobbled slowly, muttering vacantly:

'I cannot quite remember . . . There were five
Dropt dead beside me in the trench, and three
Whispered their dying messages to me . . .

'Their friends are waiting, wondering how they thrive— 10
Waiting a word in silence patiently . . .
But what they said, or who their friends may be

'I cannot quite remember . . . There were five
Dropt dead beside me in the trench—and three
Whispered their dying messages to me . . .'

Breakfast

We ate our breakfast lying on our backs,
Because the shells were screeching overhead.
I bet a rasher to a loaf of bread
That Hull United would beat Halifax°
When Jimmy Stainthorp played full-back instead
Of Billy Bradford. Ginger raised his head
And cursed, and took the bet; and dropt back dead.
We ate our breakfast lying on our backs,
Because the shells were screeching overhead.

Hit

Out of the sparkling sea
I drew my tingling body clear, and lay
On a low ledge the livelong summer day,
Basking, and watching lazily
White sails in Falmouth Bay.°

My body seemed to burn
Salt in the sun that drenched it through and through
Till every particle glowed clean and new
And slowly seemed to turn
To lucent amber in a world of blue . . . °   10

I felt a sudden wrench—
A trickle of warm blood—
And found that I was sprawling in the mud
Among the dead men in the trench.

Between the Lines

When consciousness came back, he found he lay
Between the opposing fires, but could not tell
On which hand were his friends; and either way
For him to turn was chancy—bullet and shell
Whistling and shrieking over him, as the glare
Of searchlights scoured the darkness to blind day.
He scrambled to his hands and knees ascare,°
Dragging his wounded foot through puddled clay,
And tumbled in a hole a shell had scooped
At random in a turnip-field between   10
The unseen trenches where the foes lay cooped
Through that unending battle of unseen,
Dead-locked, league-stretching armies; and quite spent
He rolled upon his back within the pit,
And lay secure, thinking of all it meant—
His lying in that little hole, sore hit,
But living, while across the starry sky
Shrapnel and shell went screeching overhead—
Of all it meant that he, Tom Dodd, should lie
Among the Belgian turnips, while his bed . . .   20

If it were he, indeed, who'd climbed each night,
Fagged with the day's work, up the narrow stair,
And slipt his clothes off in the candle-light,
Too tired to fold them neatly on a chair
The way his mother'd taught him—too dog-tired
After the long day's serving in the shop,
Inquiring what each customer required,
Politely talking weather, fit to drop . . .

And now for fourteen days and nights, at least,
He hadn't had his clothes off, and had lain   30
In muddy trenches, napping like a beast
With one eye open, under sun and rain
And that unceasing hell-fire . . .
                              It was strange
How things turned out—the chances! You'd just got

To take your luck in life, you couldn't change
Your luck.
        And so here he was lying shot
Who just six months ago had thought to spend
His days behind a counter. Still, perhaps . . .
And now, God only knew how he would end!

He'ld like to know how many of the chaps   40
Had won back to the trench alive, when he
Had fallen wounded and been left for dead,
If any! . . .
      This was different, certainly,
From selling knots of tape and reels of thread
And knots of tape and reels of thread and knots
Of tape and reels of thread and knots of tape,
Day in, day out, and answering 'Have you got's
And 'Do you keep's, till there seemed no escape
From everlasting serving in a shop,
Inquiring what each customer required,   50
Politely talking weather, fit to drop,
With swollen ankles, tired . . .
            But he was tired
Now. Every bone was aching, and had ached
For fourteen days and nights in that wet trench—
Just duller when he slept than when he waked—
Crouching for shelter from the steady drench
Of shell and shrapnel . . .
         That old trench, it seemed
Almost like home to him. He'd slept and fed
And sung and smoked in it, while shrapnel screamed
And shells went whining harmless overhead—   60
Harmless, at least, as far as he . . .
            But Dick—
Dick hadn't found them harmless yesterday,
At breakfast, when he'd said he couldn't stick
Eating dry bread, and crawled out the back way,
And brought them butter in a lordly dish—
Butter enough for all, and held it high,
Yellow and fresh and clean as you could wish—

When plump upon the plate from out the sky
A shell fell bursting . . . Where the butter went,
God only knew! . . .
                        And Dick . . . He dared not think   70
Of what had come to Dick . . . or what it meant—
The shrieking and the whistling and the stink
He'd lived in fourteen days and nights. 'Twas luck
That he still lived . . . And queer how little then
He seemed to care that Dick . . . Perhaps 'twas pluck
That hardened him—a man among the men—
Perhaps . . . Yet, only think things out a bit,
And he was rabbit-livered, blue with funk!°
And he'd liked Dick . . . and yet when Dick was hit,
He hadn't turned a hair. The meanest skunk   80
He should have thought would feel it when his mate
Was blown to smithereens—Dick, proud as punch,
Grinning like sin, and holding up the plate—
But he had gone on munching his dry hunch,°
Unwinking, till he swallowed the last crumb.

Perhaps 'twas just because he dared not let
His mind run upon Dick, who'd been his chum.
He dared not now, though he could not forget.

Dick took his luck. And, life or death, 'twas luck
From first to last; and you'd just got to trust   90
Your luck and grin. It wasn't so much pluck
As knowing that you'd got to, when needs must,
And better to die grinning . . .
                        Quiet now
Had fallen on the night. On either hand
The guns were quiet. Cool upon his brow
The quiet darkness brooded, as he scanned
The starry sky. He'd never seen before
So many stars. Although, of course, he'd known
That there were stars, somehow before the war
He'd never realised them—so thick-sown,   100
Millions and millions. Serving in the shop,
Stars didn't count for much; and then at nights

Strolling the pavements, dull and fit to drop,
You didn't see much but the city lights.
He'd never in his life seen so much sky
As he'd seen this last fortnight. It was queer
The things war taught you. He'd a mind to try
To count the stars—they shone so bright and clear.
One, two, three, four . . . Ah, God, but he was tired . . .
Five, six, seven, eight . . .

                Yes, it was number eight.   110
And what was the next thing that she required?
(Too bad of customers to come so late,
At closing-time!) Again within the shop
He handled knots of tape and reels of thread,
Politely talking weather, fit to drop . . .

When once again the whole sky overhead
Flared blind with searchlights, and the shriek of shell
And scream of shrapnel roused him. Drowsily
He stared about him wondering. Then he fell
Into deep dreamless slumber.

           *   *   *   *   *

                He could see   120
Two dark eyes peeping at him, ere he knew
He was awake, and it again was day—
An August morning burning to clear blue.
The frightened rabbit scuttled . . .

                Far away,
A sound of firing . . . Up there, in the sky
Big dragon-flies hung hovering . . . Snowballs burst
About them . . .
          Flies and snowballs! With a cry
He crouched to watch the airmen pass—the first
That he'd seen under fire. Lord, that was pluck—
Shells bursting all about them—and what nerve!   130
They took their chance, and trusted to their luck.
At such a dizzy height to dip and swerve,
Dodging the shell-fire . . .

                    Hell! but one was hit,
And tumbling like a pigeon, plump . . .
                           Thank Heaven,
It righted, and then turned; and after it
The whole flock followed safe—four, five, six, seven,
Yes, they were all there safe. He hoped they'ld win
Back to their lines in safety. They deserved,
Even if they were Germans . . . 'Twas no sin
To wish them luck. Think how that beggar swerved   140
Just in the nick of time!
                  He, too, must try
To win back to the lines, though, likely as not,
He'ld take the wrong turn: but he couldn't lie
Forever in that hungry hole and rot,
He'd got to take his luck, to take his chance
Of being sniped by foes or friends. He'ld be
With any luck in Germany or France
Or Kingdom-come, next morning . . .
                          Drearily
The blazing day burnt over him. Shot and shell
Whistling and whining ceaselessly. But light   150
Faded at last, and as the darkness fell
He rose, and crawled away into the night.

Strawberries

Since four she had been plucking strawberries:
And it was only eight now; and the sun
Already blazing. There'ld be little ease
For her until the endless day was done . . .
Yet, why should she have any ease, while he—
While he . . .
                 But there, she mustn't think of him,
Fighting beneath that burning sun, maybe,—
His rifle nigh red-hot, and every limb
Aching for sleep, the sweat dried on his brow,
And baking in the blaze, and such a thirst,   10

Prickly and choking, she could feel it now
In her own throat. He'd said it was the worst,
In his last letter, worst of all to bear,
That burning thirst—that, and the hellish noise . . .

And she was plucking strawberries: and there
In the cool shadow of the elm their boys,
Their baby-boys, were sleeping quietly . . .

But she was aching too: her head and back
Were one hot blinding ache; and dizzily
Sometimes across her eyes the light swam black   20
With dancing spots of red . . .
                              So ripe and sweet
Among their fresh green leaves the strawberries lay,
Although the earth was baking in the heat,
Burning her soles—and yet the summer day
Was young enough!
                  If she could only cram
A handful of fresh berries sweet and cool
Into his mouth, while he . . .
                          A red light swam
Before her eyes . . .
                  She mustn't think, poor fool,
What he'ld be doing now, or she'ld go crazed . . .
Then what would happen to them left alone—   30
The little lads!
              And he would be fair mazed,°
When he came back, to see how they had grown,
William and Dick, and how they talked. Two year,
Since he had gone—and he had never set
His eyes upon his youngest son. 'Twas queer
To think he hadn't seen his baby yet,—
And it nigh fourteen months old.
                              Everything
Was queer in these days. She could never guess
How it had come about that he could bring
Himself to go and fight. 'Twas little less   40
Than murder to have taken him, and he

So mild and easy-tempered, never one
For drink or picking quarrels hastily . . .
And now he would be fighting in that sun . . .
'Twas quite beyond her. Yet, somehow, it seemed
He'd got to go. She couldn't understand . . .
When they had married, little had they dreamed
What things were coming to! In all the land
There was no gentler husband . . .
                              It was queer:
She couldn't get the rights of it, no way.   50
She thought and thought, but couldn't get it clear
Why he'd to leave his own work—making hay
'Twould be this weather—leave his home, and all—
His wife and his young family, and go
To fight in foreign lands, and maybe fall,
Fighting another lad he didn't know,
And had no quarrel with . . .
                              The world was mad,
Or she was going crazy. Anyhow
She couldn't see the rights of it . . . Her lad°
Had thought it right to go, she knew . . .
                              But now   60
She mustn't think about it all . . . And so
She'd best stop puzzling, and pluck strawberries . . .

And every woman plucking in the row
Had husband, son, or brother overseas.

Men seemed to see things differently: and still
She wondered sore if even they knew why
They went themselves, almost against their will . . .

But sure enough, that was her baby's cry.
'Twas feeding time: and she'ld be glad to rest
Her back a bit. It always gave her ease,   70
To feel her baby feeding at her breast,
And pluck to go on gathering strawberries.

Otterburn

The lad who went to Flanders—°
Otterburn, Otterburn—
The lad who went to Flanders,
And never will return—

Though low he lies in Flanders,
Beneath the Flemish mud,
He hears through all his dreaming
The Otterburn in flood.

And though there be in Flanders
No clear and singing streams,   10
The Otterburn runs singing
Of summer through his dreams.

And when peace comes to Flanders,
Because it comes too late,
He'll still lie there, and listen
To the Otterburn in spate—

The lad who went to Flanders—
Otterburn, Otterburn—
The lad who went to Flanders,
And never will return.   20

Air-Raid

Night shatters in mid-heaven: the bark of guns,
The roar of planes, the crash of bombs, and all
The unshackled skiey pandemonium stuns
The senses to indifference, when a fall
Of masonry nearby startles awake,
Tingling, wide-eyed, prick-eared, with bristling hair,
Each sense within the body, crouched aware
Like some sore-hunted creature in the brake.°

Yet side by side we lie in the little room
Just touching hands, with eyes and ears that strain   10
Keenly, yet dream-bewildered, through tense gloom,
Listening, in helpless stupor of insane
Drugged nightmare panic, fantastically wild,
To the quiet breathing of our sleeping child.

MARY BORDEN
(1886–1968)

━━━

MARY BORDEN is best remembered as the author of *The Forbidden Zone* (1929), a 'collection of fragments' (as she called it) based on her experiences of running field hospitals in France during the War. She was also a prolific novelist, and after losing most of her fortune in the financial crash of 1929, she turned increasingly to fiction as a way of earning money.

Borden was born in Chicago and educated at Vassar College. She was independently wealthy, her father having made his fortune as a prospector and a property speculator. On a tour after college she met her first husband, the Scottish missionary Douglas Turner, and when he enlisted at the start of the War she volunteered as a nurse for the French Red Cross. Having given birth to her third child in November 1914, she was in Belgium the following January, speaking little French and with no nursing experience. However, she was dissatisfied with the way that the military hospital was run, and in July 1915 she established her own under French military authority. Her hospital's mortality rate, she claimed, was the lowest of the entire front. As the areas of intense fighting moved, so Borden pleaded to relocate, and in October 1916 she founded a new hospital near Bray-sur-Somme. The three parts of 'At the Somme' were written there, and the prose of *The Forbidden Zone* (withheld from publication in 1917 because of the concerns of military censors) conveyed her conditions: 'Looking back, I do not understand that woman—myself—standing in that confused goods yard filled with bundles of broken human flesh. The place by one o'clock in the morning was a shambles. The air was thick with steaming sweat, with the effluvia of mud, dirt, blood.'[1]

For her medical work, sometimes carried out while the hospital was under bombardment, Borden was awarded the *Croix de guerre* and made a member of the *Légion d'honneur*. Her marriage had disintegrated during the War, and after divorce in 1918 she married Edward Louis Spears (originally Spiers), a liaison officer with the

---

[1] Borden, *The Forbidden Zone*, repr. (2008), 98.

French army, later a British MP, diplomat, and baronet. During the
Second World War, Borden set up a field hospital in France—and
barely managed to escape to England as the country was overrun—
then founded a mobile unit for the Free French in Palestine and
Egypt. Even so, the memories of the French *poilus* of 1914–1918
endured: 'I see them still, marching up the long roads of France in
their clumsy boots and their heavy grey-blue coats that were too big
for them; dogged, patient, steady men, plodding to death in defence
of their land. I shall never forget them.'[2]

[2] Quoted by Hazel Hutchison, 'Introduction', in Borden, *The Forbidden Zone* (repr. 2008), p. xvi.

At the Somme[1]

WHERE IS JEHOVAH?

Where is Jehovah, the God of Israel, with his Ark and his
    Tabernacle and his Pillars of Fire?°
He ought to be here—This place would suit him.
Here is a people pouring through a wilderness—
Here are armies camping in a desert—
Their little tents are like sheep flocking over the prairie—
It's all in the style of the God of Israel.
Here is a land that was silent and desolate, suddenly covered with
    noise and confusion,
The wide, white plains and the shallow grey valleys are smeared
    over with the disorder of armies.
Picardy is shaking with a fever,°
Picardy's hills are wounded and broken,   10
Picardy's fields are scarred as with small-pox—
What a chance for His prophets!
What a playground for miracles!
A host of men at the end of their strength, fighting death, fighting
    terror, with no one to worship—
He need but lift his finger—
Here are all his pet properties ready to hand, the thunder, the
    lightning, the clouds and the fire—

[1] Under the Tricolour [Borden's note]

This is His hour, but Jehovah has missed it.
This is not His thunder nor His lightning—
These are not His people—
These are the armies of France and of England—   20
The thunder is the thunder of their guns, and the lightning that
   runs along the horizon is the flare and the flash of the battle
   that's raging; Moses is dead—and Joshua, who led His people
   into the promised land, is dead, and there are no more prophets
   to cry through the wilderness to comfort these people—°
They must look after themselves.
All the host of them, each one of them, quite alone each one of
   them, every one of the hundred thousand of them, alone, must
   stand up to meet the war.
With the sky cracking—
With creatures of wide metal wings tearing the sky over his head—°
With the earth shaking—
With the solid earth under his feet giving way—
With the hills covered with fire and the valleys smoking, and the
   few bare trees spitting bullets, and the long roads like liquid
   torrents, rolling up with guns and munitions and men, always
   men and more men, with these long roads rolling up like a
   river to drown him and no way of escape.
With the few houses broken, no walls, no enclosure, no protection.
With all of the universe crushing upon him, rain, sun, cold, dark,
   death, coming full on him.   30
With the men near him going mad, jibbering, bleeding, twisting,
With his comrade lying dead under his feet,
With the enemy beyond there, unseen, curious,
With eternity waiting, whispering to him through the noise of the
   cannon,
With the memory of his home haunting him, and the face of a
   woman who is waiting,
With the soft echoes of his children's sweet laughter sounding, and
   shells bursting with roars near him, but not drowning those voices,
He stands there.
He keeps on standing. He stands solid.
He is so small in the landscape as to be almost invisible. We see
   him as a speck there—
He is dirty. He is tired. His stomach is empty—   40

He is stupid. His life has been stupid—
He has lived a few years without understanding,
He does not understand now—he will never understand—
He is bigger than all the world.
He is more important than all the army.
He is more terrible than all the war.
He stands there—

*   *   *   *   *

But where is Jehovah, the God of the great drama, the God of
    Vengeance, the Lord of Hosts?°
Here the scene is set for His acting—a desert, a promised land,
    a nation in agony waiting—
Jehovah's not here—   50
There's only a man standing,—quite still.

THE SONG OF THE MUD

This is the song of the mud,
The pale yellow glistening mud that covers the naked hills like satin,
The grey gleaming silvery mud that is spread like enamel over the
    valleys,
The frothing, squirting, spurting liquid mud that gurgles along the
    road-beds,
The thick elastic mud that is kneaded and pounded and squeezed
    under the hoofs of horses,
The invincible, inexhaustible mud of the War Zone.

This is the song of the mud, the uniform of the *poilu*.°
His coat is of mud, his poor great flapping coat that is too big for
    him and too heavy,
His coat that once was blue, and now is grey and stiff with the mud
    that cakes it.
This is the mud that clothes him—   10
His trousers and boots are of mud—
And his skin is of mud—
And there is mud in his beard.
His head is crowned with a helmet of mud,
And he wears it—oh, he wears it well!

He wears it as a King wears the ermine that bores him—
He has set a new style in clothing,
He has introduced the *chic* of mud.

This is the song of the mud that wriggles its way into battle,
The impertinent, the intrusive, the ubiquitous, the unwelcome.   20
The slimy, inveterate nuisance,
That fills the trenches,
That mixes in with the food of the soldiers,
That spoils the working of motors and crawls into their
    secret parts,
That spreads itself over the guns,
That sucks the guns down and holds them fast in its slimy,
    voluminous lips,
That has no respect for destruction and muzzles the bursting
    of shells,
And slowly, softly, easily,
Soaks up the fire, the noise, soaks up the energy and the courage,
Soaks up the power of armies,   30
Soaks up the battle—
Just soaks it up and thus stops it.

This is the song of the mud, the obscene, the filthy, the putrid,
The vast liquid grave of our Armies—
It has drowned our men—
Its monstrous distended belly reeks with the undigested dead—
Our men have gone down into it, sinking slowly, and struggling
    and slowly disappearing.
Our fine men, our brave, strong young men,
Our glowing, red, shouting, brawny men,
Slowly, inch by inch, they have gone down into it.   40
Into its darkness, its thickness, its silence,
Relentlessly it drew them down, sucking them down,
They have been drowned there in thick, bitter, heaving mud—
It hides them—oh, so many of them!
Under its smooth glistening surface it is hiding them blandly,
There is not a trace of them—
There is no mark where they went down.
The mute, enormous mouth of the mud has closed over them.

This is the song of the mud,
The beautiful, glistening, golden mud that covers the hills
 like satin;   50
The mysterious, gleaming, silvery mud that is spread like enamel
 over the valleys.
Mud, the fantastic disguise of the War Zone;
Mud, the extinguishing mantle of battles;
Mud, the smooth, fluid grave of our soldiers.
This is the song of the mud.

THE HILL

From the top of the hill I looked down upon the marvellous
 landscape of the war, the beautiful, the romantic landscape of
 the superb, exulting war.
The crests of the wide surging hills were golden, and the red tents
 clustering on their naked sides were like flowers in a shining
 desert of hills.
It was evening. The long shallow valley was bathed in blue shadow,
 and through the shadow, as if swimming, I saw the armies moving.
The long convoys of their motors passed down the road, an
 endless line of mysterious energy rolling, and the troops
 spreading over the wide basin of the valley people the wilderness
 with a phantom host.
Camp fires gleamed down there.
The sun was setting, and against the brilliant sky, along the clear crest
 of the hills to the west, a regiment of cavalry went filing. A flock of
 aeroplanes was flying home with a great whirring of proud wings.
Dizzy with the marvellous spectacle of the war, I looked down
 across the rough foreground that dropped away in darkness
 beneath my feet.
A path, the deserted way of peaceful cattle, showed below, beyond
 the gaping caverns of abandoned trenches, and along the path a
 German prisoner was coming, driven by a black man on a horse.
The black man wore a turban, and he drove the prisoner before him
 as one drives an animal to market.
The German stumbled on heavily beneath the nose of his captor's
 horse. I could see the pallid disc of his face thrust forward and
 the exhausted lurching of his clumsy body. I could feel the
 heaviness of his despair.   10

Along the path that he travelled were piles of rubbish, old
  shell-cases, and boots, and battered helmets.
Two wooden crosses showed, sticking out of the rough ground.
And as I watched him disappear beneath the hill it seemed to me that
  his hate was like a curse crawling through the grave of our nation.
But beyond, in the deepening shadow of the valley, the marvellous
  spectacle of invincible phantom armies moved, as if swimming; and
  as I watched I heard, through the echoing of the guns, the faint
  crying music of bagpipes; the song of an unseen regiment marching.
The crests of the surging hills were still golden, and above the
  slumbering exultation of the prodigious war the fragile crescent
  of the new moon hung serene in the perfect sky.

Unidentified

Look well at this man. Look!
Come up out of your graves, philosophers,
And you who founded churches, and all you
Who for ten thousand years have talked of God.
Come up out of your silent, sheltering tombs
You scientists who died unsatisfied,
For you have something interesting to learn
By looking at this man.
Stand all about, you many legioned ghosts!
He will not notice you.
Fill up the desert with your shadowy forms,   10
And in this vast resounding waste of death
Be for him an unseen retinue,
For he is going to die.

Look at his ugliness.
See how he stands there, planted in the mud like some old battered
  image of a faith forgotten by its God.
Look at his grizzled head jammed up into that round, close hat
  of iron.
See how he hunches up his shoulders;
How his spine is bent under his clumsy coat like the hard bending
  of a taut strung bow;

And how he leans, gripping with grimy fists the muzzle of his gun
    that digs its butt end down into the mud between the solid
    columns of his legs.   20
Look close—come close, pale ghosts,
Come back out of the dim unfinished past,
Crowd up across the edges of the earth
Where the horizon like a red-hot wire writhes, smoking, underneath
    tremendous blows.
Come up, come up across the quaking ground that gapes in sudden
    holes beneath your feet—
Come fearlessly across the twisting field where bones of men stick
    through the tortured mud.
Ghosts have no need to fear,
Look close at this man—Look!

He waits for death—
He knows—   30
He watches it approach—
He hears it coming—
He can feel it underneath his feet—
Death bearing down on him from every side,
Violent death, death that tears the sky to shrieking pieces,
Death that suddenly explodes out of the dreadful bowels of
    the earth.
He hears it screaming through the frantic air,
He hears it burrowing underneath the ground,
He feels the impact of it on his back, his chest, his legs, his belly,
    and his arms,
He does not move.   40
In all the landscape there is just one thing that does not move,
The figure of the man.

The sky long since has fallen from its dome.
Terror let loose like a gigantic wind has torn it from the ceiling of
    the world
And it is flapping down in frantic shreds.
The earth, ages ago, leaped screaming up; out of the fastness of its
    ancient laws,
There is no centre now to hold it down;

It rolls and writhes, a shifting, tortured thing, a floating mass of
    matter, set adrift.
And in between the flapping, suffering remnants of the sky and the
    convulsions of the maddened earth
The man stands solid.   50
Something holds him there.

What holds him, timid ghosts?
What do you say, you shuddering spirits dragged from secure vaults?
You who once died in kindly quiet rooms,
You who were companioned to the end by friends,
And closed your eyes in languor on a world
That you had fashioned for your peaceful selves?

Some of you scorned this man.
He was for you the ordinary man.
You thought him pitiable; contemptible or worse;   60
You gave him idols, temples, formulas of conduct, prisons, laws;
Some of you pitied him, and wept over his sins.
Some were horrified at what you called his passions, lust of women,
    food, drink, laughter, all such simple things.
And some of you were afraid;
Wanted to beat him down, break his spirit,
Muzzle his ideas, and bind with bands of hopelessness his energy.
None of you trusted him—
No! Not a single one of you trusted him.
Look at him now. Look well—look long.
Your giant—your brute—your ordinary man—   70
Your fornicator, drunkard, anarchist,
Your ruthless, seed-sowing male,
Your covetous and greedy egoist,
Come close and look into his haggard face.
It is too late to do him justice now.

But look!—look at the stillness of that face
Made up of little fragile bones and flesh,
Tissued of quivering muscles, fine as silk,
Exquisite nerve endings and scarlet blood
That travels smoothly through the tender veins;   80

One blow—one moment more—and that man's face will be
  a mass of matter, horrid slime—and little brittle bits—
He knows—
He waits—
His face remains quite still.
And underneath the bullet-spattered helmet on his head his steady
  eyes look out.
What is it that looks out?
What is there mirrored there in those deep, bloodshot eyes?
Terror? No!
Despair? Perhaps.
But what else?   90
Ah, poor ghosts—poor, blind, unseeing ghosts—
It is his self you see—His self that does remember what he loved
  and what he wanted, and what he never had—His self that can
  regret, that can reproach his own self now—His self that gave
  its self, let loose its hold of all but just its self—
Is that then nothing, just his naked self, inviolate; pinning down
  a shaking world like a single nail that holds;
A single rivet driven down to hold a universe together—

Go back, poor ghosts—go back into your graves.
He has no need of you, this nameless man.
You philosophers, you scientists, you men of God, leave this man
  alone.
Leave him the grandeur of obscurity,
Leave in darkness the dumb anguish of his soul.
Leave him the great loss of his identity.   100
Let the guns chant his death-song down the world;
Let the flare of cannon light his dying;
Let those remnants of men beneath his feet welcome him mutely
  when he falls beside them in the mud.
Take one last look and leave him standing there,
Unfriended—Unrecognised—Unrewarded and Unknown.

SIEGFRIED SASSOON
(1886–1967)

BORN in Kent and educated at Marlborough and Cambridge—which he left without completing his degree—Sassoon in pre-war years lived the life of a country gentleman. His favourite pursuits were hunting and cricket. He kept his homosexuality secret, and his poetry hardly less so, although he did publish pamphlets of verse privately. One of these came to the attention of Edward Marsh, who had recently edited the first Georgian poetry anthology, and it was through Marsh that Sassoon met Rupert Brooke—younger but more accomplished, it seemed, in almost every way. Sassoon's dissatisfaction with his own life was a factor in the decision to enlist: he joined the Sussex Yeomanry on the day that Britain declared war on Germany. By the following May, he had transferred to the Royal Welch Fusiliers. That was to have momentous consequences for his poetry, because in November 1915 began the first of his important literary friendships, when he was introduced to a fellow officer of the regiment, Robert Graves.

Sassoon's relationship with Graves would descend into decades-long acrimony after the War, but at the time he credited his new ally with teaching him how to write naturally and idiomatically. Graves had seen action, and had tried to write realistically about his experiences; Sassoon's poetry, by contrast, had seemed to consist chiefly of *fin-de-siècle* dreaminess. It was not until early 1916 that Sassoon began to write what he called his 'outspoken' war poems. After the death of David Thomas—a friend from Cambridge days, with whom he was in love—Sassoon finally saw fighting in March, and was awarded the Military Cross for rescuing an injured soldier under heavy fire. This was the first glimpse of 'Mad Jack' Sassoon: he swore that 'since they shot [David] I would gladly stick a bayonet into a German by daylight'.[1] The next month, after attending a lecture on the use of the bayonet, Sassoon imagined exactly that in 'The Kiss'.

[1] Sassoon, *Diaries, 1915–1918*, 52.

The poem encapsulated divided feelings about the War, which he found 'beautiful or terrifying, or both . . . I had no idea I should enjoy it so much'.[2] At Mametz Wood in July he single-handedly emptied a German trench, shouting the hunting cry 'View Halloa!' and urged on by the ambition to 'kill someone at close quarters'.[3] Yet these episodes of extraordinary derring-do came in the same week as Sassoon's poem 'A Night Attack', with its agonized description of a dead Prussian 'with a decent face' who had no doubt 'loathed the war and longed for peace'.

In the poems he wrote subsequently—many of them while recovering from a bullet wound high in his back—it was less often the realities of war that angered Sassoon than the complacency, ignorance, and jingoism that he encountered on leave. *The Old Huntsman* (1917) contained few enough of these denunciations to avoid controversy, but Sassoon by now considered himself a pacifist, and aided by Bertrand Russell and John Middleton Murry, in June 1917 he wrote his 'Declaration' against the conduct of the War as 'an act of wilful defiance of military authority'. Sassoon argued that a negotiated peace was available, and that the 'fighting men' were being sacrificed by politicians for whom the War had become an opportunity for conquest, not liberation. Worst of all was the 'callous complacence with which the majority of those at home regard the continuance of the agonies which they do not share, and which they have not sufficient imagination to realise'.[4] In July he sent the 'Declaration' to his commanding officer, stating that he would refuse any further military duties. Most of Sassoon's friends—soldiers and civilians alike—were appalled, and several decades later Sassoon wondered whether his protest had been a way of becoming 'martyrised' without being 'sent to the front again'.[5] Rather than court-martialling him, a medical board decided that Sassoon was suffering from a nervous breakdown, and sent him to Craiglockhart War Hospital near Edinburgh. There, in August, he met Wilfred Owen.

Sassoon's friendship with Owen proved far more important to the younger, and still unpublished, poet than to him. As mentor and editor, Sassoon showed Owen how to write realistically about

[2] Quoted by Max Egremont, *Siegfried Sassoon*, 91.
[3] Sassoon, *Memoirs of an Infantry Officer*, 93.
[4] Sassoon, *Diaries, 1915–1918*, 173–4.
[5] Quoted by Max Egremont, *Siegfried Sassoon*, 144–5.

war—just as Graves had previously shown Sassoon—but he was slow to recognize his protégé's genius: 'I am sure he will be a very good poet some day',[6] Sassoon wrote to Graves about Owen in November 1917. More immediately significant was Sassoon's relationship with W. H. R. Rivers, the psychiatrist who treated him and became a father figure. A paper by Rivers on the treatment of shell shock gave Sassoon the title for his poem 'Repression of War Experience', and while at Craiglockhart under Rivers's supervision he wrote much of what would become *Counter-Attack and Other Poems* (1918).

Having insisted that he would leave the army if not allowed to return to the front, Sassoon was passed fit in late November and rejoined his regiment—as part of the Egyptian Expeditionary Force—in February 1918. His war ended in France the following July, when he was shot and wounded in the head by friendly fire. He never experienced, and did not write about, the Advance to Victory.

Rupert Hart-Davis has argued that 'the First World War turned [Sassoon] from a versifier into a poet'.[7] It would hardly be unfair to suggest that after the War he reverted: the War made and marred him as a poet. The animating anger of 'On Passing the New Menin Gate' creates an all-too-rare exception to the mediocrity of his later work. Sassoon showed more flair as a writer of autobiography, but even there his account of the war years attracted the most admiration. His greatest legacy, as Max Egremont has pointed out, is to have dictated the terms by which the War has been remembered:

Sassoon's war means a callous, out-of-touch High Command and the sacrifice of innocents in the apparently ceaseless hell of the Western Front: a vision so haunting that twentieth-century British warfare still seems to be defined by futile offensives, exhausted men impaled upon wire or trapped in mud before an immovable enemy a mere few yards away across a dark, lunar landscape. More than anyone, even more than Owen, Siegfried Sassoon created this, through his poetry and his prose, turning it into one of the most resonant myths of our time.[8]

    [6] Sassoon, *Diaries, 1915–1918*, 196.
    [7] Rupert Hart-Davis, 'Sassoon, Siegfried Loraine (1886–1967)', rev. *Oxford Dictionary of National Biography*, Oxford University Press, 2004; online edn, Oct 2009 <http://www.oxforddnb.com/view/article/35953>.
    [8] Egremont, *Siegfried Sassoon*, p. xi.

The Redeemer

Darkness: the rain sluiced down; the mire was deep;
It was past twelve on a mid-winter night,
When peaceful folk in beds lay snug asleep;
There, with much work to do before the light,
We lugged our clay-sucked boots as best we might
Along the trench; sometimes a bullet sang,
And droning shells burst with a hollow bang;
We were soaked, chilled and wretched, every one;
Darkness; the distant wink of a huge gun.

I turned in the black ditch, loathing the storm;   10
A rocket fizzed and burned with blanching flare,
And lit the face of what had been a form
Floundering in mirk. He stood before me there;°
I say that He was Christ; stiff in the glare,
And leaning forward from his burdening task,
Both arms supporting it; His eyes on mine
Stared from the woeful head that seemed a mask
Of mortal pain in Hell's unholy shine.

No thorny crown, only a woollen cap°
He wore—an English soldier, white and strong,   20
Who loved his time like any simple chap,
Good days of work and sport and homely song;
Now he has learned that nights are very long,
And dawn a watching of the windowed sky.
But to the end, unjudging, he'll endure
Horror and pain, not uncontent to die
That Lancaster on Lune may stand secure.°

He faced me, reeling in his weariness,
Shouldering his load of planks, so hard to bear.
I say that He was Christ, who wrought to bless   30
All groping things with freedom bright as air,
And with His mercy washed and made them fair.
Then the flame sank, and all grew black as pitch,
While we began to struggle along the ditch;

And someone flung his burden in the muck,
Mumbling: 'O Christ Almighty, now I'm stuck!'

A Working Party

Three hours ago he blundered up the trench,
Sliding and poising, groping with his boots;
Sometimes he tripped and lurched against the walls
With hands that pawed the sodden bags of chalk.°
He couldn't see the man who walked in front;
Only he heard the drum and rattle of feet
Stepping along barred trench boards, often splashing°
Wretchedly where the sludge was ankle-deep.

Voices would grunt 'Keep to your right—make way!'
When squeezing past some men from the front-line: 10
White faces peered, puffing a point of red;
Candles and braziers glinted through the chinks
And curtain-flaps of dug-outs; then the gloom
Swallowed his sense of sight; he stooped and swore
Because a sagging wire had caught his neck.

A flare went up; the shining whiteness spread°
And flickered upward, showing nimble rats
And mounds of glimmering sand-bags, bleached with rain;
Then the slow silver moment died in dark.
The wind came posting by with chilly gusts   20
And buffeting at corners, piping thin.
And dreary through the crannies; rifle-shots
Would split and crack and sing along the night,
And shells came calmly through the drizzling air
To burst with hollow bang below the hill.
Three hours ago he stumbled up the trench;
Now he will never walk that road again:
He must be carried back, a jolting lump
Beyond all needs of tenderness and care.

He was a young man with a meagre wife   30
And two small children in a Midland town;°
He showed their photographs to all his mates,
And they considered him a decent chap
Who did his work and hadn't much to say,
And always laughed at other people's jokes
Because he hadn't any of his own.

That night when he was busy at his job
Of piling bags along the parapet,°
He thought how slow time went, stamping his feet
And blowing on his fingers, pinched with cold.   40
He thought of getting back by half-past twelve,
And tot of rum to send him warm to sleep
In draughty dug-out frowsty with the fumes°
Of coke, and full of snoring weary men.°

He pushed another bag along the top,
Craning his body outward; then a flare
Gave one white glimpse of No Man's Land and wire;°
And as he dropped his head the instant split
His startled life with lead, and all went out.

The Kiss

To these I turn, in these I trust—
Brother Lead and Sister Steel.
To his blind power I make appeal,
I guard her beauty clean from rust.

He spins and burns and loves the air,
And splits a skull to win my praise;
But up the nobly marching days
She glitters naked, cold and fair.

Sweet Sister, grant your soldier this:
That in good fury he may feel   10
The body where he sets his heel
Quail from your downward darting kiss.

A Night Attack

The rank stench of those bodies haunts me still,
And I remember things I'd best forget.
For now we've marched to a green, trenchless land
Twelve miles from battering guns: along the grass
Brown lines of tents are hives for snoring men;
Wide, radiant water sways the floating sky
Below dark, shivering trees. And living-clean
Comes back with thoughts of home and hours of sleep.

To-night I smell the battle; miles away
Gun-thunder leaps and thuds along the ridge;   10
The spouting shells dig pits in fields of death,
And wounded men are moaning in the woods.
If any friend be there whom I have loved,
God speed him safe to England with a gash.

It's sundown in the camp; some youngster laughs,
Lifting his mug and drinking health to all
Who come unscathed from that unpitying waste.
(Terror and ruin lurk behind his gaze.)
Another sits with tranquil, musing face,
Puffing his pipe and dreaming of the girl   20
Whose last scrawled letter lies upon his knee.
The sunlight falls, low-ruddy from the west,
Upon their heads; last week they might have died;
And now they stretch their limbs in tired content.

One says 'The bloody Bosche has got the knock;°
And soon they'll crumple up and chuck their games.
We've got the beggars on the run at last!'
    Then I remembered someone that I'd seen
Dead in a squalid, miserable ditch,
Heedless of toiling feet that trod him down.   30
He was a Prussian with a decent face,°
Young, fresh, and pleasant, so I dare to say.
No doubt he loathed the war and longed for peace,
And cursed our souls because we'd killed his friends.

One night he yawned along a half-dug trench°
Midnight; and then the British guns began
With heavy shrapnel bursting low, and 'hows'
Whistling to cut the wire with blinding din.°
   He didn't move; the digging still went on;
Men stooped and shovelled; someone gave a grunt,   40
And moaned and died with agony in the sludge.
Then the long hiss of shells lifted and stopped.

He stared into the gloom; a rocket curved,
And rifles rattled angrily on the left
Down by the wood, and there was noise of bombs.
   Then the damned English loomed in scrambling haste
Out of the dark and struggled through the wire,
And there were shouts and curses; someone screamed
And men began to blunder down the trench
Without their rifles. It was time to go: 50
He grabbed his coat; stood up, gulping some bread;
Then clutched his head and fell.
                        I found him there
In the gray morning when the place was held.
His face was in the mud; one arm flung out
As when he crumpled up; his sturdy legs
Were bent beneath his trunk; heels to the sky.

Christ and the Soldier

I

The straggled soldier halted—stared at Him—
Then clumsily dumped down upon his knees,
Gasping, 'O blessed crucifix, I'm beat!'
And Christ, still sentried by the seraphim,
Near the front-line, between two splintered trees,
Spoke him: 'My son, behold these hands and feet.'

The soldier eyed Him upward, limb by limb,
Paused at the Face; then muttered, 'Wounds like these
Would shift a bloke to Blighty just a treat!'°

Christ, gazing downward, grieving and ungrim,   10
Whispered, 'I made for you the mysteries,
Beyond all battles moves the Paraclete.'°

II

The soldier chucked his rifle in the dust,
And slipped his pack, and wiped his neck, and said—
'O Christ Almighty, stop this bleeding fight!'
Above that hill the sky was stained like rust
With smoke. In sullen daybreak flaring red
The guns were thundering bombardment's blight.

The soldier cried, 'I was born full of lust,
With hunger, thirst, and wishfulness to wed.   20
Who cares today if I done wrong or right?'
Christ asked all pitying, 'Can you put no trust
In my known word that shrives each faithful head?°
Am I not resurrection, life and light?'

III

Machine-guns rattled from below the hill;
High bullets flicked and whistled through the leaves;
And smoke came drifting from exploding shells.
Christ said, 'Believe; and I can cleanse your ill.
I have not died in vain between two thieves;°
Nor made a fruitless gift of miracles.'   30

The soldier answered, 'Heal me if you will,
Maybe there's comfort when a soul believes
In mercy, and we need it in these hells.
But be you for both sides? I'm paid to kill
And if I shoot a man his mother grieves.
Does that come into what your teaching tells?'

A bird lit on the Christ and twittered gay;
Then a breeze passed and shook the ripening corn.
A Red Cross waggon bumped along the track.°

Forsaken Jesus dreamed in the desolate day—   40
Uplifted Jesus, Prince of Peace forsworn—
An observation post for the attack.

'Lord Jesus, ain't you got no more to say?'
Bowed hung that head below the crown of thorns.°
The soldier shifted, and picked up his pack,
And slung his gun, and stumbled on his way.
'O God,' he groaned, 'why ever was I born?' . . .
The battle boomed, and no reply came back.

'They'

The Bishop tells us: 'When the boys come back
They will not be the same; for they'll have fought
In a just cause: they lead the last attack
On Anti-Christ; their comrades' blood has bought
New right to breed an honourable race,
They have challenged Death and dared him face to face.'

'We're none of us the same!' the boys reply.
'For George lost both his legs; and Bill's stone blind;
Poor Jim's shot through the lungs and like to die;
And Bert's gone syphilitic: you'll not find°   10
A chap who's served that hasn't found *some* change.'
And the Bishop said: 'The ways of God are strange!'°

The Poet as Hero

You've heard me, scornful, harsh, and discontented,
    Mocking and loathing War: you've asked me why
Of my old, silly sweetness I've repented—
    My ecstasies changed to an ugly cry.°

You are aware that once I sought the Grail,
    Riding in armour bright, serene and strong;
And it was told that through my infant wail
    There rose immortal semblances of song.

But now I've said good-bye to Galahad,°
   And am no more the knight of dreams and show: 10
For lust and senseless hatred make me glad,
   And my killed friends are with me where I go.
Wound for red wound I burn to smite their wrongs;°
And there is absolution in my songs.°

'Blighters'

The House is crammed: tier beyond tier they grin°
And cackle at the Show, while prancing ranks
Of harlots shrill the chorus, drunk with din;
'We're sure the Kaiser loves our dear old Tanks!'°

I'd like to see a Tank come down the stalls,
Lurching to rag-time tunes, or 'Home, sweet Home',°
And there'd be no more jokes in Music-halls°
To mock the riddled corpses round Bapaume.°

Base Details

If I were fierce, and bald, and short of breath,
   I'd live with scarlet Majors at the Base,
And speed glum heroes up the line to death.
   You'd see me with my puffy petulant face,
Guzzling and gulping in the best hotel,
   Reading the Roll of Honour. 'Poor young chap,'°
I'd say—'I used to know his father well;
   Yes, we've lost heavily in this last scrap.'
And when the war is done and youth stone dead,
I'd toddle safely home and die—in bed.   10

The Rear-Guard

(Hindenburg Line, April 1917)

Groping along the tunnel, step by step,
He winked his prying torch with patching glare
From side to side, and sniffed the unwholesome air.

Tins, boxes, bottles, shapes too vague to know;
A mirror smashed, the mattress from a bed;
And he, exploring fifty feet below
The rosy gloom of battle overhead.

Tripping, he grabbed the wall; saw someone lie
Humped at his feet, half-hidden by a rug,
And stooped to give the sleeper's arm a tug.   10
'I'm looking for headquarters.' No reply.
'God blast your neck!' (For days he'd had no sleep,)
'Get up and guide me through this stinking place.'°

Savage, he kicked a soft, unanswering heap,
And flashed his beam across the livid face°
Terribly glaring up, whose eyes yet wore
Agony dying hard ten days before;
And fists of fingers clutched a blackening wound.

Alone he staggered on until he found
Dawn's ghost that filtered down a shafted stair   20
To the dazed, muttering creatures underground
Who hear the boom of shells in muffled sound.
At last, with sweat of horror in his hair,
He climbed through darkness to the twilight air,
Unloading hell behind him step by step.

The General

'Good-morning; good-morning!' the General said
When we met him last week on our way to the line.
Now the soldiers he smiled at are most of 'em dead,
And we're cursing his staff for incompetent swine.

'He's a cheery old card,' grunted Harry to Jack
As they slogged up to Arras with rifle and pack.°

*   *   *   *   *

But he did for them both by his plan of attack.

Repression of War Experience

Now light the candles; one; two; there's a moth;
What silly beggars they are to blunder in
And scorch their wings with glory, liquid flame—
No, no, not that,—it's bad to think of war,
When thoughts you've gagged all day come back to scare you;
And it's been proved that soldiers don't go mad
Unless they lose control of ugly thoughts
That drive them out to jabber among the trees.

Now light your pipe; look, what a steady hand.
Draw a deep breath; stop thinking; count fifteen,   10
And you're as right as rain . . .
                              Why won't it rain? . . .
I wish there'd be a thunder-storm to-night,
With bucketsful of water to sluice the dark,
And make the roses hang their dripping heads.
Books; what a jolly company they are,
Standing so quiet and patient on their shelves,
Dressed in dim brown, and black, and white, and green,
And every kind of colour. Which will you read?
Come on; O *do* read something; they're so wise.
I tell you all the wisdom of the world   20
Is waiting for you on those shelves; and yet
You sit and gnaw your nails, and let your pipe out,
And listen to the silence: on the ceiling
There's one big, dizzy moth that bumps and flutters;
And in the breathless air outside the house
The garden waits for something that delays.

There must be crowds of ghosts among the trees,—
Not people killed in battle,—they're in France,—
But horrible shapes in shrouds—old men who died
Slow, natural deaths,—old men with ugly souls,   30
Who wore their bodies out with nasty sins.

*   *   *   *   *

You're quiet and peaceful, summering safe at home;
You'd never think there was a bloody war on! . . .
O yes, you would . . . why, you can hear the guns.
Hark! Thud, thud, thud,—quite soft . . . they never cease—
Those whispering guns—O Christ, I want to go out
And screech at them to stop—I'm going crazy;
I'm going stark, staring mad because of the guns.

Counter-Attack

We'd gained our first objective hours before
While dawn broke like a face with blinking eyes,
Pallid, unshaved and thirsty, blind with smoke.
Things seemed all right at first. We held their line,
With bombers posted, Lewis guns well placed,°
And clink of shovels deepening the shallow trench.
  The place was rotten with dead; green clumsy legs
  High-booted, sprawled and grovelled along the saps
  And trunks, face downward, in the sucking mud,
  Wallowed like trodden sand-bags loosely filled;   10
  And naked sodden buttocks, mats of hair,
  Bulged, clotted heads slept in the plastering slime.
  And then the rain began,—the jolly old rain!

A yawning soldier knelt against the bank,
Staring across the morning blear with fog;
He wondered when the Allemands would get busy;°
And then, of course, they started with five-nines°
Traversing, sure as fate, and never a dud.°

Mute in the clamour of shells he watched them burst
Spouting dark earth and wire with gusts from hell,   20
While posturing giants dissolved in drifts of smoke.
He crouched and flinched, dizzy with galloping fear,
Sick for escape,—loathing the strangled horror
And butchered, frantic gestures of the dead.

An officer came blundering down the trench:
'Stand–to and man the fire–step!' On he went . . . °
Gasping and bawling, 'Fire–step . . . counter–attack!'
    Then the haze lifted. Bombing on the right
    Down the old sap: machine–guns on the left;°
    And stumbling figures looming out in front.   30
    'O Christ, they're coming at us!' Bullets spat,
And he remembered his rifle . . . rapid fire . . .
And started blazing wildly . . . then a bang
Crumpled and spun him sideways, knocked him out
To grunt and wriggle: none heeded him; he choked
And fought the flapping veils of smothering gloom,
Lost in a blurred confusion of yells and groans . . .
Down, and down, and down, he sank and drowned,
Bleeding to death. The counter–attack had failed.

How to Die

    Dark clouds are smouldering into red
        While down the craters morning burns.°
    The dying soldier shifts his head
        To watch the glory that returns;
    He lifts his fingers toward the skies
        Where holy brightness breaks in flame;
    Radiance reflected in his eyes,
        And on his lips a whispered name.

    You'd think, to hear some people talk,
        That lads go West with sobs and curses,°   10
    And sullen faces white as chalk,
        Hankering for wreaths and tombs and hearses.

But they've been taught the way to do it
    Like Christian soldiers; not with haste
And shuddering groans, but passing through it
    With due regard for decent taste.

Glory of Women

You love us when we're heroes, home on leave,
Or wounded in a mentionable place.
You worship decorations; you believe
That chivalry redeems the war's disgrace.
You make us shells. You listen with delight,°
By tales of dirt and danger fondly thrilled.°
You crown our distant ardours while we fight,
And mourn our laurelled memories when we're killed.
You can't believe that British troops 'retire'
When hell's last horror breaks them, and they run,   10
Trampling the terrible corpses—blind with blood.
    O German mother dreaming by the fire,
    While you are knitting socks to send your son
    His face is trodden deeper in the mud.

Everyone Sang

Everyone suddenly burst out singing;
And I was filled with such delight
As prisoned birds must find in freedom,
Winging wildly across the white
Orchards and dark-green fields; on—on—and out of sight.

Everyone's voice was suddenly lifted;
And beauty came like the setting sun:
My heart was shaken with tears; and horror
Drifted away . . . O, but Everyone
Was a bird; and the song was wordless; the singing will never be
    done.   10

On Passing the New Menin Gate

Who will remember, passing through this Gate,
The unheroic Dead who fed the guns?
Who shall absolve the foulness of their fate,—
Those doomed, conscripted, unvictorious ones?
   Crudely renewed, the Salient holds its own.°
   Paid are its dim defenders by this pomp;
   Paid, with a pile of peace-complacent stone,
   The armies who endured that sullen swamp.

Here was the world's worst wound. And here with pride
'Their name liveth for ever,' the Gateway claims.°   10
Was ever an immolation so belied°
As these intolerably nameless names?
Well might the Dead who struggled in the slime
Rise and deride this sepulchre of crime.

RUPERT BROOKE
(1887–1915)

UNDOUBTEDLY the most influential and renowned of the soldier–poets during the War and for several decades afterwards, Rupert Brooke has come to be characterized as the naïve voice of 1914, patriotic and innocent. This does him a considerable disservice. Brooke knew more than most of his contemporaries about war, having been present at the siege and fall of Antwerp. The five sonnets that comprise '1914' constitute Brooke's rallying cry to a nation which, he wrote in November of that year, did not yet realize 'what we're in for, and what great sacrifices—active or passive—everyone must make'.[1]

Of all the soldier–poets, Brooke alone had built a literary reputation before the War. He was educated at Rugby and King's College, Cambridge, where he read Classics. However, his passion was for English literature, especially Elizabethan and Jacobean drama; and primarily on the strength of his dissertation on John Webster he was appointed to a fellowship at King's in 1913. He had already published his first volume of poetry in 1911, and was instrumental in establishing the Georgian poetry anthologies under the editorship of Edward Marsh. The first and second of these featured his work prominently.

Brooke had a genius for friendship, which brought into his orbit Winston Churchill, Virginia Stephen (later Woolf), E. M. Forster, Frances Cornford, the Asquiths, and poets such as Wilfrid Gibson and Edward Thomas. He was also a great traveller: he spent the first few months of 1911 in Munich, in the unfulfilled hope of improving his German, and returned to Germany twice before the War; and a year of travel beginning in May 1913 saw visits to Canada, the United States, and the South Pacific. His affair with a woman in Tahiti produced some of his finest poetry and—although biographers are not certain—probably a daughter. Small wonder that when Siegfried

[1] Brooke, *The Letters of Rupert Brooke*, 629.

Sassoon met Brooke in July 1914 he was 'agog with excitement': 'his idea of adventure was to go half across the world and write vividly about it, while mine was to go somewhere in Warwickshire, gallop after a pack of hounds, and stop being a writer altogether!'[2]

The complexity of Brooke's relationships with women—he was always passionately in love with several at the same time—prompted regular crises in his mental health. Early in 1912 he suffered what his Harley Street doctor described as a 'severe mental breakdown'. The War offered a distraction: 'If Armageddon is *on*, I suppose one should be there.'[3] Exploiting his friendship with Winston Churchill, Brooke was granted a commission in a new unit of Churchill's own devising: the Royal Naval Division, an amphibious unit designed to be conveyed by sea and to fight on land. Its first task, in October 1914, was to reinforce Antwerp against German advance, but its failure under the weight of enemy bombardment persuaded Brooke of the necessity of total British engagement in the War. He reported the effects of what he considered to have been 'one of the greatest crimes in history': 'Hundreds of thousands of refugees, their goods on barrows and hand-carts and perambulators and wagons . . . the old men mostly weeping, the women with hard drawn faces, the children playing or crying or sleeping. That's what Belgium is now: the country where three civilians have been killed to every one soldier.' Writing the first of his famous sonnets back in England later that month, Brooke was painfully aware that, although 'incessant mechanical slaughter' had begun, Prussian militarism must be defeated: 'I've seen the half million refugees in the night'.[4]

Brooke joined the RND's Hood battalion that November, and in February 1915 his division set sail for the Dardanelles. Like his friend Patrick Shaw Stewart, he was delighted at the prospect of fighting near the plains of Troy. But the ambition was not fulfilled. Brooke became ill in April, and died on St George's Day having contracted septicaemia from a mosquito bite. He was buried the same day on the Greek island of Skyros, said to have been the birthplace of Achilles. Among his burial party were Shaw Stewart, the composer Denis Browne, and the Prime Minister's son, Oc Asquith. Churchill's obituary appeared in *The Times* three days later, celebrating a man who

[2] Quoted by Harry Ricketts, *Strange Meetings*, 13.
[3] Quoted by William E. Laskowski, *Rupert Brooke* (New York: Twayne, 1994), 27.
[4] Brooke, *The Letters of Rupert Brooke*, 632–3, 627.

'expected to die; he was willing to die for the dear England whose
beauty and majesty he knew; and he advanced to the brink in perfect
serenity, with absolute conviction of the rightness of his country's
cause'. In death, Brooke became an icon, leaving every soldier–poet
of any significance the task of confronting his legacy.

1914

I. PEACE

Now, God be thanked Who has matched us with His hour,°
   And caught our youth, and wakened us from sleeping,
With hand made sure, clear eye, and sharpened power,
   To turn, as swimmers into cleanness leaping,
Glad from a world grown old and cold and weary,
   Leave the sick hearts that honour could not move,
And half-men, and their dirty songs and dreary,
   And all the little emptiness of love!

Oh! we, who have known shame, we have found release there,°
   Where there's no ill, no grief, but sleep has mending,   10
     Naught broken save this body, lost but breath;
Nothing to shake the laughing heart's long peace there
   But only agony, and that has ending;
     And the worst friend and enemy is but Death.

II. SAFETY

Dear! of all happy in the hour, most blest°
   He who has found our hid security,
Assured in the dark tides of the world that rest,
   And heard our word, 'Who is so safe as we?'°
We have found safety with all things undying,
   The winds, and morning, tears of men and mirth,
The deep night, and birds singing, and clouds flying,
   And sleep, and freedom, and the autumnal earth.
We have built a house that is not for Time's throwing.
   We have gained a peace unshaken by pain for ever.   10

War knows no power. Safe shall be my going,
   Secretly armed against all death's endeavour;
Safe though all safety's lost; safe where men fall;
And if these poor limbs die, safest of all.

III. THE DEAD

Blow out, you bugles, over the rich Dead!
   There's none of these so lonely and poor of old,°
   But, dying, has made us rarer gifts than gold.
These laid the world away; poured out the red
Sweet wine of youth; gave up the years to be
   Of work and joy, and that unhoped serene,
   That men call age; and those who would have been,
Their sons, they gave, their immortality.

Blow, bugles, blow! They brought us, for our dearth,
   Holiness, lacked so long, and Love, and Pain.   10
Honour has come back, as a king, to earth,
   And paid his subjects with a royal wage;
And Nobleness walks in our ways again;
   And we have come into our heritage.

IV. THE DEAD

These hearts were woven of human joys and cares,
   Washed marvellously with sorrow, swift to mirth.
The years had given them kindness. Dawn was theirs,
   And sunset, and the colours of the earth.
These had seen movement, and heard music; known
   Slumber and waking; loved; gone proudly friended;
Felt the quick stir of wonder; sat alone;
   Touched flowers and furs and cheeks. All this is ended.

There are waters blown by changing winds to laughter
And lit by the rich skies, all day. And after,   10
   Frost, with a gesture, stays the waves that dance
And wandering loveliness. He leaves a white
   Unbroken glory, a gathered radiance,
A width, a shining peace, under the night.

V. THE SOLDIER

If I should die, think only this of me:
   That there's some corner of a foreign field
That is for ever England. There shall be
   In that rich earth a richer dust concealed;
A dust whom England bore, shaped, made aware,
   Gave, once, her flowers to love, her ways to roam,
A body of England's, breathing English air,
   Washed by the rivers, blest by suns of home.

And think, this heart, all evil shed away,
   A pulse in the eternal mind, no less   10
      Gives somewhere back the thoughts by England given;
Her sights and sounds; dreams happy as her day;
   And laughter, learnt of friends; and gentleness,
      In hearts at peace, under an English heaven.

[Fragment]

I strayed about the deck, an hour, to-night
Under a cloudy moonless sky; and peeped
In at the windows, watched my friends at table,
Or playing cards, or standing in the doorway,
Or coming out into the darkness. Still
No one could see me.

            I would have thought of them
—Heedless, within a week of battle—in pity,
Pride in their strength and in the weight and firmness
And link'd beauty of bodies, and pity that
This gay machine of splendour 'ld soon be broken,   10
Thought little of, pashed, scattered . . .

                 Only, always,
I could but see them—against the lamplight—pass
Like coloured shadows, thinner than filmy glass,

Slight bubbles, fainter than the wave's faint light,
That broke to phosphorus out in the night,°
Perishing things and strange ghosts—soon to die
To other ghosts—this one, or that, or I.

April 1915.

JULIAN GRENFELL
(1888–1915)

═══

JULIAN GRENFELL was the eldest son of Baron Desborough and his wife Ethel (Ettie), the leading society hostess of her day. Educated at Eton and Oxford, he excelled at sport, enjoyed boxing, and considered hunting to be his favourite pastime. After university he joined the Royal Dragoons, seeing service in India and South Africa.

Grenfell loved the experience of battle. When war broke out he was sent to France, and reported back to his parents that he had 'never felt so well, or so happy'—'The fighting-excitement vitalizes everything.'[1] His hunting expertise proved invaluable when he stalked the German lines and killed three 'Pomeranians', duly recorded in his 'game book' alongside the partridges.

'Into Battle', one of the finest and most problematic poems of the War, is a celebration of the Homeric 'fighting man'. As Elizabeth Vandiver has written, Grenfell 'excludes the Christian idea of altruistic sacrifice in favour of a deeply Homeric presentation of individual achievement in battle, where battle is its own justification and a valiant death its own reward'.[2] The poem was first published in *The Times* on 27 May 1915, the day after Grenfell had succumbed to head injuries from a shell splinter.

[1] Quoted by Viola Meynell, *Julian Grenfell* (London: Burns & Oates, 1917), 11.
[2] Vandiver, *Stand in the Trench, Achilles*, 186.

═══

Prayer for Those on the Staff

Fighting in mud, we turn to Thee,
   In these dread times of battle, Lord,
To keep us safe, if so may be,
   From shrapnel, snipers, shell, and sword.

Yet not on us—(for we are men
　　Of meaner clay, who fight in clay)—
But on the Staff, the Upper Ten,°
　　Depends the issue of the day.

The Staff is working with its brains,
　　While we are sitting in the trench,   10
The Staff the universe ordains
　　(Subject to Thee and General French).°

God, help the Staff—especially
　　The young ones, many of them sprung
From our high aristocracy;
　　Their task is hard, and they are young.

O Lord, Who mad'st all things to be,
　　And madest some things very good,
Please keep the Extra A.D.C.°
　　From horrid scenes, and sights of blood.   20

See that his eggs are newly laid,
　　Not tinged—as some of them—with green;
And let no nasty draughts invade
　　The windows of his limousine.

When he forgets to buy the bread,
　　When there are no more minerals,
Preserve his smooth well–oiled head
　　From wrath of costive generals.°

O Lord, Who mad'st all things to be
　　And hatest nothing thou hast made,   30
Please keep the Extra A.D.C.
　　Out of the sun and in the shade.

Into Battle

The naked earth is warm with spring,
And with green grass and bursting trees
Leans to the sun's kiss glorying,
And quivers in the loving breeze;
And Life is Colour and Warmth and Light,
And a striving evermore for these;
And he is dead who will not fight;
And who dies fighting has increase.

The fighting man shall from the sun
Take warmth, and life from the glowing earth;   10
Speed with the light-foot winds to run,
And with the trees a newer birth;
And when his fighting shall be done,
Great rest, and fulness after dearth.

All the bright company of Heaven
Hold him in their high comradeship—
The Dog-star, and the Sisters Seven,
Orion's Belt and sworded hip.°

The woodland trees that stand together,
They stand to him each one a friend;   20
They gently speak in the windy weather,
They guide to valley and ridge's end.

The kestrel hovering by day,
And the little owls that call by night,
Bid him be swift and keen as they—
As keen of sound, as swift of sight.

The blackbird sings to him 'Brother, brother,
If this be the last song you shall sing,
Sing well, for you will not sing another;
Brother, sing!'   30

In dreary doubtful waiting hours,
Before the brazen frenzy starts,
The horses show him nobler powers;
O patient eyes, courageous hearts!

And when the burning moment breaks,
And all things else are out of mind,
And Joy of Battle only takes
Him by the throat, and makes him blind—

Through joy and blindness he shall know,
Not caring much to know, that still   40
Nor lead nor steel shall reach him so
That it be not the Destined Will.

The thundering line of battle stands,
And in the air death moans and sings;
But Day shall clasp him with strong hands,
And Night shall fold him in soft wings.

T. P. CAMERON WILSON
(1888–1918)

T. P. CAMERON WILSON left a substantial body of work. He was the author of two novels, a long essay written 'among the entanglements of war', at least nine articles for *Punch*, some short stories, and a volume of verse—the title poem of which, 'Magpies in Picardy', has proven to be his sole claim on posterity. The only book to appear during his lifetime was his first novel, which he published under his own name; individual poems were printed under a pseudonym ('Tipuca'). Introducing *Magpies in Picardy* in 1919, his friend Harold Monro remembered that Wilson had been 'extremely shy about his verse', and was 'always disinclined to let it be seen, or discussed, by his friends'.

After Oxford, Wilson became a teacher at a prep school, but he quickly enlisted when war broke out. Serving as a Sherwood Forester in early 1915, he had already seen enough to become settled in his views: 'War is indescribably disgusting', he wrote home on 1 March, and the following year he denounced the 'picturesque phrases of war writers' which 'show nothing of the individual horror, nothing of the fine personalities smashed suddenly into red beastliness, nothing of the sick fear that is tearing at the hearts of brave boys who ought to be laughing at home'.[1]

Wilson spent some time away from the front line as a staff officer, but he returned to the Sherwood Foresters in November 1917, and was killed during the great German assault of March 1918.

[1] Quoted by Merryn Williams, *T. P. Cameron Wilson* (London: Cecil Woolf, 2006), 11–12.

Magpies in Picardy

The magpies in Picardy
Are more than I can tell.
They flicker down the dusty roads
And cast a magic spell
On the men who march through Picardy,
Through Picardy to hell.

(The blackbird flies with panic,
The swallow goes like light,
The finches move like ladies,
The owl floats by at night;   10
But the great and flashing magpie
He flies as artists might.)

A magpie in Picardy
Told me secret things—
Of the music in white feathers,
And the sunlight that sings
And dances in deep shadows—
He told me with his wings.

(The hawk is cruel and rigid,
He watches from a height;   20
The rook is slow and sombre,
The robin loves to fight;
But the great and flashing magpie
He flies as lovers might.)

He told me that in Picardy,
An age ago or more,
While all his fathers still were eggs,
These dusty highways bore
Brown singing soldiers marching out
Through Picardy to war.°   30

He said that still through chaos
Works on the ancient plan,

And two things have altered not
Since first the world began—
The beauty of the wild green earth
And the bravery of man.

(For the sparrow flies unthinking
And quarrels in his flight.
The heron trails his legs behind,
The lark goes out of sight;   40
But the great and flashing magpie
He flies as poets might.)

Song of Amiens

Lord! How we laughed in Amiens!
For here were lights and good French drink,
And Marie smiled at everyone,
And Madeleine's new blouse was pink,
And Petite Jeanne (who always runs)
Served us so charmingly, I think
That we forgot the unsleeping guns.

Lord! How we laughed in Amiens!
Till through the talk there flashed the name
Of some great man we left behind.   10
And then a sudden silence came,
And even Petite Jeanne (who runs)
Stood still to hear, with eyes aflame,
The distant mutter of the guns.

Ah! How we laughed in Amiens!
For there were useless things to buy,
Simply because Irène, who served,
Had happy laughter in her eye;
And Yvonne, bringing sticky buns,
Cared nothing that the eastern sky   20
Was lit with flashes from the guns.

And still we laughed in Amiens,
As dead men laughed a week ago.
What cared we if in Delville Wood°
The splintered trees saw hell below?
We cared . . . We cared . . . But laughter runs
The cleanest stream a man may know
To rinse him from the taint of guns.

PATRICK SHAW STEWART
(1888–1917)

PATRICK SHAW STEWART was born near Llanbedr, Gwynedd, in 1888, the fourth child of a British general. Educated at Eton and Oxford, he moved in elite circles, and numbered among his friends the Asquiths, Winston Churchill, Julian Grenfell, Rupert Brooke, and Lady Diana Manners. Despite an exhausting merry-go-round of social events, he developed a reputation as one of the most brilliant classicists of his generation, driven in part by rivalry with another friend, Ronald Knox.

Eschewing academia, Shaw Stewart seemed destined to make his fortune as a managing director at Barings Bank. But when war intervened, he enlisted as an officer in the Royal Naval Volunteer Reserve, then (with Rupert Brooke) in the Hood battalion of the Royal Naval Division. Like many public-school-educated men of his generation, he welcomed the news that he would be sent to Gallipoli: 'It is the luckiest thing and the most romantic. Think of fighting in the Chersonese . . . or alternatively, if it's the Asiatic side they want us on, on the plains of Troy itself! I am going to take my Herodotus as a guide-book.'[1] In February 1915, he embarked with his battalion on the *Grantully Castle* to the Dardanelles, and would later lead Brooke's burial party on Skyros. Shaw Stewart survived Gallipoli, but was killed by a shell at Cambrai on 30 December 1917.

'[I saw a man this morning]', Shaw Stewart's only extant poem except for some schoolboy verse, was found written on the back fly-leaf of his copy of A. E. Housman's *A Shropshire Lad* after his death.

[1] Quoted by Ronald Knox, *Patrick Shaw-Stewart* (London: Collins, 1920), 112.

[I saw a man this morning]

I saw a man this morning
    Who did not wish to die:
I ask and cannot answer,
    If otherwise wish I.

Fair broke the day this morning
    Against the Dardanelles;°
The breeze blew soft, the morn's cheeks
    Were cold as cold sea-shells.

But other shells are waiting
    Across the Aegean Sea,   10
Shrapnel and high explosive,
    Shells and hells for me.

O hell of ships and cities,
    Hell of men like me,
Fatal second Helen,
    Why must I follow thee?°

Achilles came to Troyland
    And I to Chersonese:°
He turned from wrath to battle,°
    And I from three days' peace.   20

Was it so hard, Achilles,
    So very hard to die?
Thou knewest, and I know not—
    So much the happier I.

I will go back this morning
    From Imbros over the sea;°
Stand in the trench, Achilles,
    Flame-capped, and shout for me.°

IVOR GURNEY
(1890–1937)

━━━

IVOR GURNEY, poet and composer, was born into a Gloucester family of modest means. Benefiting from the patronage of his god-father—a local vicar who gave the young boy free access to his library—Gurney became a chorister at Gloucester Cathedral, and was already composing music in his early teens. Among his Gloucestershire friends were the poet F. W. Harvey and the composer Herbert Howells. In 1911 he won a scholarship to the Royal College of Music, where he was taught by Charles Stanford. For all his obvious talents, Gurney could be obstinate and idiosyncratic: although Stanford also counted Bliss, Holst, Ireland, and Vaughan Williams among his pupils, he would later remember Gurney as potentially 'the biggest', but least teachable, of them all.[1]

Gurney fell ill in the spring of 1913, suffering from a form of depression. It may have been the first appearance of an undiagnosed mental illness which would cause him to be institutionalized less than a decade later. On this occasion, a return home to Gloucestershire brought recovery, despite severe mood swings which he endured into the following year. When war broke out Gurney volunteered immediately but was turned down because of poor eyesight. As a result of rising casualties, the authorities had become less fussy by February 1915, when Gurney successfully enlisted as a private with the Gloucesters. His motivation was to swap 'nervous exhaustion' for 'healthy' fatigue: as he told his friend, the musicologist Marion Scott, 'fatigue from body brings rest to the soul—not so mental fatigue'.[2] The discipline of military life, with its fixed schedules and regular meals, together with the comradeship of Gloucestershire soldiers who knew and loved the same landscapes, ensured that Gurney was happier during the War than before or after. This did not imply any militaristic enthusiasm: Gurney told Scott that he was not a soldier

---

[1] Quoted by Herbert Howells, 'Ivor Gurney: The Musician', *Music and Letters*, 19.1 (1938), 14.

[2] Gurney, *Collected Letters*, 36.

but a dirty civilian, and on at least one occasion he was severely reprimanded while searching for the biscuit tin during a heavy bombardment.

Gurney would not arrive in France until May 1916. By then he was writing poems in earnest; his first collection, *Severn & Somme* (1917), was politely received, but with the exception of 'Pain' it showed little originality. On Good Friday 1917 Gurney was wounded in the shoulder, his immediate response being to curse 'the double | Treachery of Fritz to Europe and to English music'. He would have to wait until later that year for the sought-after 'Blighty': in September he was gassed at Saint-Julien, and he never returned to the front. The reasons for his discharge were at least as much mental as physical: he suffered a breakdown while convalescing in early 1918, and was suicidal after his relationship with a nurse came to an end. His government pension was temporarily reduced to reflect the fact that his illness had been 'aggravated but not caused' by the War.

Gurney's second volume, *War's Embers*, appeared in 1919. Despite including what has become his best-known poem, 'To His Love', it marked no great advance on *Severn & Somme*. Yet this constituted the high point of Gurney's public career as a poet. His music continued to be performed and published: two Housman song cycles, *Ludlow and Teme* and *The Western Playland*, would appear in 1923 and 1926 respectively, and Gurney lived just long enough to see an advance copy of an edition of twenty songs published by Oxford University Press. His poetry fared less well, and was rejected repeatedly by editors in the 1920s until he gave up trying. It gradually came into print in the decades after his death, bringing Gurney proper if belated recognition as one of the most important poets of his age.

The reasons for Gurney's neglect are interlinked with his mental illness. After a return to the Royal College of Music petered out, between 1920 and 1922 he led a largely peripatetic existence, working variously as a farm labourer, a cinema pianist, and a tax officer. His family became increasingly concerned about his erratic behaviour, and he himself admitted that 'something is more wrong than formerly'. Suicidal and suffering from delusions, in 1922 he was incarcerated first at Barnwood House in Gloucester (from which he promptly escaped) and then at the City of London Mental Hospital at Dartford. The poems and letters from this time are harrowing: 'Do not leave me here, I pray . . . Death would be rest from torment.

The use of life is so far from here.'[3] He would remain at Dartford until his death from tuberculosis fifteen years later.

Gurney's productivity in the early years of his incarceration was astonishing. The single month of March 1925, for example, saw the completion of seven song settings and four volumes of poetry. These were uneven and contained inconsistencies that a good editor would have remedied, but at their strongest they rank alongside the best poetry of the war. ('The Retreat' is an extraordinary example of how the best and worst of Gurney exists side by side.) Gurney considered himself to be 'the first of the war poets', and constantly upbraided his nation for refusing to honour him.[4] Individual poems were published occasionally, courtesy of J. C. Squire at the *London Mercury*; otherwise his work went unseen except among a small group of friends who ensured its preservation. Dispirited, Gurney seems to have stopped writing after 1926 save for one or two stray poems.

[3] Gurney, *Collected Letters*, 516, 355.
[4] 'To his Lordship the Bishop of Liverpool', unpublished manuscript, Gloucestershire Archives, D10500/1/P/4/12.

━━

Pain

Pain, pain continual; pain unending;
Hard even to the roughest, but to those
Hungry for beauty . . . Not the wisest knows,
Nor most pitiful-hearted, what the wending
Of one hour's way meant. Grey monotony lending
Weight to the grey skies, grey mud where goes
An army of grey bedrenched scarecrows in rows
Careless at last of cruellest Fate-sending.
Seeing the pitiful eyes of men foredone,°
Or horses shot, too tired merely to stir,   10
Dying in shell-holes both, slain by the mud.
Men broken, shrieking even to hear a gun.—
Till pain grinds down, or lethargy numbs her,
The amazed heart cries angrily out on God.

To the Prussians of England

When I remember plain heroic strength
And shining virtue shown by Ypres pools,°
Then read the blither written by knaves for fools°
In praise of English soldiers lying at length,°
Who purely dream what England shall be made
Gloriously new, free of the old stains
By us, who pay the price that must be paid,
Will freeze all winter over Ypres plains.
Our silly dreams of peace you put aside
And Brotherhood of man, for you will see°   10
An armed Mistress, braggart of the tide
Her children slaves, under your mastery.
We'll have a word there too, and forge a knife,
Will cut the cancer threatens England's life.°

To His Love

He's gone, and all our plans°
    Are useless indeed.
We'll walk no more on Cotswold°
    Where the sheep feed
    Quietly and take no heed.

His body that was so quick
    Is not as you
Knew it, on Severn river°
    Under the blue
    Driving our small boat through.   10

You would not know him now . . .
    But still he died
Nobly, so cover him over
    With violets of pride
    Purple from Severn side.

Cover him, cover him soon!°
  And with thick-set
Masses of memoried flowers—°
  Hide that red wet
  Thing I must somehow forget.   20

The Bugle

High over London
Victory floats
And high, high, high,
Harsh bugle notes
Rend and embronze the air.°
Triumph is there
With sombre sunbeams mixed of Autumn rare.
Over and over the loud brass makes its cry,
Summons to exultancy
Of past in Victory.   10
Yet in the gray street women void of grace
Chatter of trifles
Hurry to barter, wander aimlessly
The heedless town,
Men lose their souls in care of business,
As men had not been mown
Like corn swathes East of Ypres or the Somme°
Never again home
Or beauty most beloved to see, for that
London Town might still be busy at   20
Its sordid cares
Traffic of wares.
O Town, O Town
In soldiers' faces one might see the fear
That once again they should be called to bear
Arms, and to save England from her own.

Billet

O, but the racked clear tired strained frames we had!
Tumbling in the new billet on to straw bed,
Dead asleep in eye shutting. Waking as sudden
To a golden and azure roof, a golden ratcheted
Lovely web of blue seen and blue shut, and cobwebs and tiles,
And gray wood dusty with time. June's girlish kindest smiles.
Rest at last and no danger for another week, a seven-day week.
But one Private took on himself a Company's heart to speak,
'I wish to bloody Hell I was just going to Brewery—surely°
To work all day (in Stroud) and be free at tea-time—allowed°   10
Resting when one wanted, and a joke in season,
To change clothes and take a girl to Horsepool's turning,°
Or drink a pint at "Travellers Rest", and find no cloud.
Then God and man and war and Gloucestershire would have
    a reason,
But I get no good in France, getting killed, cleaning off mud.'
He spoke the heart of all of us—the hidden thought burning,
    unturning.

First Time In

After the dread tales and red yarns of the Line°
Anything might have come to us; but the divine
Afterglow brought us up to a Welsh colony
Hiding in sandbag ditches, whispering consolatory
Soft foreign things. Then we were taken in
To low huts candle-lit shaded close by slitten°
Oilsheets, and there but boys gave us kind welcome;
So that we looked out as from the edge of home.
Sang us Welsh things, and changed all former notions
To human hopeful things. And the next days' guns   10
Nor any line-pangs ever quite could blot out
That strangely beautiful entry to War's rout,
Candles they gave us precious and shared over-rations—
Ulysses found little more in his wanderings without doubt.°

'David of the White Rock', the 'Slumber Song' so soft, and that°
Beautiful tune to which roguish words by Welsh pit boys
Are sung—but never more beautiful than here under the guns'
   noise.°

Strange Hells

There are strange Hells within the minds War made
Not so often, not so humiliatingly afraid
As one would have expected—the racket and fear guns made.
One Hell the Gloucester soldiers they quite put out;
Their first bombardment, when in combined black shout
Of fury, guns aligned, they ducked lower their heads—
And sang with diaphragms fixed beyond all dreads,
That tin and stretched-wire tinkle, that blither of tune;°
'Après la guerre fini' till Hell all had come down.°
12 inch—6 inch and 18 pounders hammering Hell's thunders.°   10

Where are they now on State-doles, or showing shop-patterns°
Or walking town to town sore in borrowed tatterns°
Or begged. Some civic routine one never learns.
The heart burns—but has to keep out of face how heart burns.

Farewell

What! to have had gas, and to expect
No more than a week's sick, and to get Blighty—°
This is the gods' gift, and not anyway exact—
To Ypres, or bad St Julien or Somme Farm.°
Don Hancox, shall I no more see your face frore,°
Gloucester-good in the first light (But you are dead!)
Shall I see no more Monger with india rubber°
Twisted face—(But machine gun caught him and his grimace.)
No more to march happy with such good comrades,
Watching the sky, the brown land, the bayonet blades   10

Moving—to muse on music forgetting the pack.
Nor to hear Gloucester with Stroud debating the lack
Of goodliness or virtue in girls or farmlands.
Nor to hear Cheltenham hurling at Cotswold demands
Of civilization; nor West Severn joking at East Severn?°
No more—across the azure and the brown lands
The morning mist, or high day clear of rack
Shall move my dear knees—or feel them frosted, shivering
By Somme or Aubers—or to have a courage from faces°
Full of all West England, Her God given graces.   20
There was not one of all that Battalion
Loved his comrades as well as I—but kept shy.
Or said in verse, what his voice would not rehearse.
So gassed I went back—to Northlands where voices speak soft as
    in verse.°
And after to meet evil not fit for the thought one touch to dwell on.°
Dear Battalion, the dead of you would not have let
Your comrade be so long—prey for the unquiet
Black evil of the unspoken and concealed pit.
You would have had me safe—dead or free happy alive.
They bruise my head and torture with their own past-hate   30
Sins of the past, and lie so as earth moves at it—°
You dead ones—I lay with you under the unbroken wires once.°

La Rime

Fritz caught a sight of a fatigue party going down—°
Probably just ended—having escaped observation,
So this offended Fritz and he let fly
With everything of powder, cordite or T.N.T.°
One did his bootlace up, one lit his pipe and cursed
Ration tobacco, and said 'Boys this is war at the worst,'
One blew his nose, one plucked at a dead nettle
Growing above the trench side—and one made rattle
The breech of his rifle in ragtime, nobody ran.°
One having written seven lines to rhyme and scan,   10
(So to say) raised his umbrella and cursed Fritz—

Who never had, nor never would produce poets,
And at the Red House, said sudden, 'I see that's the one,'°
Finished his eighth line and blasted home-critics to bits.°

Serenade

It was after the Somme, our line was quieter,°
Wires mended, neither side daring attacker
Or aggressor to be—the guns equal, the wires a thick hedge,
When there sounded, (O past days for ever confounded!)
The tune of Schubert which belonged to days mathematical,°
Effort of spirit bearing fruit worthy, actual.
The gramophone for an hour was my quiet's mocker,
Until I cried, 'Give us "Heldenleben", "Heldenleben",'°
The Gloucesters cried out 'Strauss is our favourite wir haben°
Sich geliebt'. So silence fell, Aubers' front slept,°   10
And the sentries an unsentimental silence kept.
True, the size of the rum ration was still a shocker
But at last over Aubers the majesty of the dawn's veil swept.

Joyeuse et Durandal

Joyeuse, O lovely bayonet of the Old Army°
Why have they given us this gray thing wherewith to slay?
Durandal, you are longer, certainly not stronger,
And have no looks to speak of—we would risk the danger
Of an extra three inches of German weapon
If they would grant that bare bright steel again.
War Office, with spare green envelopes we would charm thee,°
And do worrying fatigues on Rest for a day,°
Entreat the Colonel and the Sergeant major
So we might joyously have our gaze upon   10
This bright and fashioned sword, not for honour, in vain . . .
For they would fight with formulae and with figures,
But we with songs and praises, and more soldiers;
Having caressed that fair blade with long fingers.

The Stokes Gunners

When Fritz and we were nearly on friendly terms—°
Of mornings, furtively, (O moral insects, O worms!)
A group of khaki people would saunter into
Our sector and plant a stove-pipe directed on to°
Fritz trenches, insert black things, shaped like Ticklers jams—°
The stove pipe hissed a hundred times and one might count to
A hundred damned unexpected explosions,
Which was all very well, but the group having finished
    performance
And hissed and whistled, would take their contrivance down to
Head quarters to report damage, and hand in forms   10
While the Gloucesters who desired peace or desired battle°
Were left to pay the piper—Cursing Stokes to Hell, Montreal
    and Seattle.°

The Bohemians

Certain people would not clean their buttons,
Nor polish buckles after latest fashions,
Preferred their hair long, putties comfortable,°
Barely escaping hanging, indeed hardly able
In Bridge and smoking without army cautions
Spending hours that sped like evil for quickness,
(While others burnished brasses, earned promotions)
These were those ones who jested in the trench,
While others argued of army ways, and wrenched
What little soul they had still further from shape,   10
And died off one by one, or became officers
Without the first of dream, the ghost of notions
Of ever becoming soldiers, or smart and neat,
Surprised as ever to find the army capable
Of sounding 'Lights out' to break a game of Bridge,°
As to fear candles would set a barn alight.
In Artois or Picardy they lie—free of useless fashions.°

The Retreat

After three weeks of freezing and thawing over
Against Chaulnes; mud dreadful; with water cover°
Of gumboots in the low places; and ice of nights;
They marched us out sore footed to far billets;
Straw and warm tea; more bread; letters more . . .
Where for a week we recovered; and now less sore
Our feet were—beer there was; a little bread, wine;
But not the strength they asked of making roads fine
With weak bodies; sore feet; and hungry bellies.
Warmth there was, and sleep—the barn a Palace.   10
When suddenly the news came, Fritz has retreated . . . °
What! from Chaulnes wired yard deep—where a shot greeted
Any patrol at midnight moving strict ways,
None else to take: it was a most strict terrible maze.
It was true—we marched three days—to our old place,
Passed through a hedge of No mans land and saw far°
Other lines, Pillboxes; Headquarters; and farther
Artillery wired positions, Heads of Divisions—
Passed; came to Omiecourt; found billets; it was but the fractions°
Of Farms—but wood in plenty, and water pure   20
Fire warm; billets warm while the North wind sheer
Tore a space round corners of our one small room.
There was a Mass book, great Plain Song in the gloom
Of the broken church with German Journals and such . . .
I found a score of postcards in a billet, to catch
All of them, and to be sorry afterwards . . .
But first finding den and souvenirs as rewards.
After that onward slowly till roads we had mended;
Weak, hungry; feeling the heart labour bended;
To come to the last rise, see Somme azure of blaze°   30
(Soft March . . . it was warm of sun), and go onwards; across
The pioneer mending of the arch broken; by planking
Laid across, rattling but standing strain, Transport clanking,
Artillery. We passed Y, and another huge mined destroyed place;°
(Terribly huge) and on till Caulaincourt valley of grace,°
Home of the dead men of Napoleon's man

Lay in the Mausoleum, expecting never invasion,
Nor to see Gloucesters guarding a place that few°
Should touch, but of the old rule Rousseau or Le Sage knew—°
But Caulaincourt glad enough boys were there who had stuff   40
Of such within them communion with the smooth and rough
Of road and valley gleaming with lit sapling water
Young Artois sister to become Somme's one daughter°
Glimmering beauty before 'Lights Out' stirring heart out°
To tears. (I climbed weak kneed, I saw Fallow unploughed
And the darling valley . . .) German prisoners passed, defiantly;
One gaily; and we went on to artillery before the town
Vermand: where (road mending) our Captain rode too far shown°
And got a blast of gun barrage—frightened his horse—
    A Company
Took Vermand—two prisoners; and our first trophy   50
A machine-gun . . . So further to high banks France had raised
Long ago against the Eastward threat, nobly placed
To be the guard of Vermand—Caulaincourt, Somme's Land;
Free men making, cursing, arms-taking to Hell out of hand;
Digging with sulky vigour; or in furious paced
Frenzy; promised dismissal and an early end.
(We knew) Fine mounds of Roman sort—we saw looming
First through the dim night . . . then one miserable week;
Through displeasure of the weather; body sick; heart sick
Saw change from green to white, white to golden;   60
With sleet and sunshine changing—with storm and sun frowning.

First night I lay forward freezing, while others dug pits—
A lump of panged ice—Two hours watching keen for Fritz:
Who saw no more than flurries of snow against the spinneys°
Or bare ridge . . . Next day rested—at night advanced
To the near wood searched and left; nothing but fancies
Of shadows; nothing but dry leaves rustling fortissimo.°
Left again—spent one day of before Spring sun.
But next to be bombarded by Fritz while guarded
Our own feeble guns with a third of such.   70
So we dug in, under the trunks and brush.
Stayed—in holes—with a sheet to get warmth and shelter
(On which the winter leaves pattered helter skelter

And the trees dripped.) I was sentry—with two others;
When suddenly two hundred off three great Germans
Appeared . . . the sentry (duty) ran quietly off
To warn the others. His friend went off in the smothers
Of embarrassment . . . I alone (good shot) in the foreground?
Now Ivor Gurney lonely, make no sound wait.
The others are at the wood end; now waste no shot.   80
No noise, no noise . . . To find (as in once; a mine)
My equipment tangled up in my right ear; the bayonet
Hurting my ribs; the foresight; O where the foresight
Against the woods gunmetal, most lively shine?
They touched the wood, I fired straight at the middle one
No move; now at the right side of the left one.
No move; again between the right one and middle one . . .
When up there dashed my Platoon crashing branches down;°
And off went Germans as swift as deer as soon
To turn; great, well fed men to our hungry: 90
Two Corporals; one over fed, lusty Lance Corporal
I should guess . . . How did I miss them! How did I miss?
But I refuse to believe (flatly refuse)
And believe that men may be shot through middle bodies
Before enemies without dropping—I who had hit posts
As hard as ghosts to hit in Verey lights of Laventie . . . °
Posts and any echoing thing . . . It was, and yet is
Absurd to me to think the belly may not be wholly
Shot through—by a tiny Bullet of our Army
And the man not stand up without sign of folly   100
Or wound . . . The nicest men I had seen for six
Weeks; to our poor scarecrows of weak pulses . . .

Moving by will—hungry, yet comradely;
While these comfortable Burghers came over like country squires°
To see the work of the farm hand; happy after white coffee;
And a good gossip before glowing half wood fires . . .
(O! O! Newspapers Anglais, Français Papers daily,
What have you told us of hungry or cowed Bavaria, Saxony?°
What yarns of three course dinners, when here the sinners
Come overland 8 mile an hour, and do it easily?   110
And walk off indigestion after meals like millionaires

For size (and accomplishment) O Wurtemburgherie,
Is this the population you fake your figures on?
Is this the beaten horde of conscripts, beginners?°
(Two as nice men as I'd ever meet again . . .))
So we talked over . . . they cursed me . . . the little skirmish;
Cursed also and felt excitement and watched them vanish—
Like record breakers, over the chalk slope borders.
'Good bye'—'You chaps, I'm sure I hit them in the guts.
Bang through or near . . . You know I have hit dark posts,   120
My equipment round my neck . . .' To which only jests
Were answer; and 'no excuses for a miss at twelve yards, Sir!'

Next night to trench again—and they told us we were going
Over the top to take some unseen damned wiring
Over the crest . . . They bombarded, and our guns cutting were
    trying.
At seven the drizzle began; at 10 we formed in Line . . .
And (they too fast) went over across Country
I grumbling, and half running; while silence sombrely
Hung over all things—the air misty almost rainy.
I weak as a rabbit—'How much longer, dammit?'   130
They said 'Shut up'. I said 'I wish this were over!'
They said 'Shut up'. When suddenly up went a cheer.
The men on the left had hit it . . . I stumbled on and struck it
Blind eyed, upfaced . . . fearing wire high and to be scratch faced,
Hit wire—and lay down . . . seeing fires—whether of theirs
Or ours, cutting the wires I knew not—only from behind
The impatient second line shot past my helmet,
And the machine guns blazed away, lower lower
(O Christ, what pain—) and lower till my body did cower
Stuck to the mire—and no holes at all in the wire.   140
So much for artillery fire . . .

The Company jester and my little lieutenant
Crept about; snipping odd wires . . . ten yards I guessed went
Before us (or over ten foot) and shells came down, and that damned
    machine gun
Sprayed us . . . O down; further down; Vermand,
You are too chalky a land . . . We retreated . . . dug shallow

Pits—the moon above the mist made a mellow
Light, transfused—we could see an old machine gun post . . .
And nothing more—we were a little down in the hollow.
Again returning, to catch the same—lighter now, see wires   150
Thick against dares; and no more forrader; to retreat again;
When suddenly my arm went blazing with bright ardour of pain;
The end of music . . . I knelt down and cursed the double
Treachery of Fritz to Europe and to English music;°
Cursed Pomerania, Saxony, Wurtemburg, Bavaria,
Prussia, Rheinland, Mecklenburg, Pomerania
Again . . . (But had forgotten Franconia, Swabia,)°
Then said 'You chaps, she's beginning to move again';
Borrowed a rifle—shot one shot to say 'These things were so'.
'My arm—she'll stay on yet: I believe it's a Blighty . . .'°   160
And the stretcher bearers bound it up carefully, neatly . . .
In the darkness whitely . . . And I left them all, vulgar soldiers to
   brawl;
Passed through reserve in the sunken Road . . . Oxfords
   I just could°
See, who asked me news 'O wires, wires, wires, sticks, wood . . .
Machine guns, machine guns, shells . . . Nothing else: goodnight'
And went off through a barrage spraying the hillside
(Machine-guns) risking so much . . . tired out and careless;
Having a Blighty; hunger; weakness; by disgust fearless;
And saw the downward slope to Blighty and new hope.

                                                    23 April 1925

Signallers

To be signallers and to be relieved two hours
Before the common infantry—and to come down
Hurriedly to where estaminet's friendliest doors°
Opened—where before the vulgar brawling common crew
Could take the seats for tired backs, or take the wine
Best suited for palates searching for delicate flavours
(Or pretty tints) to take from the mind trench ways and strain,
Though it be on tick, with delicately wangled sly flavours.°

Then having obtained grace from the lady of the inn—
How good to sit still and sip with all appreciative lip,   10
(After the grease and skilly of line-cookhouse tea,)°
The cool darkling texture of the heavenly dew
Of wine—to smoke as one pleased in a house of courtesy—
Signallers gentlemen all away from the vulgar
Infantry—so dull and dirty and so underpaid,
So wont to get killed and leave the cautious signallers
To signal down the message that they were dead.°
Anyway, distinction or not—there was a quiet
Hour or so before the Company fours halted, and were°
Formed two deep, and dismissed and paid after leaden dilatory   20
Hanging around, to bolt (eager) to find those apparently
Innocent signallers drinking on tick, at last beer.

It is Near Toussaints

It is near Toussaints, the living and dead will say,
'Have they ended it? What has happened to Gurney?'
And along the leaf-strewed roads of France many brown shades
Will go, recalling singing, and a comrade for whom also they
Had hoped well. His Honour them had happier made.
Curse all that hates good. When I spoke of my breaking
(Not understood) in London, they imagined of the taking°
Vengeance, and seeing things were different in future.
(A musician was a cheap honourable and nice creature.)
Kept sympathetic silence; heard their packs creaking   10
And burst into song—Hilaire Belloc was all our Master.°
On the night of all the dead, they will remember me,
Pray Michael, Nicholas, Maries, lost in Novembery°
River-mist in the old City of our dear love, and batter°
At doors about the farms crying 'Our war poet is lost'
'Madame, no bon!'—and cry his two names, warningly,
    sombrely.°

The Silent One

Who died on the wires, and hung there, one of two—
Who for his hours of life had chattered through
Infinite lovely chatter of Bucks accent;°
Yet faced unbroken wires; stepped over, and went,
A noble fool, faithful to his stripes—and ended.°
But I weak, hungry, and willing only for the chance
Of line—to fight in the line, lay down under unbroken
Wires, and saw the flashes, and kept unshaken.
Till the politest voice—a finicking accent, said:°
'Do you think you might crawl through, there; there's a hole;'
   In the afraid   10
Darkness, shot at; I smiled, as politely replied—
'I'm afraid not, Sir.' There was no hole, no way to be seen.
Nothing but chance of death, after tearing of clothes
Kept flat, and watched the darkness, hearing bullets whizzing—
And thought of music—and swore deep heart's deep oaths.
(Polite to God—) and retreated and came on again.
Again retreated—and a second time faced the screen.°

ISAAC ROSENBERG
(1890–1918)

━━━

ISAAC ROSENBERG was born in 1890 to impoverished Jewish refu-
gees, his father having fled Lithuania four years before to escape con-
scription into the Russian army. The Rosenbergs spoke little English,
and enjoyed few if any social advantages: Isaac's father scraped a
living as a pedlar, which his mother supplemented through sewing
and embroidery. When Rosenberg was seven, his family moved from
Bristol to east London, and at 14 he left school to become apprentice
to an engraver. Aged 20 he joined the Slade School of Art with the
generous support of a patron. Around this time, he became part of a
brilliant network of radical Jewish artists and writers—later known as
the Whitechapel Boys—who included among their number David
Bomberg, Mark Gertler, Joseph Leftwich, and John Rodker.

During the years leading up to the outbreak of war, Rosenberg
vacillated between poetry and painting, unsure where his real gifts
lay. In a letter probably from 1910, he expressed the ambition to 'take
up painting seriously; I think I might do something at that; but
poetry—I despair of ever writing excellent poetry'. By 1915 he had
changed his mind: 'I believe in myself more as a poet than a painter.'
That same year, Rosenberg enlisted in the Bantam Battalion of the
Suffolk Regiment. (Accepting men under five feet three, it was, he
reported, 'the only regiment my build allowed'.)[1] From that moment,
he had little opportunity to paint.

Rosenberg was an unlikely soldier. Sharing his family's pacifist
ideals and lacking any feelings of patriotism, he argued from the start
that war was 'against all [his] principles of justice', and that he 'would
be doing the most criminal thing a man can do'. Yet as he explained
in an unsent letter, 'There is certainly a strong temptation to join
when you are making no money.'[2] Having arrived in France in June
1916, Rosenberg found himself the target of anti-Semitic bullying:
'Why do they sneer at me?', he asked in a short lyric, 'The Jew'.

[1] Rosenberg, *Isaac Rosenberg*, ed. Noakes, 228, 280.
[2] Ibid., 274.

Rosenberg's acute awareness that Jews faced each other across no-man's-land, fighting a bloody civil war, shaped his best-known poem, 'Break of Day in the Trenches', in which the 'cosmopolitan' rat (a common symbol in anti-Semitic discourse) has 'touched this English hand' and will soon 'do the same to a German'. Published in the Chicago journal *Poetry* at Ezra Pound's instigation, it was one of very few poems by Rosenberg to reach a wide audience during his lifetime.

Rosenberg considered 'Break of Day in the Trenches' to be 'as simple as ordinary talk', but he admitted that he could be obscure, much against his own desire for 'Simple *Poetry* that is where an interesting complexity of thought is kept in tone and right value to the dominating idea so that it is understandable and still ungraspable.' Economy of expression sometimes slipped into mannerism and became an effective impediment to understanding. Yet Rosenberg's best poems create a disturbing phantasmagoria out of their compression. The compound words of 'Dead Man's Dump'—'God-ancestralled essences', 'blood-dazed intelligence', 'quivering-bellied mules'— came naturally to a Yiddish-speaking poet. When Rosenberg complained that Walt Whitman's diction was 'so diffused', he was criticizing a writer who, in this respect, worked at the opposite pole.[3]

In January 1918 Rosenberg described his conditions in lines to Edward Marsh, some of which the military censor saw fit to delete:

I am back in the trenches which are terrible now. We spend most of our time pulling each other out of the mud. I am not fit at all now and am more in the way than any use. You see I appear in excellent health and a doctor will make no distinction between health and strength. I am not strong. ~~What is happening to me now is more tragic than the 'passion play'. Christ never endured what I endure. It is breaking me completely.~~[4]

He was killed while on night patrol just over two months later.

[3] Ibid., 305, 353.   [4] Ibid., 356.

[A worm fed on the heart of Corinth]

A worm fed on the heart of Corinth,
Babylon and Rome.°
Not Paris raped tall Helen,°
But this incestuous worm
Who lured her vivid beauty
To his amorphous sleep.°
England! famous as Helen
Is thy betrothal sung.
To him the shadowless,
More amorous than Solomon.° 10

Break of Day in the Trenches

The darkness crumbles away.
It is the same old Druid Time as ever.°
Only a live thing leaps my hand,
A queer sardonic rat,
As I pull the parapet's poppy°
To stick behind my ear.
Droll rat, they would shoot you if they knew
Your cosmopolitan sympathies.
Now you have touched this English hand
You will do the same to a German° 10
Soon, no doubt, if it be your pleasure
To cross the sleeping green between.
It seems, odd thing, you grin as you pass
Strong eyes, fine limbs, haughty athletes,
Less chanced than you for life,
Bonds to the whims of murder,
Sprawled in the bowels of the earth,
The torn fields of France.
What do you see in our eyes
At the shrieking iron and flame 20
Hurl'd through still heavens?
What quaver—what heart aghast?

Poppies whose roots are in man's veins
Drop, and are ever dropping,°
But mine in my ear is safe—
Just a little white with the dust.

August 1914

What in our lives is burnt
In the fire of this?
The heart's dear granary?
The much we shall miss?

Three lives hath one life—
Iron, honey, gold.
The gold, the honey gone—
Left is the hard and cold.

Iron are the lives
Molten right through our youth.   10
A burnt space through ripe fields,
A fair mouth's broken tooth.

Louse Hunting

Nudes—stark aglisten
Yelling in lurid glee. Grinning faces of fiends
And raging limbs
Whirl over the floor one fire,
For a shirt verminously busy
Yon soldier tore from his throat
With oaths
Godhead might shrink at, but not the lice.°
And soon the shirt was aflare
Over the candle he'd lit while we lay.   10
Then we all sprung up and stript
To hunt the vermin brood.
Soon like a devils' pantomime

The place was raging.
See the silhouettes agape,
See the gibbering shadows
Mixed with the battled arms on the wall.
See gargantuan hooked fingers
Dug in supreme flesh
To smutch the supreme littleness.°   20
See the merry limbs in hot Highland fling
Because some wizard vermin
Charmed from the quiet this revel
When our ears were half lulled
By the dark music
Blown from Sleep's trumpet.

From France

The spirit drank the Café lights;
All the hot life that glittered there,
And heard men say to women gay,
'Life is just so in France'.

The spirit dreams of Café lights,
And golden faces and soft tones,
And hears men groan to broken men,
'This is not Life in France'.

Heaped stones and a charred signboard shows
With grass between and dead folk under,°   10
And some birds sing, while the spirit takes wing.°
And this is life in France.

Returning, we hear the larks

Sombre the night is.
And though we have our lives, we know
What sinister threat lurks there.

Dragging these anguished limbs, we only know
This poison-blasted track opens on our camp—
On a little safe sleep.

But hark! joy—joy—strange joy.
Lo! heights of night ringing with unseen larks.°
Music showering our upturned list'ning faces.

Death could drop from the dark   10
As easily as song—
But song only dropped,°
Like a blind man's dream on the sand
By dangerous tides,
Like a girl's dark hair for she dreams no ruin lies there,
Or her kisses where a serpent hides.

Dead Man's Dump

The plunging limbers over the shattered track°
Racketed with their rusty freight,
Stuck out like many crowns of thorns,°
And the rusty stakes like sceptres old
To stay the flood of brutish men°
Upon our brothers dear.

The wheels lurched over sprawled dead
But pained them not, though their bones crunched,
Their shut mouths made no moan,
They lie there huddled, friend and foeman,   10
Man born of man, and born of woman,°
And shells go crying over them
From night till night and now.

Earth has waited for them
All the time of their growth
Fretting for their decay:
Now she has them at last!
In the strength of their strength
Suspended—stopped and held.

What fierce imaginings their dark souls lit   20
Earth! have they gone into you?
Somewhere they must have gone,
And flung on your hard back
Is their soul's sack,
Emptied of God-ancestralled essences.
Who hurled them out? Who hurled?

None saw their spirits' shadow shake the grass,°
Or stood aside for the half used life to pass
Out of those doomed nostrils and the doomed mouth,
When the swift iron burning bee   30
Drained the wild honey of their youth.

What of us, who flung on the shrieking pyre,
Walk, our usual thoughts untouched,
Our lucky limbs as on ichor fed,°
Immortal seeming ever?
Perhaps when the flames beat loud on us,
A fear may choke in our veins
And the startled blood may stop.

The air is loud with death,
The dark air spurts with fire   40
The explosions ceaseless are.

Timelessly now, some minutes past,
These dead strode time with vigorous life,
Till the shrapnel called 'an end!'
But not to all. In bleeding pangs
Some borne on stretchers dreamed of home,
Dear things, war-blotted from their hearts.

A man's brains splattered on
A stretcher-bearer's face;
His shook shoulders slipped their load,   50
But when they bent to look again
The drowning soul was sunk too deep
For human tenderness.

They left this dead with the older dead,
Stretched at the cross roads.

Burnt black by strange decay
Their sinister faces lie
The lid over each eye,
The grass and coloured clay
More motion have than they,   60
Joined to the great sunk silences.

Here is one not long dead;
His dark hearing caught our far wheels,
And the choked soul stretched weak hands
To reach the living word the far wheels said,
The blood-dazed intelligence beating for light,
Crying through the suspense of the far torturing wheels
Swift for the end to break,
Or the wheels to break,
Cried as the tide of the world broke over his sight.   70

Will they come? Will they ever come?
Even as the mixed hoofs of the mules,
The quivering-bellied mules,
And the rushing wheels all mixed
With his tortured upturned sight,
So we crashed round the bend,
We heard his weak scream,
We heard his very last sound,
And our wheels grazed his dead face.°

Daughters of War

Space beats the ruddy freedom of their limbs—
Their naked dances with man's spirit naked
By the root side of the tree of life
(The underside of things
And shut from earth's profoundest eyes).

I saw in prophetic gleams
These mighty daughters in their dances
Beckon each soul aghast from its crimson corpse
To mix in their glittering dances.
I heard the mighty daughters' giant sighs   10
In sleepless passion for the sons of valour,
And envy of the days of flesh
Barring their love with mortal boughs across,—
The mortal boughs—the mortal tree of life,
The old bark burnt with iron wars
They blow to a live flame
To char the young green days
And reach the occult soul;—they have no softer lure—
No softer lure than the savage ways of death.
We were satisfied of our Lords the moon and the sun   20
To take our wage of sleep and bread and warmth—
These maidens came—these strong everliving Amazons,°
And in an easy might their wrists
Of night's sway and noon's sway the sceptres brake,
Clouding the wild—the soft lustres of our eyes.

Clouding the wild lustres, the clinging tender lights;
Driving the darkness into the flame of day,
With the Amazonian wind of them
Over our corroding faces
That must be broken—broken for evermore   30
So the soul can leap out
Into their huge embraces.
Tho' there are human faces
Best sculptures of Deity,
And sinews lusted after
By the Archangels tall,
Even these must leap to the love-heat of these maidens
From the flame of terrene days,°
Leaving grey ashes to the wind—to the wind.

One (whose great lifted face,   40
Where wisdom's strength and beauty's strength
And the thewed strength of large beasts°
Moved and merged, gloomed and lit)

Was speaking, surely, as the earth-men's earth fell away;
Whose new hearing drunk the sound
Where pictures lutes and mountains mixed
With the loosed spirit of a thought,
Essenced to language, thus—

'My sisters force their males
From the doomed earth, from the doomed glee   50
And hankering of hearts.
Frail hands gleam up through the human quagmire, and lips of ash
Seem to wail, as in sad faded paintings
Far sunken and strange.
My sisters have their males
Clean of the dust of old days
That clings about those white hands,
And yearns in those voices sad.
But these shall not see them,
Or think of them in any days or years,   60
They are my sisters' lovers in other days and years.'

[Through these pale cold days]

Through these pale cold days
What dark faces burn
Out of three thousand years,°
And their wild eyes yearn,

While underneath their brows
Like waifs their spirits grope
For the pools of Hebron again—°
For Lebanon's summer slope.°

They leave these blond still days
In dust behind their tread   10
They see with living eyes
How long they have been dead.

ARTHUR GRAEME WEST
(1891–1917)

▬▬

ARTHUR GRAEME WEST'S legacy is problematic. *The Diary of a Dead Officer* (1919), comprising his literary remains, contains just ten poems, along with letters and diary entries covering the period from his enlistment in early 1915 until his death near Bapaume on 3 April 1917. These were selectively edited by the pacifist philosopher Cyril Joad, who had passed through Blundell's in Tiverton and then Balliol College, Oxford, a year ahead of West. Until Nazism changed his mind in 1940, Joad passionately believed that total subjugation was preferable to resistance. He foregrounded a pacifist narrative in West's writings, omitting inconvenient facts (such as West's voluntary membership of the Officer Training Corps at Oxford), and losing or destroying the original diaries.

Even allowing for Joad's manipulations, West's disillusionment with the War is clearly audible. From December 1915 until the following April he endured heavy fighting, but felt 'a spirit of amiable fraternity' with an enemy which 'has to sit just like us and do all the horrible and useless things that we do'. However, his crisis was provoked less by front-line horrors of the sort he described in 'The Night Patrol' than by the brutality of an officer training camp that he attended in Scotland between April and July 1916. It was probably while on leave during August, staying with Cyril Joad, that West wrote his best-known poem, 'God! How I Hate You, You Young Cheerful Men!', which scourged the patriotism and religious sentiment typical of the memorial volumes of soldier versifiers. Having by now lost both his Christian faith and his belief in the war effort, West considered refusing to rejoin the army after his leave, but eventually acquiesced: 'I do ill to go. I ought to fight no more. But death, I suppose, is the penalty.'[1] Editing *The Diary of a Dead Officer*, Joad insisted that that penalty, when it came early in April 1917, had been delivered in unheroic form. 'He died, it seems, in no blaze of glory,

---

[1] West, *The Diary of a Dead Officer*, 12, 54.

he died leading no forlorn hope, but struck by a chance sniper's bullet as he was leaving his trench.'[2]

² C. J., 'Introduction', in *The Diary of a Dead Officer*, p. xiv.

═══

The Night Patrol

France, March 1916.

Over the top! The wire's thin here, unbarbed
Plain rusty coils, not staked, and low enough:
Full of old tins, though—'When you're through, all three,
Aim quarter left for fifty yards or so,
Then straight for that new piece of German wire;
See if it's thick, and listen for a while
For sounds of working; don't run any risks;
About an hour; now, over!'
            And we placed
Our hands on the topmost sand-bags, leapt, and stood
A second with curved backs, then crept to the wire,   10
Wormed ourselves tinkling through, glanced back, and dropped.
The sodden ground was splashed with shallow pools,
And tufts of crackling cornstalks, two years old,
No man had reaped, and patches of spring grass.
Half-seen, as rose and sank the flares, were strewn
With the wrecks of our attack: the bandoliers,°
Packs, rifles, bayonets, belts, and haversacks,
Shell fragments, and the huge whole forms of shells
Shot fruitlessly—and everywhere the dead.
Only the dead were always present—present   20
As a vile sickly smell of rottenness;
The rustling stubble and the early grass,
The slimy pools—the dead men stank through all,
Pungent and sharp; as bodies loomed before,
And as we passed, they stank: then dulled away
To that vague fœtor, all encompassing,
Infecting earth and air. They lay, all clothed,
Each in some new and piteous attitude

That we well marked to guide us back: as he,
Outside our wire, that lay on his back and crossed   30
His legs Crusader-wise; I smiled at that,°
And thought on Elia and his Temple Church.°
From him, at quarter left, lay a small corpse,
Down in a hollow, huddled as in bed,
That one of us put his hand on unawares.
Next was a bunch of half a dozen men
All blown to bits, an archipelago°
Of corrupt fragments, vexing to us three,
Who had no light to see by, save the flares.
On such a trail, so lit, for ninety yards   40
We crawled on belly and elbows, till we saw
Instead of lumpish dead before our eyes,
The stakes and crosslines of the German wire.
We lay in shelter of the last dead man,
Ourselves as dead, and heard their shovels ring
Turning the earth, then talk and cough at times.
A sentry fired and a machine-gun spat;
They shot a flare above us, when it fell
And spluttered out in the pools of No Man's Land,
We turned and crawled past the remembered dead: 50
Past him and him, and them and him, until
For he lay some way apart, we caught the scent
Of the Crusader and slid past his legs,
And through the wire and home, and got our rum.

God! How I Hate You, You Young Cheerful Men!

On a University Undergraduate moved to verse by the war.

*Phrases from H. Rex Feston's "Quest of Truth": Poems on Doubt, War, Sorrow,
Despair, Hope, Death, Somewhere in France. He was killed in action and was an
undergraduate at Exeter.*

*His attitude is that God is good, amused, rather, at us fighting. 'Oh, happy to
have lived these epic days,' he writes (of us). This (he had been three years at
Oxford) is his address to the Atheists:*

'I know that God will never let me die.
    He is too passionate and intense for that.

See how He swings His great suns through the sky,
   See how He hammers the proud-faced mountains flat;
He takes a handful of a million years
   And flings them at the planets; or He throws
His red stars at the moon; then with hot tears
   He stoops to kiss one little earth-born rose.
Don't nail God down to rules, and think you know!
   Or God, Who sorrows all a summer's day
Because a blade of grass has died, will come
   And suck this world up in His lips, and lo!
Will spit it out a pebble, powdered grey,
   Into the whirl of Infinity's nothingless foam.'

This ruined the reputation of all English Atheists for months!

God! How I hate you, you young cheerful men,
Whose pious poetry blossoms on your graves
As soon as you are in them, nurtured up
By the salt of your corruption, and the tears
Of mothers, local vicars, college deans,
And flanked by prefaces and photographs
From all your minor poet friends—the fools—
Who paint their sentimental elegies°
Where sure, no angel treads; and, living, share
The dead's brief immortality.
                  Oh Christ!   10
To think that one could spread the ductile wax°
Of his fluid youth to Oxford's glowing fires
And take her seal so ill! Hark how one chants—
'Oh happy to have lived these epic days'—°
'These epic days'! And *he'd* been to France,°
And seen the trenches, glimpsed the huddled dead
In the periscope, hung in the rusting wire:°
Choked by their sickly fœtor, day and night
Blown down his throat: stumbled through ruined hearths,
Proved all that muddy brown monotony,   20
Where blood's the only coloured thing. Perhaps
Had seen a man killed, a sentry shot at night,
Hunched as he fell, his feet on the firing-step,°
His neck against the back slope of the trench,

And the rest doubled up between, his head
Smashed like an egg-shell, and the warm grey brain
Spattered all bloody on the parados:°
Had flashed a torch on his face, and known his friend,
Shot, breathing hardly, in ten minutes—gone!
Yet still God's in His heaven, all is right   30
In the best possible of worlds. The woe,°
Even His scaled eyes *must* see, is partial, only
A seeming woe, we cannot understand.
God loves us, God looks down on this our strife
And smiles in pity, blows a pipe at times
And calls some warriors home. We do not die,
God would not let us, He is too 'intense,'
Too 'passionate,' a whole day sorrows He
Because a grass-blade dies. How rare life is!°
On earth, the love and fellowship of men,   40
Men sternly banded: banded for what end?
Banded to maim and kill their fellow men—
For even Huns are men. In heaven above°
A genial umpire, a good judge of sport,
Won't let us hurt each other! Let's rejoice
God keeps us faithful, pens us still in fold.
Ah, what a faith is ours (almost, it seems,
Large as a mustard-seed)—we trust and trust,°
Nothing can shake us! Ah, how good God is
To suffer us be born just now, when youth   50
That else would rust, can slake his blade in gore,°
Where very God Himself does seem to walk
The bloody fields of Flanders He so loves!°

WILFRED OWEN
(1893–1918)

———

WILFRED OWEN was born near Oswestry, and grew up in Birkenhead and Shrewsbury. His early passions were more religious than literary, but Owen's discovery of Keats's work in 1911 came with the force of revelation. The poems that followed were obsessed with Keats in both style and subject; even in the trenches, he would never entirely shake off his formative influence.

Having narrowly missed a scholarship to London University, Owen funded his studies by spending sixteen months from October 1911 as lay assistant to a vicar near Reading, who shared his family's Evangelical beliefs. But he became increasingly unhappy, finding himself forced to choose between a life of 'imagination, physical sensation, aesthetic philosophy' and what seemed to him like a narrow and doctrinaire Christianity.[1] He left the vicarage when instructed to renounce worldly pleasures such as 'verse-making'. The religious quest was not completely abandoned: as Owen told his mother, 'I have murdered my false creed. If a true one exists, I shall find it.'[2] Such a creed would be required to accommodate the aestheticism that had replaced the faith of his upbringing.

Owen was acting as a private tutor in south-west France when war was declared. His letters were heavily censored by his brother before publication, but the surviving correspondence implies that Owen's two years in France allowed him to pursue the aesthetic life more freely than at home. His friendship with the poet Laurent Tailhade opened new avenues of French literature, and Owen's own poetry during this period became increasingly Decadent in language and subject. It is possible that Owen also began to enjoy a new sexual freedom in France: Robert Graves—whose accounts were not always reliable—reported after the War that Owen had told him of brief liaisons with men picked up in Bordeaux.

Owen first glimpsed something of war's pain when he observed

---

[1] Quoted by Dominic Hibberd, *Wilfred Owen*, 98.
[2] Owen, *Collected Letters*, 175.

surgical operations at a military hospital, writing unflinching descrip-
tions (with sketches) to his brother and explaining that 'I deliberately
tell you all this to educate you to the actualities of the war.' A trip
back to England in the summer of 1915 exposed him for the first time
to recruitment campaigns, which were effective enough for Owen to
declare: 'I *now do* most *intensely want to fight*.'[3] He enlisted with the
Artists' Rifles the following October. Training was a drawn-out pro-
cess, but Owen took advantage of time spent in London to attend
readings at Harold Monro's Poetry Bookshop and seek advice about
his poems from its proprietor.

Owen eventually arrived in the trenches of the Western Front as a
second lieutenant of the Manchester Regiment, in the bitter cold of
January 1917. Within days he came under ferocious bombardment,
cooped up with his men in an old German dugout; later that month,
one of them froze to death. Owen would return to these experiences
a year later in 'The Sentry', 'Futility', and 'Exposure', but what little
poetry dates from this time makes no reference to the War. Owen's
transformation into war poet was still some months off, and it was
initiated by particular circumstances. In March, Owen fell in the
dark into a ruined cellar, suffering severe concussion; the following
month, several days after experiencing the 'extraordinary exultation'
of going over the top, he was blown into the air by a shell and landed
amid the exploded remains of a fellow officer whose corpse had been
disinterred by the blast.[4] Suffering from delayed shock, Owen was
hospitalized in May, and sent to Craiglockhart War Hospital near
Edinburgh for further treatment. There, in August 1917, he met
Siegfried Sassoon, and the most important literary friendship of the
War began.

Sassoon's example gave Owen licence to make subject matter of
his experiences: 'Nothing like [Sassoon's] trench life sketches has
ever been written,' Owen told his mother, and he found the older
poet's work 'perfectly truthfully descriptive of war'.[5] Yet after sev-
eral attempts at imitation, Owen realized that his strengths did not
lie in satire, and that he must find ways of marrying Keatsian
gorgeousness with its shocking opposite: the horrors that he had
experienced in the trenches. From September 1917 the poems came
quickly: 'Anthem for Doomed Youth', 'Disabled' and 'Dulce et

---

[3] Ibid., 285, 341.   [4] Ibid., 458.   [5] Ibid., 484, 489.

Decorum Est' were all Craiglockhart poems, with Sassoon on hand as adviser. During this time, Owen published one of his own poems in *The Hydra*, the hospital magazine of which he edited several issues. It was the first of only five poems to appear in his lifetime.

There were signs, even before he met Sassoon, that Owen had been growing increasingly disillusioned with the war effort. In letters home he had argued that Christianity was incompatible with patriotism, that its message was pacifist, and that 'Christ is literally in no man's land.'[6] Sassoon introduced a political dimension to Owen's incipient radicalism, having publicly declared that the War had changed from one of 'defence and liberation' to 'a war of aggression and conquest'.[7] Sassoon believed—unlike most soldiers at the time and most historians subsequently—that a negotiated truce was possible, and that the politicians were wilfully prolonging the War. Together, he and Owen were in large measure responsible for a public perception of the War's futility which is still prevalent today.

Through Sassoon, Owen met Robert Graves, and formed the view that his poet friends were 'already as many Keatses'. On leave after Craiglockhart, he briefly moved in London literary society, encountering old-guard luminaries like H. G. Wells and Arnold Bennett. Before Christmas he rejoined the Manchester Regiment in Scarborough, and the following March transferred to Ripon. By now his poetry had become—as he believed that every poem should be—'a *matter of experience*'. Writing poems of witness, he was able to navigate between two rival philosophies: Keats's insistence that poetry should have no palpable design on the reader, and the tendency that Owen detected in Sassoon to turn poetry into 'a mere vehicle of propaganda'.[8] His own ambition, as expressed in the draft preface to a volume of poems that he would not live to publish, was to 'warn': 'That is why the true Poets must be truthful.'[9]

At Scarborough and Ripon, Owen revised his work and experimented with pararhyme, of which 'Miners' and 'Strange Meeting' (the poem described by Sassoon as Owen's 'passport to immortality')[10]

[6] Ibid., 461.

[7] Sassoon, *Diaries, 1915–1918*, 173–4.

[8] Owen, *Collected Letters*, 553, 510, 520.

[9] Owen, *The Complete Poems and Fragments*, II, 535.

[10] Siegfried Sassoon, 'Wilfred Owen: A Personal Appreciation', BBC Third Programme, 22 August 1948.

were among the early examples. Ignoring opportunities to stay in England, and convinced that he must lead his men so that he could 'speak of them as well as a pleader can', he returned to France in September 1918.[11] After heroics under intense fire the following month, he was awarded the Military Cross for 'inflict[ing] considerable losses on the enemy'. On 4 November, a week before the Armistice, Owen was killed while helping his men to cross the Sambre and Oise Canal.

[11] Owen, *Collected Letters*, 580.

―――――

Anthem for Doomed Youth

What passing-bells for these who die as cattle?°
   ―Only the monstrous anger of the guns.
   Only the stuttering rifles' rapid rattle
Can patter out their hasty orisons.°
No mockeries now for them; no prayers nor bells;
   Nor any voice of mourning save the choirs,―
The shrill, demented choirs of wailing shells;°
   And bugles calling for them from sad shires.

What candles may be held to speed them all?
   Not in the hands of boys but in their eyes   10
Shall shine the holy glimmers of goodbyes.
   The pallor of girls' brows shall be their pall;°
Their flowers the tenderness of patient minds,
And each slow dusk a drawing-down of blinds.°

The Sentry

We'd found an old Boche dug-out, and he knew,°
And gave us hell; for shell on frantic shell
Lit full on top, but never quite burst through.
Rain, guttering down in waterfalls of slime,
Kept slush waist-high and rising hour by hour,
And choked the steps too thick with clay to climb.

What murk of air remained stank old, and sour
With fumes from whizz-bangs, and the smell of men°
Who'd lived there years, and left their curse in the den,
If not their corpses . . .

                  There we herded from the blast   10
Of whizz-bangs; but one found our door at last,—
Buffeting eyes and breath, snuffing the candles,
And thud! flump! thud! down the steep steps came thumping
And sploshing in the flood, deluging muck,
The sentry's body; then his rifle, handles
Of old Boche bombs, and mud in ruck on ruck.
We dredged it up, for dead, until he whined,
'O sir—my eyes,—I'm blind,—I'm blind,—I'm blind.'
Coaxing, I held a flame against his lids
And said if he could see the least blurred light   20
He was not blind; in time they'd get all right.
'I can't,' he sobbed. Eyeballs, huge-bulged like squids',
Watch my dreams still,—yet I forgot him there
In posting Next for duty, and sending a scout
To beg a stretcher somewhere, and flound'ring about
To other posts under the shrieking air.

Those other wretches, how they bled and spewed,
And one who would have drowned himself for good,—°
I try not to remember these things now.
Let Dread hark back for one word only: how,   30
Half-listening to that sentry's moans and jumps,
And the wild chattering of his shivered teeth,
Renewed most horribly whenever crumps
Pummelled the roof and slogged the air beneath,—
Through the dense din, I say, we heard him shout
'I see your lights!'—But ours had long gone out.

Dulce et Decorum Est

Bent double, like old beggars under sacks,
Knock-kneed, coughing like hags, we cursed through sludge,
Till on the haunting flares we turned our backs
And towards our distant rest began to trudge.

Men marched asleep. Many had lost their boots
But limped on, blood-shod. All went lame; all blind;
Drunk with fatigue; deaf even to the hoots
Of tired, outstripped Five-Nines that dropped behind.°

Gas! GAS! Quick, boys!—An ecstasy of fumbling,
Fitting the clumsy helmets just in time;   10
But someone still was yelling out and stumbling,
And flound'ring like a man in fire or lime . . .
Dim, through the misty panes and thick green light,
As under a green sea, I saw him drowning.

In all my dreams, before my helpless sight,
He plunges at me, guttering, choking, drowning.

If in some smothering dreams you too could pace
Behind the wagon that we flung him in,
And watch the white eyes writhing in his face,
His hanging face, like a devil's sick of sin;   20
If you could hear, at every jolt, the blood
Come gargling from the froth-corrupted lungs,
Obscene as cancer, bitter as the cud
Of vile, incurable sores on innocent tongues,—
My friend, you would not tell with such high zest°
To children ardent for some desperate glory,
The old Lie: Dulce et decorum est
Pro patria mori.°

Insensibility

I

Happy are men who yet before they are killed°
Can let their veins run cold.
Whom no compassion fleers°
Or makes their feet
Sore on the alleys cobbled with their brothers.
The front line withers.
But they are troops who fade, not flowers,

For poets' tearful fooling:
Men, gaps for filling:°
Losses, who might have fought   10
Longer; but no one bothers.

2

And some cease feeling
Even themselves or for themselves.
Dullness best solves
The tease and doubt of shelling,
And Chance's strange arithmetic
Comes simpler than the reckoning of their shilling.°
They keep no check on armies' decimation.°

3

Happy are these who lose imagination:
They have enough to carry with ammunition.   20
Their spirit drags no pack.
Their old wounds, save with cold, can not more ache.
Having seen all things red,
Their eyes are rid
Of the hurt of the colour of blood for ever.
And terror's first constriction over,
Their hearts remain small-drawn.
Their senses in some scorching cautery of battle°
Now long since ironed,
Can laugh among the dying, unconcerned.   30

4

Happy the soldier home, with not a notion
How somewhere, every dawn, some men attack,
And many sighs are drained.
Happy the lad whose mind was never trained:
His days are worth forgetting more than not.
He sings along the march
Which we march taciturn, because of dusk,
The long, forlorn, relentless trend
From larger day to huger night.

5

We wise, who with a thought besmirch   40
Blood over all our soul,
How should we see our task
But through his blunt and lashless eyes?
Alive, he is not vital overmuch;
Dying, not mortal overmuch;
Nor sad, nor proud,
Nor curious at all.
He cannot tell
Old men's placidity from his.

6

But cursed are dullards whom no cannon stuns,   50
That they should be as stones.
Wretched are they, and mean
With paucity that never was simplicity.
By choice they made themselves immune
To pity and whatever moans in man
Before the last sea and the hapless stars;
Whatever mourns when many leave these shores;
Whatever shares
The eternal reciprocity of tears.

Greater Love

Red lips are not so red
   As the stained stones kissed by the English dead.
Kindness of wooed and wooer
Seems shame to their love pure.
O Love, your eyes lose lure°
   When I behold eyes blinded in my stead!

Your slender attitude
   Trembles not exquisite like limbs knife-skewed,
Rolling and rolling there

Where God seems not to care;   10
Till the fierce love they bear
   Cramps them in death's extreme decrepitude.

Your voice sings not so soft,—
   Though even as wind murmuring through raftered loft,—
Your dear voice is not dear,
Gentle, and evening clear,
As theirs whom none now hear,
   Now earth has stopped their piteous mouths that coughed.

Heart, you were never hot
   Nor large, nor full like hearts made great with shot;   20
And though your hand be pale,
Paler are all which trail
Your cross through flame and hail:
   Weep, you may weep, for you may touch them not.°

Disabled

He sat in a wheeled chair, waiting for dark,°
And shivered in his ghastly suit of grey,
Legless, sewn short at elbow. Through the park
Voices of boys rang saddening like a hymn,
Voices of play and pleasure after day,
Till gathering sleep had mothered them from him.

*   *   *   *   *

About this time Town used to swing so gay
When glow-lamps budded in the light blue trees,
And girls glanced lovelier as the air grew dim,—
In the old times, before he threw away his knees.   10
Now he will never feel again how slim
Girls' waists are, or how warm their subtle hands.
All of them touch him like some queer disease.

*   *   *   *   *

There was an artist silly for his face,
For it was younger than his youth, last year.
Now, he is old; his back will never brace;
He's lost his colour very far from here,
Poured it down shell-holes till the veins ran dry,
And half his lifetime lapsed in the hot race
And leap of purple spurted from his thigh.   20

                    *   *   *   *   *

One time he liked a blood-smear down his leg,
After the matches, carried shoulder-high.°
It was after football, when he'd drunk a peg,°
He thought he'd better join.—He wonders why.
Someone had said he'd look a god in kilts,
That's why; and maybe, too, to please his Meg,
Aye, that was it, to please the giddy jilts°
He asked to join. He didn't have to beg;
Smiling they wrote his lie: aged nineteen years.°
Germans he scarcely thought of, all their guilt,   30
And Austria's, did not move him. And no fears
Of Fear came yet. He thought of jewelled hilts
For daggers in plaid socks; of smart salutes;
And care of arms; and leave; and pay arrears;
Esprit de corps; and hints for young recruits.°
And soon, he was drafted out with drums and cheers.

                    *   *   *   *   *

Some cheered him home, but not as crowds cheer Goal.
Only a solemn man who brought him fruits
Thanked him; and then enquired about his soul.

                    *   *   *   *   *

Now, he will spend a few sick years in institutes,   40
And do what things the rules consider wise,
And take whatever pity they may dole.
Tonight he noticed how the women's eyes

Passed from him to the strong men that were whole.
How cold and late it is! Why don't they come
And put him into bed? Why don't they come?°

Apologia pro Poemate Meo

I, too, saw God through mud,—°
    The mud that cracked on cheeks when wretches smiled.
    War brought more glory to their eyes than blood,
    And gave their laughs more glee than shakes a child.

Merry it was to laugh there—
    Where death becomes absurd and life absurder.
    For power was on us as we slashed bones bare
    Not to feel sickness or remorse of murder.

I, too, have dropped off Fear—
    Behind the barrage, dead as my platoon,°   10
    And sailed my spirit surging light and clear
    Past the entanglement where hopes lay strewn;

And witnessed exultation—
    Faces that used to curse me, scowl for scowl,
    Shine and lift up with passion of oblation,°
    Seraphic for an hour; though they were foul.

I have made fellowships—
    Untold of happy lovers in old song.
    For love is not the binding of fair lips
    With the soft silk of eyes that look and long,°   20

By Joy, whose ribbon slips,—
    But wound with war's hard wire whose stakes are strong;
    Bound with the bandage of the arm that drips;°
    Knit in the webbing of the rifle-thong.

I have perceived much beauty
    In the hoarse oaths that kept our courage straight;

Heard music in the silentness of duty;
Found peace where shell-storms spouted reddest spate.

Nevertheless, except you share
   With them in hell the sorrowful dark of hell,   30
   Whose world is but the trembling of a flare
   And heaven but as the highway for a shell,

You shall not hear their mirth:
   You shall not come to think them well content
   By any jest of mine. These men are worth
   Your tears. You are not worth their merriment.

The Show

   We have fallen in the dreams the ever-living
   Breathe on the tarnished mirror of the world,
   And then smooth out with ivory hands and sigh.

                              W.B. YEATS

My soul looked down from a vague height, with Death,
As unremembering how I rose or why,
And saw a sad land, weak with sweats of dearth,
Grey, cratered like the moon with hollow woe,
And pitted with great pocks and scabs of plagues.

Across its beard, that horror of harsh wire,
There moved thin caterpillars, slowly uncoiled.
It seemed they pushed themselves to be as plugs
Of ditches, where they writhed and shrivelled, killed.

By them had slimy paths been trailed and scraped   10
Round myriad warts that might be little hills.

From gloom's last dregs these long-strung creatures crept,
And vanished out of dawn down hidden holes.

(And smell came up from those foul openings
As out of mouths, or deep wounds deepening.)

On dithering feet upgathered, more and more,
Brown strings, towards strings of grey, with bristling spines,°
All migrants from green fields, intent on mire.

Those that were grey, of more abundant spawns,
Ramped on the rest and ate them and were eaten.°   20

I saw their bitten backs curve, loop, and straighten.
I watched those agonies curl, lift, and flatten.

Whereat, in terror what that sight might mean,
I reeled and shivered earthward like a feather.

And Death fell with me, like a deepening moan.
And He, picking a manner of worm, which half had hid
Its bruises in the earth, but crawled no further,°
Showed me its feet, the feet of many men,
And the fresh-severed head of it, my head.

[I saw his round mouth's crimson]

I saw his round mouth's crimson deepen as it fell,
    Like a sun, in his last deep hour;
Watched the magnificent recession of farewell,
    Clouding, half gleam, half glower,
And a last splendour burn the heavens of his cheek.
    And in his eyes
The cold stars lighting, very old and bleak,
    In different skies.

A Terre

(being the philosophy of many soldiers)

Sit on the bed. I'm blind, and three parts shell.
Be careful; can't shake hands now; never shall.
Both arms have mutinied against me,—brutes.
My fingers fidget like ten idle brats.

I tried to peg out soldierly,—no use!°
One dies of war like any old disease.
This bandage feels like pennies on my eyes.°
I have my medals?—Discs to make eyes close.
My glorious ribbons?—Ripped from my own back°
In scarlet shreds. (That's for your poetry book.)   10

A short life and a merry one, my buck!
We used to say we'd hate to live dead-old,—
Yet now . . . I'd willingly be puffy, bald,
And patriotic. Buffers catch from boys°
At least the jokes hurled at them. I suppose
Little I'd ever teach a son, but hitting,
Shooting, war, hunting, all the arts of hurting.
Well, that's what I learnt,—that, and making money.

Your fifty years ahead seem none too many?
Tell me how long I've got? God! For one year   20
To help myself to nothing more than air!
One Spring! Is one too good to spare, too long?
Spring wind would work its own way to my lung,
And grow me legs as quick as lilac-shoots.

My servant's lamed, but listen how he shouts!
When I'm lugged out, he'll still be good for that.
Here in this mummy-case, you know, I've thought
How well I might have swept his floors for ever.°
I'd ask no nights off when the bustle's over,
Enjoying so the dirt. Who's prejudiced   30
Against a grimed hand when his own's quite dust,
Less live than specks that in the sun-shafts turn,

Less warm than dust that mixes with arms' tan?
I'd love to be a sweep, now, black as Town,
Yes, or a muckman. Must I be his load?

O Life, Life, let me breathe,—a dug-out rat!
Not worse than ours the lives rats lead—
Nosing along at night down some safe rut,
They find a shell-proof home before they rot.
Dead men may envy living mites in cheese,   40
Or good germs even. Microbes have their joys,
And subdivide, and never come to death.
Certainly flowers have the easiest time on earth.
'I shall be one with nature, herb, and stone,'
Shelley would tell me. Shelley would be stunned:°
The dullest Tommy hugs that fancy now.
'Pushing up daisies' is their creed, you know.°

To grain, then, go my fat, to buds my sap,
For all the usefulness there is in soap.
D'you think the Boche will ever stew man-soup?°   50
Some day, no doubt, if . . .
                              Friend, be very sure
I shall be better off with plants that share
More peaceably the meadow and the shower.
Soft rains will touch me,—as they could touch once,
And nothing but the sun will make me ware.
Your guns may crash around me. I'll not hear;
Or, if I wince, I shall not know I wince.

Don't take my soul's poor comfort for your jest.
Soldiers may grow a soul when turned to fronds,°
But here the thing's best left at home with friends.   60

My soul's a little grief, grappling your chest,
To climb your throat on sobs; easily chased
On other sighs and wiped by fresher winds.

Carry my crying spirit till it's weaned
To do without what blood remained these wounds.

Exposure

Our brains ache, in the merciless iced east winds that knive us . . . °
Wearied we keep awake because the night is silent . . .
Low, drooping flares confuse our memory of the salient . . . °
Worried by silence, sentries whisper, curious, nervous,
    But nothing happens.

Watching, we hear the mad gusts tugging on the wire,
Like twitching agonies of men among its brambles.
Northward, incessantly, the flickering gunnery rumbles,
Far off, like a dull rumour of some other war.
    What are we doing here?   10

The poignant misery of dawn begins to grow . . .
We only know war lasts, rain soaks, and clouds sag stormy.
Dawn massing in the east her melancholy army
Attacks once more in ranks on shivering ranks of grey,°
    But nothing happens.

Sudden successive flights of bullets streak the silence.
Less deathly than the air that shudders black with snow,
With sidelong flowing flakes that flock, pause, and renew;
We watch them wandering up and down the wind's nonchalance,
    But nothing happens.   20

Pale flakes with fingering stealth come feeling for our faces—
We cringe in holes, back on forgotten dreams, and stare, snow-
    dazed,
Deep into grassier ditches. So we drowse, sun-dozed,
Littered with blossoms trickling where the blackbird fusses,
    —Is it that we are dying?

Slowly our ghosts drag home: glimpsing the sunk fires, glozed°
With crusted dark-red jewels; crickets jingle there;
For hours the innocent mice rejoice: the house is theirs;
Shutters and doors, all closed: on us the doors are closed,—
    We turn back to our dying.   30

Since we believe not otherwise can kind fires burn;
Nor ever suns smile true on child, or field, or fruit.
For God's invincible spring our love is made afraid;
Therefore, not loath, we lie out here; therefore were born,
   For love of God seems dying.

Tonight, this frost will fasten on this mud and us,
Shrivelling many hands, puckering foreheads crisp.
The burying-party, picks and shovels in shaking grasp,
Pause over half-known faces. All their eyes are ice,
   But nothing happens.   40

Miners

There was a whispering in my hearth,
   A sigh of the coal,
Grown wistful of a former earth
   It might recall.

I listened for a tale of leaves
   And smothered ferns,
Frond-forests, and the low sly lives°
   Before the fauns.°

My fire might show steam-phantoms simmer
   From Time's old cauldron,   10
Before the birds made nests in summer,
   Or men had children.

But the coals were murmuring of their mine,
   And moans down there
Of boys that slept wry sleep, and men
   Writhing for air.

And I saw white bones in the cinder-shard,
   Bones without number.
Many the muscled bodies charred,
   And few remember.   20

I thought of all that worked dark pits
    Of war, and died
Digging the rock where Death reputes
    Peace lies indeed.

Comforted years will sit soft-chaired,
    In rooms of amber;°
The years will stretch their hands, well-cheered
    By our life's ember;

The centuries will burn rich loads
    With which we groaned,   30
Whose warmth shall lull their dreaming lids,
    While songs are crooned;
But they will not dream of us poor lads,
    Left in the ground.

The Last Laugh

'Oh! Jesus Christ! I'm hit,' he said; and died.
Whether he vainly cursed or prayed indeed,
    The Bullets chirped—In vain, vain, vain!
    Machine-guns chuckled—Tut-tut! Tut-tut!
    And the Big Gun guffawed.

Another sighed—'O Mother,—Mother,—Dad!'
Then smiled at nothing, childlike, being dead.
    And the lofty Shrapnel-cloud
    Leisurely gestured,—Fool!
    And the splinters spat, and tittered.   10

'My Love!' one moaned. Love-languid seemed his mood,
Till slowly lowered, his whole face kissed the mud.
    And the Bayonets' long teeth grinned;
    Rabbles of Shells hooted and groaned;
    And the Gas hissed.

Strange Meeting

It seemed that out of battle I escaped
Down some profound dull tunnel, long since scooped
Through granites which titanic wars had groined.

Yet also there encumbered sleepers groaned,°
Too fast in thought or death to be bestirred.
Then, as I probed them, one sprang up, and stared
With piteous recognition in fixed eyes,
Lifting distressful hands, as if to bless.
And by his smile, I knew that sullen hall,—
By his dead smile I knew we stood in Hell.   10

With a thousand pains that vision's face was grained;
Yet no blood reached there from the upper ground,
And no guns thumped, or down the flues made moan.°
'Strange friend,' I said, 'here is no cause to mourn.'
'None,' said that other, 'save the undone years,
The hopelessness. Whatever hope is yours,
Was my life also; I went hunting wild
After the wildest beauty in the world,
Which lies not calm in eyes, or braided hair,
But mocks the steady running of the hour,   20
And if it grieves, grieves richlier than here.
For by my glee might many men have laughed,
And of my weeping something had been left,
Which must die now. I mean the truth untold,
The pity of war, the pity war distilled.°
Now men will go content with what we spoiled,
Or, discontent, boil bloody, and be spilled.
They will be swift with swiftness of the tigress.
None will break ranks, though nations trek from progress.
Courage was mine, and I had mystery,   30
Wisdom was mine, and I had mastery:
To miss the march of this retreating world
Into vain citadels that are not walled.
Then, when much blood had clogged their chariot-wheels,
I would go up and wash them from sweet wells,

Even with truths that lie too deep for taint.
I would have poured my spirit without stint
But not through wounds; not on the cess of war.
Foreheads of men have bled where no wounds were.

'I am the enemy you killed, my friend.°   40
I knew you in this dark: for so you frowned
Yesterday through me as you jabbed and killed.
I parried; but my hands were loath and cold.
Let us sleep now . . .'

Futility

Move him into the sun—
Gently its touch awoke him once,
At home, whispering of fields half-sown.
Always it woke him, even in France,
Until this morning and this snow.
If anything might rouse him now
The kind old sun will know.

Think how it wakes the seeds—
Woke once the clays of a cold star.°
Are limbs, so dear achieved, are sides   10
Full-nerved, still warm, too hard to stir?
Was it for this the clay grew tall?°
—O what made fatuous sunbeams toil
To break earth's sleep at all?

The Send-Off

Down the close darkening lanes they sang their way
To the siding-shed,
And lined the train with faces grimly gay.

Their breasts were stuck all white with wreath and spray
As men's are, dead.

Dull porters watched them, and a casual tramp
Stood staring hard,
Sorry to miss them from the upland camp.

Then, unmoved, signals nodded, and a lamp
Winked to the guard.   10

So secretly, like wrongs hushed-up, they went.
They were not ours:
We never heard to which front these were sent;

Nor there if they yet mock what women meant
Who gave them flowers.

Shall they return to beating of great bells
In wild train-loads?
A few, a few, too few for drums and yells,

May creep back, silent, to village wells,
Up half-known roads.   20

Mental Cases

Who are these? Why sit they here in twilight?
Wherefore rock they, purgatorial shadows,
Drooping tongues from jaws that slob their relish,
Baring teeth that leer like skulls' teeth wicked?
Stroke on stroke of pain,—but what slow panic,
Gouged these chasms round their fretted sockets?
Ever from their hair and through their hands' palms
Misery swelters. Surely we have perished
Sleeping, and walk hell; but who these hellish?

—These are men whose minds the Dead have ravished.   10
Memory fingers in their hair of murders,
Multitudinous murders they once witnessed.
Wading sloughs of flesh these helpless wander,

Treading blood from lungs that had loved laughter.°
Always they must see these things and hear them,
Batter of guns and shatter of flying muscles,
Carnage incomparable, and human squander
Rucked too thick for these men's extrication.°

Therefore still their eyeballs shrink tormented
Back into their brains, because on their sense   20
Sunlight seems a blood-smear; night comes blood-black;
Dawn breaks open like a wound that bleeds afresh.
—Thus their heads wear this hilarious, hideous,
Awful falseness of set-smiling corpses.
—Thus their hands are plucking at each other;
Picking at the rope-knouts of their scourging;
Snatching after us who smote them, brother,
Pawing us who dealt them war and madness.

The Parable of the Old Man and the Young

So Abram rose, and clave the wood, and went,
And took the fire with him, and a knife.
And as they sojourned both of them together,
Isaac the first-born spake and said, My Father,
Behold the preparations, fire and iron,
But where the lamb, for this burnt-offering?
Then Abram bound the youth with belts and straps,
And builded parapets and trenches there°
And stretchèd forth the knife to slay his son.
When lo! an Angel called him out of heaven,   10
Saying, Lay not thy hand upon the lad,
Neither do anything to him, thy son.
Behold! Caught in a thicket by its horns,
A Ram. Offer the Ram of Pride instead.

But the old man would not so, but slew his son,
And half the seed of Europe, one by one.

Spring Offensive

Halted against the shade of a last hill
They fed, and eased of pack-loads, were at ease;
And leaning on the nearest chest or knees
Carelessly slept.
                    But many there stood still
To face the stark blank sky beyond the ridge,
Knowing their feet had come to the end of the world.
Marvelling they stood, and watched the long grass swirled
By the May breeze, murmurous with wasp and midge;
And though the summer oozed into their veins
Like an injected drug for their bodies' pains,   10
Sharp on their souls hung the imminent ridge of grass,
Fearfully flashed the sky's mysterious glass.

Hour after hour they ponder the warm field
And the far valley behind, where buttercups
Had blessed with gold their slow boots coming up;
When even the little brambles would not yield
But clutched and clung to them like sorrowing arms.
They breathe like trees unstirred.

Till like a cold gust thrills the little word
At which each body and its soul begird°   20
And tighten them for battle. No alarms
Of bugles, no high flags, no clamorous haste,—
Only a lift and flare of eyes that faced
The sun, like a friend with whom their love is done.
O larger shone that smile against the sun,—
Mightier than his whose bounty these have spurned.

So, soon they topped the hill, and raced together
Over an open stretch of herb and heather
Exposed. And instantly the whole sky burned
With fury against them; earth set sudden cups   30
In thousands for their blood; and the green slope
Chasmed and deepened sheer to infinite space.

Of them who running on that last high place
Breasted the surf of bullets, or went up
On the hot blast and fury of hell's upsurge,
Or plunged and fell away past this world's verge,
Some say God caught them even before they fell.

But what say such as from existence' brink
Ventured but drave too swift to sink,
The few who rushed in the body to enter hell,   40
And there out-fiending all its fiends and flames
With superhuman inhumanities,
Long-famous glories, immemorial shames—
And crawling slowly back, have by degrees
Regained cool peaceful air in wonder—
Why speak not they of comrades that went under?

Smile, Smile, Smile

Head to limp head, the sunk-eyed wounded scanned
Yesterday's *Mail*; the casualties (typed small)
And (large) Vast Booty from our Latest Haul.°
Also, they read of Cheap Homes, not yet planned,
'For', said the paper, 'when this war is done
The men's first instincts will be making homes.
Meanwhile their foremost need is aerodromes,
It being certain war has but begun.
Peace would do wrong to our undying dead,—
The sons we offered might regret they died   10
If we got nothing lasting in their stead.
We must be solidly indemnified.°
Though all be worthy Victory which all bought,
We rulers sitting in this ancient spot
Would wrong our very selves if we forgot
The greatest glory will be theirs who fought,
Who kept this nation in integrity.'
Nation?—The half-limbed readers did not chafe
But smiled at one another curiously

Like secret men who know their secret safe.   20
(This is the thing they know and never speak,
That England one by one had fled to France,
Not many elsewhere now, save under France.)
Pictures of these broad smiles appear each week,
And people in whose voice real feeling rings
Say: How they smile! They're happy now, poor things.

MARGARET POSTGATE COLE
(1893–1980)

═══

MARGARET COLE (*née* Postgate) achieved recognition as a left-wing thinker and politician, a biographer, and as one half of a prolific novel-writing partnership with her husband, G. D. H. Cole. Together, they published more than thirty detective novels between 1925 and 1946. However, both had started their writing careers as poets. *Margaret Postgate's Poems* appeared in 1918—the year of her marriage—and she continued to write poetry, albeit with dwindling frequency, until the 1930s. 'I like what poetry I have written, but others, save a few friends, do not,' she noted lugubriously.[1] Perhaps as a consequence, Cole directed her energies towards politics and fiction. In the years leading up to the Second World War, she produced a series of studies advocating a new economics and a socialist feminism. Watching the rise of fascist ideology, she also came to reject the pacifism that she had previously espoused.

Cole was the daughter of an eminent classicist, John Percival Postgate. Educated at Roedean and Cambridge (where she studied Classics), at first she was more likely to mix in literary than political circles. She became politically active in 1916, when her brother refused non-combatant military service as a conscientious objector and was briefly imprisoned: 'I walked into a new world,' she later remembered, 'a world of doubters and protesters.'[2] Campaigning against conscription, she became an important voice in guild socialism, and it was while working in the Research Department of the Fabian Society that she met her husband-to-be. Ford Madox Ford affectionately based the character of Valentine Wallop in *Parade's End* on her: 'a pug-nosed girl' and 'hot pacifist'. Yet despite a fierce reputation, Cole retained an impartial love of poetry: Walt Whitman was praised as the greatest American poet ('a philosopher, an optimist and a lover of life'), but more surprising politically was her love

---

[1] Quoted by Betty D. Vernon, *Margaret Cole*, 37.
[2] Cole, *Growing up into Revolution*, 37–8.

of Rudyard Kipling for his 'rhythmic robustness and ability to tell a good story'.[3]

[3] Quoted by Betty D. Vernon, *Margaret Cole*, 45, 46.

════

Præmaturi

When men are old, and their friends die,
They are not so sad,
Because their love is running slow,
And cannot spring from the wound with so sharp a pain;
And they are happy with many memories,
And only a little while to be alone.

But we were young, and our friends are dead
Suddenly, and our quick love is torn in two;
So our memories are only hopes that came to nothing.
We are left alone like old men; we should be dead   10
—But there are years and years in which we shall still be young.

The Falling Leaves
November 1915

To-day, as I rode by,
I saw the brown leaves dropping from their tree
In a still afternoon,
When no wind whirled them whistling to the sky,
But thickly, silently,
They fell, like snowflakes wiping out the noon;
And wandered slowly thence
For thinking of a gallant multitude
Which now all withering lay,
Slain by no wind of age or pestilence,   10
But in their beauty strewed
Like snowflakes falling on the Flemish clay.°

Afterwards

Oh, my beloved, shall you and I
Ever be young again, be young again?
The people that were resigned said to me
—Peace will come and you will lie
Under the larches up in Sheer,°
Sleeping,
And eating strawberries and cream and cakes—
   O cakes, O cakes, O cakes, from Fuller's!°
And quite forgetting there's a train to town,
Plotting in an afternoon the new curves for the world.   10

And peace came. And lying in Sheer
I look round at the corpses of the larches
Whom they slew to make pit-props°
For mining the coal for the great armies.
And think, a pit-prop cannot move in the wind,
Nor have red manes hanging in spring from its branches,
And sap making the warm air sweet.
Though you planted it out on the hill again it would be dead.
And if these years have made you into a pit-prop,
To carry the twisting galleries of the world's reconstruction   20
(Where you may thank God, I suppose
That they set you the sole stay of a nasty corner)
What use is it to you? What use
To have your body lying here
In Sheer, underneath the larches?

MAY WEDDERBURN CANNAN

(1893–1973)

MAY WEDDERBURN CANNAN'S father was Charles Cannan, Dean of Trinity College, Oxford, and later Secretary to the Delegates of Oxford University Press. May grew up in a literary household, describing her father's library as her 'world'. Among her father's closest friends was Arthur Quiller-Couch ('Q'), poet, novelist, and literary critic. Her doomed relationship with Q's son, Bevil, would inspire much of her finest poetry.

At the outbreak of war, when so many men left to enlist, Cannan was recruited by her father to help with his firm's general catalogue. But she was desperate to get to France. In May 1915 she crossed the Channel to work in a canteen serving soldiers; this 'adventure'—as she called it—is remembered in 'Rouen', which she included in her first volume, *In War Time* (1917). None of Cannan's poems displayed anxiety about the righteousness of the war effort, despite the change in mood that she detected after the Somme: 'A saying went round, "Went to the war with Rupert Brooke and came home with Siegfried Sassoon." I had much admired some of Sassoon's verse but I was not coming home with him. Someone must go on writing for those who were still convinced of the right of the cause for which they had taken up arms.'[1]

Cannan was in France again in August 1918, this time working for a branch of MI5 in the War Office Department in Paris. There she received and transmitted news of the Armistice in November, taking dictation of the official terms down the telephone. Two days later, she became engaged to Bevil Quiller-Couch, who had come to Paris on leave to propose. She had already noticed the beginnings of the influenza pandemic: 'Paris was swept by it.'[2] Having survived the War and won the Military Cross, Quiller-Couch rejoined his battery in Germany, but became ill in early February 1919, and died of pneumonia following flu. The poems of Cannan's second volume,

---

[1] Cannan, *Grey Ghosts and Voices*, 113.
[2] Ibid., 134.

The Splendid Days (1919), map an agonizing journey from the exhilaration of the Armistice and reciprocated love to the sudden cruelty of Quiller-Couch's death.

———

August 1914

The sun rose over the sweep of the hill
  All bare for the gathered hay,
And a blackbird sang by the window-sill,
  And a girl knelt down to pray:
    'Whom Thou hast kept through the night, O Lord,
    Keep Thou safe through the day.'

The sun rose over the shell-swept height,
  The guns are over the way,
And a soldier turned from the toil of the night
  To the toil of another day,   10
    And a bullet sang by the parapet°
    To drive in the new-turned clay.

The sun sank slow by the sweep of the hill,
  They had carried all the hay,
And a blackbird sang by the window-sill,
  And a girl knelt down to pray:
    'Keep Thou safe through the night, O Lord,
    Whom Thou hast kept through the day.'

The sun sank slow by the shell-swept height,
  The guns had prepared a way,   20
And a soldier turned to sleep that night
  Who would not wake for the day,
    And a blackbird flew from the window-sill,
    When a girl knelt down to pray.

March 1915

Rouen

April 26–May 25, 1915

Early morning over Rouen, hopeful, high, courageous morning,
And the laughter of adventure and the steepness of the stair,
And the dawn across the river, and the wind across the bridges,
And the empty littered station and the tired people there.

Can you recall those mornings and the hurry of awakening,
And the long-forgotten wonder if we should miss the way,
And the unfamiliar faces, and the coming of provisions,
And the freshness and the glory of the labour of the day?

Hot noontide over Rouen, and the sun upon the city,
Sun and dust unceasing, and the glare of cloudless skies,   10
And the voices of the Indians and the endless stream of soldiers,
And the clicking of the tatties, and the buzzing of the flies.°

Can you recall those noontides and the reek of steam and coffee,
Heavy-laden noontides with the evening's peace to win,
And the little piles of woodbines, and the sticky soda bottles,°
And the crushes in the 'Parlour', and the letters coming in?

Quiet night-time over Rouen, and the station full of soldiers,
All the youth and pride of England from the ends of all the earth;
And the rifles piled together, and the creaking of the sword-belts,
And the faces bent above them, and the gay, heart-breaking
        mirth.   20

Can I forget the passage from the cool white-bedded Aid Post
Past the long sun-blistered coaches of the khaki Red Cross train°
To the truck train full of wounded, and the weariness and laughter,
And 'Good-bye, and thank you, Sister', and the empty yards again?

Can you recall the parcels that we made them for the railroad,
Crammed and bulging parcels held together by their string,
And the voices of the sergeants who called the Drafts together,
And the agony and splendour when they stood to save the King?

Can you forget their passing, the cheering and the waving,
The little group of people at the doorway of the shed,   30
The sudden awful silence when the last train swung to darkness,
And the lonely desolation, and the mocking stars o'erhead?

Can you recall the midnights, and the footsteps of night watchers,
Men who came from darkness and went back to dark again,
And the shadows on the rail-lines and the all-inglorious labour,
And the promise of the daylight firing blue the window-pane?

Can you recall the passing through the kitchen door to morning,
Morning very still and solemn breaking slowly on the town,
And the early coastways engines that had met the ships at daybreak,
And the Drafts just out from England, and the day shift coming
    down?   40

Can you forget returning slowly, stumbling on the cobbles,
And the white-decked Red Cross barges dropping seawards for
    the tide,
And the search for English papers, and the blessed cool of water,
And the peace of half-closed shutters that shut out the world
    outside?

Can I forget the evenings and the sunsets on the island,
And the tall black ships at anchor far below our balcony,
And the distant call of bugles, and the white wine in the glasses,
And the long line of the street lamps, stretching Eastwards to
    the sea?

. . . When the world slips slow to darkness, when the office fire
    burns lower,
My heart goes out to Rouen, Rouen all the world away;   50
When other men remember I remember our Adventure
And the trains that go from Rouen at the ending of the day.

                                                        November 1915

Lamplight

We planned to shake the world together, you and I
Being young, and very wise;
Now in the light of the green shaded lamp
Almost I see your eyes
Light with the old gay laughter; you and I
Dreamed greatly of an Empire in those days,
Setting our feet upon laborious ways,
And all you asked of fame
Was crossed swords in the Army List,
My Dear, against your name.°   10

We planned a great Empire together, you and I,
Bound only by the sea;
Now in the quiet of a chill Winter's night
Your voice comes hushed to me
Full of forgotten memories: you and I
Dreamed great dreams of our future in those days,
Setting our feet on undiscovered ways,
And all I asked of fame
A scarlet cross on my breast, my Dear,°
For the swords by your name.   20

We shall never shake the world together, you and I,
For you gave your life away;
And I think my heart was broken by the war,
Since on a summer day
You took the road we never spoke of: you and I
Dreamed greatly of an Empire in those days;
You set your feet upon the Western ways°
And have no need of fame—
There's a scarlet cross on my breast, my Dear,
And a torn cross with your name.   30

December 1916

'After the War'

After the War perhaps I'll sit again
Out on the terrace where I sat with you,
And see the changeless sky and hills beat blue
And live an afternoon of summer through.

I shall remember then, and sad at heart
For the lost day of happiness we knew,
Wish only that some other man were you
And spoke my name as once you used to do.

February 1917

The Armistice

In an Office, in Paris

The news came through over the telephone:
All the terms had been signed: the War was won:
And all the fighting and the agony,
And all the labour of the years were done.
One girl clicked sudden at her typewriter
And whispered, 'Jerry's safe', and sat and stared:
One said, 'It's over, over, it's the end:
The War is over: ended': and a third,
'I can't remember life without the war'.
And one came in and said, 'Look here, they say   10
We can all go at five to celebrate,
As long as two stay on, just for to-day'.

It was quite quiet in the big empty room
Among the typewriters and little piles
Of index cards: one said, 'We'd better just
Finish the day's reports and do the files'.
And said, 'It's awf'lly like *Recessional*,
Now when the tumult has all died away'.°
The other said, 'Thank God we saw it through;
I wonder what they'll do at home to-day'.   20

And said, 'You know it will be quiet to-night
Up at the Front: first time in all these years,
And no one will be killed there any more',
And stopped, to hide her tears.
She said, 'I've told you; he was killed in June'.
The other said, 'My dear, I know; I know . . .
It's over for me too . . . My Man was killed,
Wounded . . . and died . . . at Ypres . . . three years ago . . . °
And he's my Man, and I want him,' she said,
And knew that peace could not give back her Dead.   30

For a Girl

Paris, November 11 1918

Go cheering down the boulevards
And shout and wave your flags,
Go dancing down the boulevards
In all your gladdest rags:
And raise your cheers and wave your flags
And kiss the passer-by,
But let me break my heart in peace
For all the best men die.
    It was 'When the War is over
    Our dreams will all come true,   10
    When the War is over
    I'll come back to you';
    And the War is over, over,
    And they never can come true.

Go cheering down the boulevards
In all your brave array,
Go singing down the boulevards
To celebrate the day:
But for God's sake let me stay at home
And break my heart and cry,   20
I've loved and worked, and I'll be glad,
But all the best men die.

It was 'When the War is over
Our dreams will all come true,
When the War is over
I'll come back to you';
And the War is over, over,
And they never can come true.

Perfect Epilogue

Armistice Day 1933

It's when the leaves are fallen I think of you,
And the long boulevards where the ghosts walk now,
And Paris is dark again save for one great star
That's caught and held in the dark arms of a bough

And wonder, among them are two a girl and boy
Silent, because their love was greater than song,
Who whisper 'farewell' and whisper 'if it's for ever';
And did not know, poor ghosts, for ever could be so long.

It's when the leaves are fallen I think of you,
And if you're lonely too, who went with the great host;°   10
And know that Time's no mender of hearts but only
Still the divider of Light and Darkness, Ghost.

CHARLES SORLEY

(1895–1915)

CHARLES SORLEY was 20 years old when he was killed by a sniper's bullet while leading his men in an attack at the Battle of Loos. His father, the eminent Scottish philosopher William Ritchie Sorley, prepared posthumous editions of his poems and letters, which together comprise the record of an astonishingly precocious talent. Sorley, in the opinion of Siegfried Sassoon and Robert Graves, had been the first poet capable of writing the truth of war unembellished by patriotism. Graves later pronounced him 'one of the three poets of importance killed during the war' (the other two being Isaac Rosenberg and Wilfred Owen).[1]

Sorley was born in Aberdeen, and schooled at Marlborough, where he was already an accomplished poet. Because of the outbreak of the War, he was never able to take up the offer of a scholarship to read Classics at Oxford. He spent the first half of 1914 in Germany, and became a student of philosophy and politics at the University of Jena. On a walking holiday when war was declared, he was immediately arrested and (for nine hours) imprisoned at Trier. A rumour that Britain had declared war against Russia on Germany's side aided a speedy release. Back home Sorley immediately joined the Suffolk Regiment, but his love of German people and culture divided his loyalties: 'I regard the war as one between sisters, between Martha and Mary, the efficient and intolerant against the casual and sympathetic. Each side has a virtue for which it is fighting, and each that virtue's supplementary vice . . . But I think that tolerance is the larger virtue of the two, and efficiency must be her servant.'[2]

Sorley wrote several of his best poems in the first month of the War. He was unimpressed by contemporaries: even his beloved Thomas Hardy, whom he compared to Shakespeare, had written in 'Men Who March Away' an 'arid' poem which was 'untrue of the sentiments of the ranksman going to war'; while Rupert Brooke, for

---

[1] Graves, *Goodbye to All That*, rev. edn. (1957), 175.

[2] Sorley, *The Letters of Charles Sorley*, 232.

all his 'fine words', had 'taken the sentimental attitude'.³ Sorley him-
self resisted the idea of collecting his work into a book, telling his
mother in June 1915, a fortnight after he arrived in France, that the
proposal was 'premature'.⁴

Sorley was killed on 13 October 1915. Among his belongings after
his death was found the manuscript of what has become his best-
known poem, '[When you see millions of the mouthless dead]'.

³ Ibid., 246, 263.   ⁴ Ibid., 273.

[All the hills and vales along]

All the hills and vales along
Earth is bursting into song,
And the singers are the chaps
Who are going to die perhaps.
  O sing, marching men,
  Till the valleys ring again,
    Give your gladness to earth's keeping,
    So be glad, when you are sleeping.

Cast away regret and rue,
Think what you are marching to.   10
Little live, great pass.
Jesus Christ and Barabbas°
Were found the same day.
This died, that went his way.
  So sing with joyful breath,
  For why, you are going to death.
    Teeming earth will surely store
    All the gladness that you pour.

Earth that never doubts nor fears,
Earth that knows of death, not tears,   20
Earth that bore with joyful ease
Hemlock for Socrates,°
Earth that blossomed and was glad
'Neath the cross that Christ had,

Shall rejoice and blossom too
When the bullet reaches you.
  Wherefore, men marching,
  On the road to death, sing!
  Pour your gladness on earth's head,
  So be merry, so be dead.   30

From the hills and valleys earth
Shouts back the sound of mirth,
Tramp of feet and lilt of song
Ringing all the road along.
All the music of their going,
Ringing swinging glad song-throwing,
Earth will echo still, when foot
Lies numb and voice mute.
  On, marching men, on
  To the gates of death with song.   40
  Sow your gladness for earth's reaping,
  So you may be glad, though sleeping.
  Strew your gladness on earth's bed,
  So be merry, so be dead.

To Germany

You are blind like us. Your hurt no man designed,
And no man claimed the conquest of your land.
But gropers both through fields of thought confined
We stumble and we do not understand.
You only saw your future bigly planned,
And we, the tapering paths of our own mind,
And in each other's dearest ways we stand,
And hiss and hate. And the blind fight the blind.

When it is peace, then we may view again
With new-won eyes each other's truer form   10
And wonder. Grown more loving-kind and warm
We'll grasp firm hands and laugh at the old pain,
When it is peace. But until peace, the storm
The darkness and the thunder and the rain.

[A hundred thousand million mites we go]

A hundred thousand million mites we go
Wheeling and tacking o'er the eternal plain,
Some black with death—and some are white with woe.
Who sent us forth? Who takes us home again?

And there is sound of hymns of praise—to whom?
And curses—on whom curses?—snap the air.
And there is hope goes hand in hand with gloom,
And blood and indignation and despair.

And there is murmuring of the multitude
And blindness and great blindness, until some   10
Step forth and challenge blind Vicissitude°
Who tramples on them: so that fewer come.

And nations, ankle-deep in love or hate,
Throw darts or kisses all the unwitting hour
Beside the ominous unseen tide of fate;
And there is emptiness and drink and power.

And some are mounted on swift steeds of thought
And some drag sluggish feet of stable toil.
Yet all, as though they furiously sought,
Twist turn and tussle, close and cling and coil.   20

A hundred thousand million mites we sway
Writhing and tossing on the eternal plain,
Some black with death—but most are bright with Day!
Who sent us forth? Who brings us home again?

                                        September 1914

Two Sonnets

I

Saints have adored the lofty soul of you.
Poets have whitened at your high renown.
We stand among the many millions who
Do hourly wait to pass your pathway down.
You, so familiar, once were strange: we tried
To live as of your presence unaware.
But now in every road on every side
We see your straight and steadfast signpost there.

I think it like that signpost in my land,
Hoary and tall, which pointed me to go   10
Upward, into the hills, on the right hand,
Where the mists swim and the winds shriek and blow,
A homeless land and friendless, but a land
I did not know and that I wished to know.

II

Such, such is Death: no triumph: no defeat:
Only an empty pail, a slate rubbed clean,
A merciful putting away of what has been.

And this we know: Death is not Life effete,°
Life crushed, the broken pail. We who have seen
So marvellous things know well the end not yet.

Victor and vanquished are a–one in death:
Coward and brave: friend, foe. Ghosts do not say
'Come, what was your record when you drew breath?'
But a big blot has hid each yesterday   10
So poor, so manifestly incomplete.
And your bright Promise, withered long and sped,
Is touched, stirs, rises, opens and grows sweet
And blossoms and is you, when you are dead.

                                        12 June 1915

[*When you see millions of the mouthless dead*]

When you see millions of the mouthless dead
Across your dreams in pale battalions go,
Say not soft things as other men have said,
That you'll remember. For you need not so.°
Give them not praise. For, deaf, how should they know
It is not curses heaped on each gashed head?
Nor tears. Their blind eyes see not your tears flow.
Nor honour. It is easy to be dead.
Say only this, 'They are dead.' Then add thereto,
'Yet many a better one has died before.'°   10
Then, scanning all the o'ercrowded mass, should you
Perceive one face that you loved heretofore,
It is a spook. None wears the face you knew.°
Great death has made all his for evermore.

ROBERT GRAVES
(1895–1985)

━━

ROBERT GRAVES was the author of more than 130 books—of fiction, poetry, literary criticism, history, and mythology. The range and profusion of his interests ensured that, unlike many of his contemporaries, he avoided being defined by war writing. In later years Graves did not greatly value his soldier poetry, suppressing much of it. Better known was his brilliant and contentious prose account of his war experience in *Good-bye to All That* (1929), which attracted threats of lawsuits, and caused a decades-long rupture in his friendships with Siegfried Sassoon and Edmund Blunden.

Graves was born into an artistic family. His father was the minor Irish poet Alfred Perceval Graves, and his German mother the daughter of a professor of medicine and the great-niece of the historian Leopold von Ranke. Graves began writing poetry at Charterhouse, and would have taken a scholarship to Oxford had the War not intervened. Appalled at reports of German atrocities in Belgium, in August 1914 he accepted a commission with the Royal Welch Fusiliers. This, Graves noted, put right the 'family balance', with 'ten members fighting on each side'.[1] He arrived at the front in May 1915, and in November he first met Sassoon. Drawn together by their poetry and their homosexuality—Graves would apologize to his uncomprehending friend when he got engaged in late 1917—the two men inspired in each other a surge of creativity. Most of Graves's war poetry is collected in *Over the Brazier* (1916), *Goliath and David* (1916), and *Fairies and Fusiliers* (1917), the last of these taking part of its title from a poem celebrating the tight bonds of the 'lovely friendship' with Sassoon which had 'blossom[ed] from mud'.

Graves was so badly injured at the Somme in July 1916 that he was assumed dead; he read his obituary in *The Times*, and pointedly asked for a correction to be published. Back at the front the following January he suffered a nervous collapse, and was sent home to England

[1] Graves, *Goodbye to All That*, rev. edn. (1957), 289.

for the rest of the War. The summer of 1917 was spent rescuing
Sassoon from court martial after he had made public his 'Declaration'
against the continuation of hostilities; and later that year, while visit-
ing Sassoon at Craiglockhart, Graves met and befriended Wilfred
Owen, who attended his wedding in January 1918. Having lost so
many friends and relatives during the War—latterly Owen himself—
Graves received news of the Armistice by 'cursing and sobbing and
thinking of the dead'. His next collection of poems, *Country Sentiment*
(1920), would be 'a book of romantic poems and ballads' intended, he
confessed, to make him 'forget about the war'.[2]

[2] Ibid.

It's a Queer Time

It's hard to know if you're alive or dead
When steel and fire go roaring through your head.

One moment you'll be crouching at your gun
Traversing, mowing heaps down half in fun:
The next, you choke and clutch at your right breast—
No time to think—leave all—and off you go . . .
To Treasure Island where the Spice winds blow,°
To lovely groves of mango, quince and lime—
Breathe no goodbye, but ho, for the Red West!°
       It's a queer time.   10

You're charging madly at them yelling 'Fag!'°
When somehow something gives and your feet drag.
You fall and strike your head; yet feel no pain
And find . . . you're digging tunnels through the hay
In the Big Barn, 'cause it's a rainy day.
Oh springy hay, and lovely beams to climb!
You're back in the old sailor suit again.°
       It's a queer time.

Or you'll be dozing safe in your dug-out—
A great roar—the trench shakes and falls about—   20

You're struggling, gasping, struggling, then . . . hullo!
Elsie comes tripping gaily down the trench,
Hanky to nose—that lyddite makes a stench—°
Getting her pinafore all over grime.
Funny! because she died ten years ago!
        It's a queer time.

The trouble is, things happen much too quick;
Up jump the Bosches, rifles thump and click,°
You stagger, and the whole scene fades away:
Even good Christians don't like passing straight   30
From Tipperary or their Hymn of Hate°
To Alleluiah-chanting, and the chime
Of golden harps . . . and . . . I'm not well to-day . . .
        It's a queer time.

A Dead Boche

To you who'd read my songs of War
   And only hear of blood and fame,
I'll say (you've heard it said before)
   'War's Hell!' and if you doubt the same,°
To-day I found in Mametz Wood°
A certain cure for lust of blood:

Where, propped against a shattered trunk,
   In a great mess of things unclean,
Sat a dead Boche; he scowled and stunk
   With clothes and face a sodden green,   10
Big-bellied, spectacled, crop-haired,
Dribbling black blood from nose and beard.

Corporal Stare

Back from the Line one night in June
I gave a dinner at Béthune:°

Seven courses, the most gorgeous meal
Money could buy or batman steal.°
Five hungry lads welcomed the fish
With shouts that nearly cracked the dish;
Asparagus came with tender tops,
Strawberries in cream, and mutton chops.
Said Jenkins, as my hand he shook,
'They'll put this in the history book.'   10
We bawled Church anthems *in choro*°
Of Bethlehem and Hermon snow,°
And drinking songs, a mighty sound
To help the good red Pommard round.°
Stories and laughter interspersed,
We drowned a long La Bassée thirst—°
Trenches in June make throats damned dry.
Then through the window suddenly,
Badge, stripes and medals all complete,
We saw him swagger up the street,   20
Just like a live man—Corporal Stare!
    Stare! Killed last month at Festubert,°
Caught on patrol near the Boche wire,
Torn horribly by machine-gun fire!
He paused, saluted smartly, grinned,
Then passed away like a puff of wind,
Leaving us blank astonishment.
The song broke, up we started, leant
Out of the window—nothing there,
Not the least shadow of Corporal Stare,   30
Only a quiver of smoke that showed
A fag-end dropped on the silent road.

A Child's Nightmare

Through long nursery nights he stood
By my bed unwearying,
Loomed gigantic, formless, queer,
Purring in my haunted ear

That same hideous nightmare thing,
Talking, as he lapped my blood,
In a voice cruel and flat,
Saying for ever, 'Cat! . . . Cat! . . . Cat! . . .'

That one word was all he said,
That one word through all my sleep,   10
In monotonous mock despair.
Nonsense may be light as air,
But there's Nonsense that can keep
Horror bristling round the head,
When a voice cruel and flat
Says for ever, 'Cat! . . . Cat! . . . Cat! . . .'

He had faded, he was gone
Years ago with Nursery Land,
When he leapt on me again
From the clank of a night train,   20
Overpowered me foot and hand,
Lapped my blood, while on and on
The old voice cruel and flat
Purred for ever, 'Cat! . . . Cat! . . . Cat! . . .'

Morphia drowsed, again I lay°
In a crater by High Wood:°
He was there with straddling legs,
Staring eyes as big as eggs,
Purring as he lapped my blood,
His black bulk darkening the day,   30
With a voice cruel and flat,
'Cat! . . . Cat! . . . Cat! . . .' he said,
    'Cat! . . . Cat! . . .'

When I'm shot through heart and head,
And there's no choice but to die,
The last word I'll hear, no doubt,
Won't be 'Charge!' or 'Bomb them out!'
Nor the stretcher-bearer's cry,
'Let that body be, he's dead!'

But a voice cruel and flat   40
Saying for ever, 'Cat! . . . Cat! . . . Cat!'

Two Fusiliers

And have we done with War at last?
Well, we've been lucky devils both,
And there's no need of pledge or oath
To bind our lovely friendship fast,
By firmer stuff
Close bound enough.

By wire and wood and stake we're bound,
By Fricourt and by Festubert,°
By whipping rain, by the sun's glare,
By all the misery and loud sound,   10
By a Spring day,
By Picard clay.°

Show me the two so closely bound
As we, by the wet bond of blood,
By friendship blossoming from mud,
By Death: we faced him, and we found
Beauty in Death,
In dead men, breath.

Sergeant–Major Money
(1917)

It wasn't our battalion, but we lay alongside it,
    So the story is as true as the telling is frank.
They hadn't one Line–officer left, after Arras,°
    Except a batty major and the Colonel, who drank.

'B' Company Commander was fresh from the Depôt,
    An expert on gas drill, otherwise a dud;
So Sergeant-Major Money carried on, as instructed,
    And that's where the swaddies began to sweat blood.°

His Old Army humour was so well-spiced and hearty°
   That one poor sod shot himself, and one lost his wits;   10
But discipline's maintained, and back in rest-billets°
   The Colonel congratulates 'B' Company on their kits.

The subalterns went easy, as was only natural
   With a terror like Money driving the machine,
Till finally two Welshmen, butties from the Rhondda,°
   Bayoneted their bugbear in a field-canteen.

Well, we couldn't blame the officers, they relied on Money;
   We couldn't blame the pitboys, their courage was grand;
Or, least of all, blame Money, an old stiff surviving
   In a New (bloody) Army he couldn't understand.°   20

Recalling War

Entrance and exit wounds are silvered clean,
The track aches only when the rain reminds.
The one-legged man forgets his leg of wood,
The one-armed man his jointed wooden arm.
The blinded man sees with his ears and hands
As much or more than once with both his eyes.
Their war was fought these twenty years ago
And now assumes the nature-look of time,
As when the morning traveller turns and views
His wild night-stumbling carved into a hill.   10

What, then, was war? No mere discord of flags
But an infection of the common sky
That sagged ominously upon the earth
Even when the season was the airiest May.
Down pressed the sky, and we, oppressed, thrust out
Boastful tongue, clenched fist and valiant yard.
Natural infirmities were out of mode,
For Death was young again: patron alone
Of healthy dying, premature fate-spasm.

Fear made fine bed-fellows. Sick with delight   20
At life's discovered transitoriness,
Our youth became all-flesh and waived the mind.
Never was such antiqueness of romance,
Such tasty honey oozing from the heart.
And old importances came swimming back—
Wine, meat, log-fires, a roof over the head,
A weapon at the thigh, surgeons at call.
Even there was a use again for God—
A word of rage in lack of meat, wine, fire,
In ache of wounds beyond all surgeoning.   30

War was return of earth to ugly earth,
War was foundering of sublimities,
Extinction of each happy art and faith
By which the world had still kept head in air,
Protesting logic or protesting love,
Until the unendurable moment struck—
The inward scream, the duty to run mad.

And we recall the merry ways of guns—
Nibbling the walls of factory and church
Like a child, piecrust; felling groves of trees   40
Like a child, dandelions with a switch.
Machine-guns rattle toy-like from a hill,
Down in a row the brave tin-soldiers fall:
A sight to be recalled in elder days
When learnedly the future we devote
To yet more boastful visions of despair.

DAVID JONES
(1895–1974)

AMONG the significant poets of the War, David Jones proves by far the most difficult to anthologize. His masterpiece is *In Parenthesis* (1937), a book-length 'writing'—as Jones himself described it—which defies traditional categories. Neither wholly poetry nor wholly prose but held as if in parentheses between them, Jones's epic has been called the most important book to have been inspired by the War. T. S. Eliot, who published it at Faber, describes having been deeply moved when he first read the typescript: 'I then regarded it, and I still regard it, as a work of genius.'[1] For Eliot, Jones belonged in elite company with Ezra Pound, James Joyce, and himself.

Although born in Kent, Jones was heavily influenced by his father's Welsh heritage. From an early age he showed astonishing artistic ability, and in his teens enrolled at Camberwell Art School. When war was declared he attempted unsuccessfully to enlist with the Artists' Rifles, but in January 1915 he became a private in the Royal Welch Fusiliers. The closest he came to encountering a fellow poet was when—as the two men established when they met in old age almost fifty years later—Jones's company relieved Siegfried Sassoon's on 5 July 1916. Within days, Jones was shot in the leg during an assault on Mametz Wood. *In Parenthesis*, obliquely based on Jones's experiences, ends at that point with one of the protagonists dragging himself back towards his own lines. Jones was at the front again by October 1916, and would not escape the War until he developed a severe bout of trench fever in February 1918.

Jones portrayed himself as 'a parade's despair',[2] so it is surprising that he gave serious consideration to re-enlisting after the War. In the event, he secured a government grant to study at the Westminster School of Art, and in 1922 (having converted to Catholicism the year before) he joined Eric Gill's artistic community, first in Sussex, then in the Black Mountains. Most of his work during this period was

---

[1] T. S. Eliot, 'A Note of Introduction', in *In Parenthesis*, rev. edn. (1963), p. vii.

[2] Jones, 'Preface', *In Parenthesis*, p. xv.

as an illustrator, although he increasingly experimented with water-colours. But it was through a literary rather than a visual form that Jones would achieve artistic expression of his wartime experiences. In 1927 or 1928 he began *In Parenthesis*, attempting to make what he called 'a shape in words'.

Jones identified a change in the nature of warfare after the start of the Battle of the Somme: 'striking with a hand weapon' had given way to 'loosing poison from the sky', so that 'we doubt the decency of our own inventions'. Set in the earlier part of the War before 'whole-sale slaughter', *In Parenthesis* is still able to celebrate common decency and courage, to revel in the verbal ingenuities of its multiple voices, and to connect the War with earlier conflicts through language and allusion.[3] 'I did not intend this as a "War Book",' Jones states in his 'Preface', but 'it happens to be concerned with war. I should prefer it to be about a good kind of peace.' He dedicated *In Parenthesis* to— inter alia—'the enemy front-fighters who shared our pains against whom we found ourselves by misadventure'.

[3] Jones, 'Preface', *In Parenthesis*, p. xiv, p. ix.

━━━━━

from *In Parenthesis*

[*The march from training camp to the embarcation port, from Part 1*]

The rain increases with the light and the weight increases with the rain. In all that long column in brand-new overseas boots weeping blisters stick to the hard wool of grey government socks.

I'm a bleedin' cripple already Corporal, confides a limping child.

Kipt' that step there.°

Keep that proper distance.

Keept' y'r siction o'four—can't fall out me little darlin'.°

Corporal Quilter subsides, he too retreats within himself,   10
he has his private thoughts also.

It's a proper massacre of the innocents in a manner of speaking, no so-called seven ages o' man only this bastard military age.°

Keep that step there.
Keep that section distance.
Hand us thet gas-pipe young Saunders—let's see you shape
—you too, little Benjamin—hang him about like a goddam
Chris'us tree—use his ample shoulders for an armoury-
rack—it is his part to succour the lambs of the flock.°   20

With some slackening of the rain the band had wiped
their instruments. Broken catches on the wind-gust came
shrilly back:
Of Hector and Lysander and such great names as these°
—the march proper to them.°

[*A nocturnal march, from Part 3*]

The repeated passing back of aidful messages assumes a ca-
dency.
Mind the hole
mind the hole
mind the hole to left
hole right
step over
keep left, left.

One grovelling, precipitated, with his gear tangled, strug-
gles to feet again: 10
Left be buggered.

Sorry mate—you all right china?—lift us yer rifle—an'°
don't take it so Honey—but rather, mind
the wire here°
mind the wire
mind the wire
mind the wire.

Extricate with some care that taut strand—it may well be
you'll sweat on its unbrokenness.°

[*What the sentry hears at night, from Part 3*]

You can hear the silence of it:
You can hear the rat of no-man's-land°
rut-out intricacies,
weasel-out his patient workings,

scrut, scrut, sscrut,
harrow-out earthly, trowel his cunning paw;
redeem the time of our uncharity, to sap his own amphibi-
ous paradise.

You can hear his carrying-parties rustle our corruptions
through the night-weeds—contest the choicest morsels in his   10
tiny conduits, bead-eyed feast on us; by a rule of his nature,
at night-feast on the broken of us.

Those broad-pinioned;
blue-burnished, or brinded-back;
whose proud eyes watched
                    the broken emblems
droop and drag dust,
suffer with us this metamorphosis.

These too have shed their fine feathers; these too have
slimed their dark-bright coats, these too have condescended   20
to dig in.

The white-tailed eagle at the battle ebb,°
                    where the sea wars against the river°
the speckled kite of Maldon°
and the crow
have naturally selected to be un-winged;
to go on the belly, to
sap   sap   sap
with festered spines, arched under the moon; furrit with°
whiskered snouts the secret parts of us.   30

When it's all quiet you can hear them:
scrut scrut scrut
when it's as quiet as this is.

It's so very still.

Your body fits the crevice of the bay in the most comfor-
table fashion imaginable.

It's cushy enough.°

[*Distribution of rations, from Part 4*]

In a little while they came again, the Lance-Corporal with
his file of two, carrying a full sack.

No. 1 section gathered, bunched, in the confined traverse;°
that lance-jack balances carefully his half mess-tin of rum.°

They bring for them,
in common:
Loose tea mingled with white sugar, tied in heel of sand-
bag, pudding fashion, congealed, clinging to the hemp mesh,
and one tin of butter.

    They bring for them,   10
for each and for several;
he makes division, he ordains:
three ration biscuits,
one-third part of a loaf,
two Field Service postcards,°
one Field Service envelope,
one piece of cheese of uncertain dimension, clammy, pitted
with earth and very hairy, imprinted with the sodden hes-
sian's weft and warp; powerfully unappetising;
one tin of *Tickler's* plum and apple for three,°   20
two packets of *Trumpeter* for cigarette smokers,°
one tin of issue tobacco for pipe smokers.

[*The moments before going over the top, from Part 7*]

Perhaps they'll cancel it.
O blow fall out the officers cantcher, like a wet afternoon°
or the King's Birthday.°
    Or you read it again many times to see if it will come dif-
ferent:
you can't believe the cup won't pass from
or they won't make a better show°
in the Garden.°
Won't someone forbid the banns°
or God himself will stay their hands.   10
It just can't happen in our family°
even though a thousand
and ten thousand at thy right hand.

[*Encountering the enemy, from Part 7*]

It was largely his machine guns in Acid Copse that did it, and°
our own heavies firing by map reference, with all lines phut°
and no reliable liaison.

So you just lay where you were and shielded what you could
of your body.

It slackened a little and they try short rushes and you find
yourself alone in a denseness of hazel-brush and body high
bramble and between the bright interstices and multifarious°
green-stuff, grey textile, scarlet-edged goes and comes—and
there is another withdrawing-heel from the thicket.   10

His light stick-bomb winged above your thorn-bush, and°
aged oak-timbers shiver and leaves shower like thrown blos-
som for a conqueror.
You tug at rusted pin—
it gives unexpectedly and your fingers pressed to release
flange.°
You loose the thing into the underbrush.

Dark-faceted iron oval lobs heavily to fungus-cushioned
dank, wobbles under low leaf to lie, near where the heel drew
out just now; and tough root-fibres boomerang to top-most   20
green filigree and earth clods flung disturb fresh fragile shoots°
that brush the sky.

You huddle closer to your mossy bed
you make yourself scarce
you scramble forward and pretend not to see,
but ruby drops from young beech-sprigs—
are bright your hands and face.

And the other one cries from the breaking-buckthorn.

He calls for Elsa, for Manuela
for the parish priest of Burkersdorf in Saxe Altenburg.°   30

You grab his dropt stick-bomb as you go, but somehow you
don't fancy it and anyway you forget how it works. You defi-
nitely like the coloured label on the handle, you throw it to°
the tall wood-weeds.

So double detonations, back and fro like well-played-up-to
service at a net, mark left and right the forcing of the groves.

[*Digging in after an assault, from Part 7*]

But it's no good you cant do it with these toy spades, you want
axes, heavy iron for tough anchoring roots, tendoned deep
down.

When someone brought up the Jerry picks it was better,°
and you did manage to make some impression. And the next
one to you, where he bends to delve gets it in the middle body.
Private Ball is not instructed, and how could you stay so fast
a tide, it would be difficult with him screaming whenever
you move him ever so little, let alone try with jack-knife to
cut clear the hampering cloth.   10

The First Field Dressing is futile as frantic seaman's shift
bunged to stoved bulwark, so soon the darking flood perco-°
lates and he dies in your arms.
    And get back to that digging can't yer—
this aint a bloody Wake
        for these dead, who soon will have their dead
for burial clods heaped over.
Nor time for halsing°
nor to clip green wounds°
nor weeping Maries bringing anointments°   20
neither any word spoken
nor no decent nor appropriate sowing of this seed
nor remembrance of the harvesting
of the renascent cycle°
and return
nor shaving of the head nor ritual incising for these *viriles* un-
der each tree.°
    No one sings: Lully lully
for the mate whose blood runs down.°

EDMUND BLUNDEN
(1896–1974)

━━━

EDMUND BLUNDEN recalled his wartime self as 'a harmless young
shepherd in a soldier's coat'.[1] The soldier and the shepherd—the
martial and the pastoral—represent the twin subjects of his best
poetry. More than any of his contemporaries, Blunden was painfully
attuned to the destruction that war wrought not only on soldiers and
civilians but on an environment that constantly brought to mind his
own loved English landscapes. The collision between high Romantic
celebration of nature and the brutal horrors of the trenches inspired
his writings about the War: 'It was a beautiful world even then', he
noted of the battlescape in his memoir, *Undertones of War* (1928).

Blunden was born in London, but his family moved to Kent when
he was 4. Educated at Christ's Hospital in Horsham, where he began
to write poetry, he deferred a scholarship at Oxford because of the
outbreak of the War. In August 1915 he took a commission as second
lieutenant in the Royal Sussex Regiment, and was posted to the front
in May 1916. He came through two years at Festubert, Ypres, and
Passchendaele unscathed, and was awarded the Military Cross in
1916 after reaching the German line on a reconnaissance mission.

Many of Blunden's wartime poems vanished in the mud
('Festubert: The Old German Line' and 'Thiepval Wood' are rare
survivors). His reputation is based on poetry written subsequently,
and the temporal distance is acknowledged in titles like '1916 seen
from 1921'. The developing relationship between past and present,
war and memory, becomes part of the drama of poems from the 1920s
and later, as Blunden returns figuratively and (sometimes) literally to
the battlefields to make sense of his experiences. 'I must go over the
ground again', he confesses in the 'Preliminary' to *Undertones of War*.
That compulsion informed his prose account and the thirty-two war
poems that he published as a 'supplement' to it.

Blunden met and befriended Siegfried Sassoon in 1919, sharing

---

[1] Blunden, *Undertones of War* (repr. 2000), 191.

with his older contemporary not just war and poetry but a love of
cricket and the countryside. After several years as a literary journal-
ist, he accepted a post as professor of English in Tokyo in 1924, where
he stayed for three years. In 1931 he became a tutor at Merton
College, Oxford. There he would later include among his students
the finest poet of the Second World War, Keith Douglas, whom he
was able to assure that 'The fighting man in this as in other wars is . . .
the only man whom Truth really cares to meet.'[2]

Blunden was also a friend to war poets in other respects. During a
prestigious academic career, he edited the poetry of Wilfred Owen
(1931) and Ivor Gurney (1954)—the latter virtually unknown at the
time. The War was never far from Blunden's mind, and his last
poem, 'Ancre Sunshine', went over the ground one final time. Five
decades after his own 'fighting' had ended, Blunden admitted to an
interviewer in the 1960s: 'My experiences in the First World War
have haunted me all my life and for many days I have, it seemed, lived
in that world rather than this.'[3]

[2] Quoted by Desmond Graham in *Keith Douglas: A Prose Miscellany* (Manchester:
Carcanet, 1985), 129.
[3] Quoted by Paul Fussell, *The Great War and Modern Memory*, 256.

Festubert: The Old German Line

Sparse mists of moonlight hurt our eyes
With gouged and scourged uncertainties
Of soul and soil in agonies.

One derelict grim skeleton
That drench and dry had battened on
Still seemed to wish us malison;°

Still zipped across the gouts of lead
Or cracked like whipcracks overhead;
The gray rags fluttered on the dead.°

May 1916

Thiepval Wood

The tired air groans as the heavies swing over, the river-hollows
    boom;°
The shell-fountains leap from the swamps, and with wildfire and
    fume
    The shoulder of the chalkdown convulses.°
Then jabbering echoes stampede in the slatting wood,
Ember-black the gibbet trees like bones or thorns protrude°
    From the poisonous smoke—past all impulses.
To them these silvery dews can never again be dear,
Nor the blue javelin-flame of thunderous noons strike fear.

September 1916

1916 seen from 1921

Tired with dull grief, grown old before my day,
I sit in solitude and only hear
Long silent laughters, murmurings of dismay,
The lost intensities of hope and fear;
In those old marshes yet the rifles lie,
On the thin breastwork flutter the grey rags,
The very books I read are there—and I
Dead as the men I loved, wait while life drags

Its wounded length from those sad streets of war
Into green places here, that were my own;   10
But now what once was mine is mine no more,
I seek such neighbours here and I find none.
With such strong gentleness and tireless will
Those ruined houses seared themselves in me,
Passionate I look for their dumb story still,
And the charred stub outspeaks the living tree.

I rise up at the singing of a bird
And scarcely knowing slink along the lane,
I dare not give a soul a look or word
Where all have homes and none's at home in vain: 20

Deep red the rose burned in the grim redoubt,°
The self-sown wheat around was like a flood,
In the hot path the lizard lolled time out,
The saints in broken shrines were bright as blood.

Sweet Mary's shrine between the sycamores!°
There we would go, my friend of friends and I,
And snatch long moments from the grudging wars,
Whose dark made light intense to see them by.
Shrewd bit the morning fog, the whining shots
Spun from the wrangling wire; then in warm swoon   30
The sun hushed all but the cool orchard plots,
We crept in the tall grass and slept till noon.

Illusions

Trenches in the moonlight, in the lulling moonlight
Have had their loveliness; when dancing dewy grasses
Caressed us passing along their earthy lanes;
When the crucifix hanging over was strangely illumined,
And one imagined music, one even heard the brave bird
In the sighing orchards flute above the weedy well.
There are such moments; forgive me that I note them,
Nor gloze that there comes soon the nemesis of beauty,°
In the fluttering relics that at first glimmer wakened
Terror—the no-man's ditch suddenly forking: 10
There, the enemy's best with bombs and brains and courage!
—Softly, swiftly, at once be animal and angel—
But, O no, no, they're Death's malkins dangling in the wire°
    For the moon's interpretation.

Concert Party: Busseboom

The stage was set, the house was packed,
    The famous troop began;
Our laughter thundered, act by act;
    Time light as sunbeams ran.

Dance sprang and spun and neared and fled,
   Jest chirped at gayest pitch,
Rhythm dazzled, action sped
   Most comically rich.

With generals and lame privates both
   Such charms worked wonders, till   10
The show was over—lagging loth
   We faced the sunset chill;

And standing on the sandy way,
   With the cracked church peering past,
We heard another matinée,
   We heard the maniac blast

Of barrage south by Saint Eloi,°
   And the red lights flaming there
Called madness: Come, my bonny boy,
   And dance to the latest air.   20

To this new concert, white we stood;
   Cold certainty held our breath;
While men in tunnels below Larch Wood°
   Were kicking men to death.

Vlamertinghe: Passing the Chateau, July 1917

'And all her silken flanks with garlands drest'—
But we are coming to the sacrifice.°
Must those have flowers who are not yet gone West?
May those have flowers who live with death and lice?
This must be the floweriest place
That earth allows; the queenly face
Of the proud mansion borrows grace for grace
Spite of those brute guns lowing at the skies.

Bold great daisies, golden lights,
Bubbling roses' pinks and whites—   10
Such a gay carpet! poppies by the million;
Such damask! such vermilion!
But if you ask me, mate, the choice of colour
Is scarcely right; this red should have been much duller.

La Quinque Rue

O road in dizzy moonlight bleak and blue,
With forlorn effigies of farms besprawled,
With trees bitterly bare or snapped in two,
Why riddle me thus—attracted and appalled?
For surely now the grounds both left and right
Are tilled, and scarless houses undismayed
Glow in the lustrous mercy of sweet night
And one may hear the flute or fiddle played.
Why lead me then
Through the foul-gorged, the cemeterial fen   10
To fear's sharp sentries? Why do dreadful rags
Fur these bulged banks, and feebly move to the wind?
That battered drum, say why it clacks and brags?
Another and another! what's behind?
How is it that these flints flame out fire's tongue,
Shrivelling my thought? these collapsed skeletons,
What are they, and these iron hunks among?
Why clink those spades, why glare these startling suns
And topple to the wet and crawling grass,
Where the strange briars in taloned hedges twine?   20
What need of that stopped tread, that countersign?
O road, I know those muttering groups you pass.
I know your way of turning blood to glass.
But, I am told, to-night you safely shine
To trim roofs and cropped fields; the error's mine.

'Trench Nomenclature'

Genius named them, as I live! What but genius could compress
In a title what man's humour said to man's supreme distress?
Jacob's Ladder ran reversed, from earth to a fiery pit extending,°
With not angels but poor Angles, those for the most part
    descending.°
Thence *Brock's Benefit* commanded endless fireworks by two nations,°
Yet some voices there were raised against the rival coruscations.°
Picturedome peeped out upon a dream, not Turner could surpass,°
And presently the picture moved, and greyed with corpses and
    morass.°
So down south; and if remembrance travel north, she marvels yet
At the sharp Shakespearean names, and with sad mirth her eyes
    are wet.   10
The Great Wall of China rose, a four-foot breastwork, fronting guns°
That, when the word dropped, beat at once its silly ounces with
    brute tons;
Odd *Krab Krawl* on paper looks, and odd the foul-breathed alley
    twisted,
As one feared to twist there too, if *Minnie*, forward quean, insisted.°
Where the Yser at *Dead End* floated on its bloody waters°
Dead and rotten monstrous fish, note (east) *The Pike and Eel*
    headquarters.
Ah, such names and apparitions! name on name! what's in a name?°
From the fabled vase the genie in his shattering horror came.°

'Can you Remember?'

Yes, I still remember
   The whole thing in a way;
Edge and exactitude
   Depend on the day.

Of all that prodigious scene
   There seems scanty loss,
Though mists mainly float and screen
   Canal, spire and fosse;°

Though commonly I fail to name
    That once obvious Hill,   10
And where we went, and whence we came
    To be killed, or kill.

Those mists are spiritual
    And luminous-obscure,
Evolved of countless circumstance
    Of which I am sure;

Of which, at the instance
    Of sound, smell, change and stir,
New-old shapes for ever
    Intensely recur.   20

And some are sparkling, laughing, singing,
    Young, heroic, mild;
And some incurable, twisted,
    Shrieking, dumb, defiled.

Ancre Sunshine

In all his glory the sun was high and glowing
Over the farm world where we found great peace,
And clearest blue the winding river flowing
Seemed to be celebrating a release
From all that speed and music of its own
Which but for some few cows we heard alone.

Here half a century before might I,
Had something chanced, about this point have lain,
Looking with failing sense on such blue sky,
And then became a name with others slain.   10
But that thought vanished. Claire was wandering free°
Miraumont way in the golden tasselled lea.°

The railway trains went by, and dreamily
I thought of them as planets in their course,

Thought bound perhaps for Arras, how would we°
Have wondered once if through the furious force
Murdering our world one of these same had come,
Friendly and sensible—'the war's over, chum'.

And now it seemed Claire was afar, and I
Alone, and where she went perhaps the mill°   20
That used to be had rised again, and by
All that had fallen was in its old form still,
For her to witness, with no cold surprise,
In one of those moments when nothing dies.

EDGELL RICKWORD
(1898–1982)

▬▬▬

YOUNGEST of the soldier–poets, Edgell Rickword wrote all his war poetry after the Armistice. As a schoolboy at Colchester Grammar he had been impatient to join the army, and in July 1916 he was sworn in to the Artists' Rifles. There followed a year at training camp in Essex, and several months with his new regiment, the Berkshires, in Dublin. He arrived at the front as an officer in January 1918, and was injured by a shell blast in March. At Beaumont Hamel in May he was wounded again; during his recovery in England he read Graves and then Sassoon, whose *Counter-Attack* 'named things as one talked about them' and demonstrated to Rickword how to write 'more colloquially'.[1] Back at the front, in October Rickword carried out a dangerous reconnaissance mission, for which he would be awarded the Military Cross. He came close to death nearly two months after the Armistice, when a serious bout of septicaemia necessitated the removal of his left eye.

Rickword took a scholarship to Oxford in 1919, but did not graduate. By now he was writing and publishing in earnest; his first volume of poems, including 'Winter Warfare', 'The Soldier Addresses his Body', 'Trench Poets', and 'War and Peace', appeared in 1921. Rickword later described his war poems as 'reflecting on the experience rather than writing directly out of the experience'.[2] He also busied himself as a literary critic and editor of literary magazines. As the decade wore on, he increasingly identified with left-wing radicalism, and in 1934 he founded the *Left Review*. That same year he joined the Communist Party. Rickword's virtual abandonment of poetry after the appearance of his third volume in 1931 is often blamed on his political commitments. He eventually came to view the War as 'the result of the same human will that condemns the people

---

[1] Rickword, in Alan Young and Michael Schmidt, 'A Conversation with Edgell Rickword', http://www.poetrymagazines.org.uk/magazine/record.asp?id=1920.
[2] Ibid.

to a low and precarious standard of life whether engaged with an external foe or not'.³

³ Quoted by Michael Copp, *Edgell Rickword*, 14.

━━━

Winter Warfare

Colonel Cold strode up the Line
    (tabs of rime and spurs of ice);
stiffened all that met his glare:
    horses, men, and lice.

Visited a forward post,
    left them burning, ear to foot;
fingers stuck to biting steel,
    toes to frozen boot.

Stalked on into No Man's Land,
    turned the wire to fleecy wool,   10
iron stakes to sugar sticks
    snapping at a pull.

Those who watched with hoary eyes
    saw two figures gleaming there;
Hauptmann Kälte, Colonel Cold,°
    gaunt in the grey air.

Stiffly, tinkling spurs they moved,
    glassy-eyed, with glinting heel
stabbing those who lingered there
    torn by screaming steel.   20

The Soldier Addresses his Body

I shall be mad if you get smashed about,
we've had good times together, you and I;
although you groused a bit when luck was out,
say a girl turned us down, or we went dry.

But there's a world of things we haven't done,
countries not seen, where people do strange things;
eat fish alive, and mimic in the sun
the solemn gestures of their stone-grey kings.

I've heard of forests that are dim at noon
where snakes and creepers wrestle all day long;   10
where vivid beasts grow pale with the full moon,
gibber and cry, and wail a mad old song;

because at the full moon the Hippogriff°
with crinkled ivory snout and agate feet,°
with his green eye will glare them cold and stiff
for the coward Wyvern to come down and eat.°

Vodka and kvass, and bitter mountain wines°
we've never drunk; nor snatched the bursting grapes
to pelt slim girls among Sicilian vines,
who'd flicker through the leaves, faint frolic shapes.   20

Yes, there's a world of things we've never done,
but it's a sweat to knock them into rhyme,
let's have a drink, and give the cards a run
and leave dull verse to the dull peaceful time.

Advice to a Girl from the War

Weep for me half a day,
    then dry your eyes.
Think! is a mess of clay
    worth a girl's sighs?

Sigh three days if you can
    for my waste blood.
Think then, you love a man
    whose face is mud;

whose flesh and hair thrill not
    to any touch.   10
  Dear! best things soonest rot!
    Dream not of such!

Trench Poets

I knew a man, he was my chum,
but he grew darker day by day,
and would not brush the flies away,
nor blanch however fierce the hum
of passing shells; I used to read,
to rouse him, random things from Donne—
like 'Get with child a mandrake-root.'°
But you can tell he was far gone,
for he lay gaping, mackerel-eyed,
and stiff and senseless as a post   10
even when that old poet cried
'I long to talk with some old lover's ghost.'°

I tried the Elegies one day,
but he, because he heard me say:
'What needst thou have more covering than a man?'°
grinned nastily, so then I knew
the worms had got his brains at last.
There was one thing I still might do
to starve those worms; I racked my head
for wholesome lines and quoted *Maud*.°   20
His grin got worse and I could see
he sneered at passion's purity.
He stank so badly, though we were great chums
I had to leave him; then rats ate his thumbs.

War and Peace

In sodden trenches I have heard men speak,
  though numb and wretched, wise and witty things;

and loved them for the stubbornness that clings
longest to laughter when Death's pulleys creak;

and seeing cool nurses move on tireless feet
to do abominable things with grace,
dreamed them dear sisters in that haunted place
where, with child's voices, strong men howl or bleat.

Yet now those men lay stubborn courage by,
riding dull-eyed and silent in the train   10
to old-man stools; or sell gay-coloured socks
and listen fearfully for Death; so I
love the low-laughing girls, who now again
go daintily, in thin and flowery frocks.

Moonrise over Battlefield

After the fallen sun the wind was sad
like violins behind immense old walls.
Trees were musicians swaying round the bend
of a woman in gloomy halls.

In privacy of music she made ready
with comb and silver dust and fard;°
under her silken rest her little belly
shone like a bladder of sweet lard.

She drifted with the grand air of a punk°
on Heaven's streets soliciting white saints;   10
then lay in bright communion on a cloud-bank
as one who near extreme of pleasure faints.

Then I thought, standing in the ruined trench,
(all round, dead Boche white-shirted slumped like sheep),°
'Why does this damned entrancing bitch
choose all her lovers among them that sleep?'

MUSIC-HALL AND TRENCH SONGS

WHEN F. T. Nettleingham published *Tommy's Tunes* in 1917, he reas-
sured his readership that 'It is a peculiarity of British humour to be
derogatory to its own dignity, to wipe itself in the mud, to affect self-
satire to an alarming extent.'[1] The songs that he collected may have
demonstrated the 'lofty cynicism' and 'confirmed fatalism' of the
average Tommy, he continued, but any foreigner who—on the basis
of Tommy's musical proclivities—took the British soldier to be lack-
ing in discipline or *esprit de corps* would be dangerously mistaken.
That slippage between song and deed was also noted by Ivor Gurney,
whose regiment sang 'I Want to Go Home' in the midst of heavy
bombardment: it is not a brave song, Gurney acknowledged, but
'brave men sing it'.[2]

The sentiments heard in trench songs were not new. Several of the
best-known songs are not included here because they date from earl-
ier conflicts: 'I Don't Want to Be a Soldier' seems to have originated
in the Peninsular War, and 'When This Bloody War is Over' in the
American Civil War. 'Mademoiselle from Armenteers' is a military
heirloom, its lyrics adapted according to circumstance and audience;
the version below is different enough from predecessors to justify its
presence. Many songs have multiple versions ranging from the chaste
to the obscene, and many more are bawdy parodies of hymns or
music-hall tunes. Nettleingham apologized to his soldier–readers for
having 'purged' their favourites, and admitted that he had been
obliged to exclude some songs as beyond all possibility of purging.
The trench songs among the selection below also err on the side of
decorum—Mademoiselle from Armenteers 'hasn't been *kissed* for
forty years'.

[1] Nettleingham (ed.), *Tommy's Tunes*, 14.
[2] Gurney, *Collected Letters*, 106.

Never Mind

(Air: 'Never Mind')

If the sergeant drinks your rum, *never mind*;
And your face may lose its smile, *never mind*.
He's entitled to a tot but not the bleeding lot,
If the sergeant drinks your rum, *never mind*.

When old Jerry shells the trench, *never mind*;°
When old Jerry shells the trench, *never mind*.
Though the sandbags bust and fly you have only once to die,
If old Jerry shells the trench, *never mind*.

If you get stuck on the wire, *never mind*;
If you get stuck on the wire, *never mind*.   10
Though you're stuck there all the day, they count you dead and
    stop your pay,
If you get stuck on the wire, *never mind*.

If the sergeant says you're mad, *never mind*;
P'raps you are a little bit, *never mind*.
Just be calm, don't answer back, 'cause the sergeant stands
    no 'slack',
So if he says you're mad, well—you are.

Mademoiselle from Armenteers

Mademoiselle from Armenteers, parlay-voo,°
Mademoiselle from Armenteers, parlay-voo,
Mademoiselle from Armenteers,
She hasn't been kissed for forty years,
Hinky pinky, parlay-voo.

Our top kick in Armenteers, parlay-voo,°
Our top kick in Armenteers, parlay-voo,
Our top kick in Armenteers
Soon broke the spell of forty years,
Hinky pinky, parlay-voo.   10

The officers get all the steak, parlay-voo,
The officers get all the steak, parlay-voo,
The officers get all the steak
And all we get is a belly ache,
Hinky pinky, parlay-voo.

From gay Paree we heard guns roar, parlay-voo,°
From gay Paree we heard guns roar, parlay-voo,
From gay Paree we heard guns roar,
But all we heard was 'Je t'adore',°
Hinky pinky, parlay-voo.   20

You might forget the gas and shell, parlay-voo,
You might forget the gas and shell, parlay-voo,
You might forget the gas and shell,
You'll never forget the mademoiselle,
Hinky pinky, parlay-voo.

Pack up your troubles in your old kit-bag

Private Perks is a funny little codger°
With a smile—a funny smile.
Five-feet-none, he's an artful little dodger°
With a smile—a sunny smile.
Flush or broke, he'll have his little joke,°
He can't be suppress'd.
All the other fellows have to grin
When he gets this off his chest, Hi!

CHORUS
'Pack up your troubles in your old kit bag,
And smile, smile, smile.   10
While you've a lucifer to light your fag,°
Smile, boys, that's the style.
What's the use of worrying?
It never was worth while, so
Pack up your troubles in your old kit-bag,
And smile, smile, smile.'

Private Perks went a-marching into Flanders°
With his smile—his funny smile.
He was lov'd by the privates and commanders
For his smile—his sunny smile.   20
When a throng of Germans came along
With a mighty swing,
Perks yell'd out, 'This little bunch is mine!
Keep your heads down, boys, and sing, Hi!

CHORUS
'Pack up your troubles in your old kit-bag, (etc.)

Private Perks he came back from Bosche shooting°
With his smile—his funny smile.
Round his home he then set about recruiting
With his smile—his sunny smile.
He told all his pals, the short, the tall,
What a time he'd had;   30
And as each enlisted like a man,
Private Perks said 'Now my lad, Hi!

CHORUS
'Pack up your troubles in your old kit-bag, (etc.)

Fred Karno's Army

(Air: 'Aurelia', sung to the hymn 'The Church's
One Foundation')

We are Fred Karno's Army,
What bloody use are we?
We cannot fight, we cannot shoot,
So we joined the infantry.
But when we get to Berlin,
The Kaiser he will say,°
'Hoch! Hoch! Mein Gott,°
What a jolly fine lot
Are the ragtime infantry.'°

We are Fred Karno's Army,   10
A jolly lot are we,
Fred Karno is our Captain,
Charlie Chaplin our O.C.°
But when we get to Berlin,
The Kaiser he will say,
'Hoch! Hoch! Mein Gott,
What a jolly fine lot
Are the ragtime infantry.'°

I Want to Go Home
(Air: Traditional)

I want to go home, I want to go home.
I don't want to go to the trenches no more,
Where whizzbangs and shrapnel they whistle and roar.°
Take me over the sea where the Alleyman can't get at me.°
Oh my, I don't want to die, I want to go home.

I want to go home, I want to go home,
I don't want to visit *la Belle France* no more,
For oh the Jack Johnsons they make such a roar.°
Take me over the sea where the snipers they can't snipe at me.
Oh my, I don't want to die, I want to go home.   10

The Bells of Hell
(Air: 'She Only Answered "Ting-A-Ling-A-Ling"')

The bells of hell go ting-a-ling-a-ling
For you but not for me:
And the little devils how they sing-a-ling-a-ling
For you but not for me.
O Death, where is thy sting-a-ling-a-ling,
O Grave, thy victor-ee?°
The bells of hell go ting-a-ling-a-ling,
For you but not for me.

If It's a German—Guns Up!
(Air: 'If It's a Lady—Thumbs Up!')

If it's a German—Guns Up!
If it's a German with hands up,
Don't start taking prisoners now,
Give it 'em in the neck and say 'Bow-wow.'
If it's a German—Guns Up!
Stick him in the leg—it is sublime.
If he whispers in your ear,
'Kamerad! Kamerad!'°
Guns Up—every time.

Après la Guerre Fini
(Air: 'Sous les Ponts de Paris')

Après la guerre fini,
Soldat Anglais parti;°
Mam'selle Fransay boko pleuray°
Après la guerre fini.

Après la guerre fini,
Soldat Anglais parti,
Mademoiselle in the family way,°
Après la guerre fini.

Après la guerre fini,
Soldat Anglais parti;   10
Mademoiselle can go to hell
Après la guerre fini.

The Old Barbed Wire
(Air: Traditional)

If you want to find the sergeant,
I know where he is, I know where he is.

If you want to find the sergeant,
I know where he is,
He's lying on the canteen floor.
I've seen him, I've seen him,
Lying on the canteen floor,
I've seen him,
Lying on the canteen floor.

If you want to find the quarter-bloke,° 10
I know where he is, I know where he is.
If you want to find the quarter-bloke,
I know where he is,
He's miles and miles behind the line.
I've seen him, I've seen him,
Miles and miles behind the line,
I've seen him,
Miles and miles behind the line.

If you want to find the sergeant-major,
I know where he is, I know where he is. 20
If you want to find the sergeant-major,
I know where he is,
He's boozing up the privates' rum.
I've seen him, I've seen him,
Boozing up the privates' rum,
I've seen him,
Boozing up the privates' rum.

If you want to find the C.O.,°
I know where he is, I know where he is.
If you want to find the C.O., 30
I know where he is,
He's down in the deep dug-outs.
I've seen him, I've seen him,
Down in the deep dug-outs,
I've seen him,
Down in the deep dug-outs.

If you want to find the old battalion,
I know where they are, I know where they are.

If you want to find the old battalion,
I know where they are,   40
They're hanging on the old barbed wire.
I've seen 'em, I've seen 'em,
Hanging on the old barbed wire,
I've seen 'em,
Hanging on the old barbed wire.

Hush! Here Comes a Whizz-Bang

(Air: 'Hush! Here Comes the Dream Man')

Hush! Here comes a whizz-bang,
Hush! Here comes a whizz-bang,
Now then soldier, get down them stairs,
Into your dug-out and say your prayers.
Hush! Here comes a whizz-bang,
And it's making straight for you:
And you'll see all the wonders of No Man's Land
If a whizz-bang (BANG!) gets you.

That Shit Shute

(Air: 'Wrap Me Up in My Tarpaulin Jacket')

The General inspecting the trenches
Exclaimed with a horrified shout,
'I refuse to command a Division
Which leaves its excreta about.'

But nobody took any notice
No one was prepared to refute,
That the presence of shit was congenial
Compared with the presence of Shute.

And certain responsible critics
Made haste to reply to his words   10
Observing that his Staff advisers
Consisted entirely of turds.

For shit may be shot at odd corners
And paper supplied there to suit,
But a shit would be shot without mourners
If somebody shot that shit Shute.

Bombed Last Night

(Air: 'Drunk Last Night and Drunk the Night Before')

Bombed last night and bombed the night before,
Going to get bombed tonight if we never get bombed anymore.
When we're bombed, we are scared as we can be.
Can't stop the bombing from old Higher Germany.°

CHORUS

They're warning us, they're warning us
One shell hole for the four of us
Thank your lucky stars there is no more of us
'Cos one of us can fill it all alone.

Gassed last night and gassed the night before,
Going to get gassed tonight if we never get gassed anymore.   10
When we're gassed we're sick as we can be.
For Phosgene and Mustard Gas is much too much for me.°

CHORUS

They're killing us, they're killing us
One respirator for the four of us.
Thank your lucky stars there is no more of us
So one of us can take it all alone.

I Wore a Tunic

(Air: 'I Wore a Tulip')

I wore a tunic,
A dirty khaki-tunic,
And you wore civilian clothes.
We fought and bled at Loos°

While you were on the booze,
The booze that no one here knows.

Oh, you were with the wenches
While we were in the trenches
Facing the German foe.
Oh, you were a-slacking   10
While we were attacking
Down the Menin Road.°

Good-bye-ee!

Brother Bertie went away
To do his bit the other day°
With a smile on his lips and his lieutenant 'pips'°
Upon his shoulder, bright and gay.
As the train mov'd out he said,
'Remember me to all the 'Birds!'°
Then he wagg'd his paw, and went away to war,
Shouting out these pathetic words,

CHORUS

'Good-bye-ee! good-bye-ee!
Wipe the tear, baby dear, from your eye-ee.   10
Tho' it's hard to part, I know,
I'll be tickled to death to go.
Don't cry-ee! don't sigh-ee!
There's a silver lining in the sky-ee.
Bonsoir, old thing! cheerio! chin-chin!
Nahpoo! Toodle-oo! Good-bye-ee!'°

Marmaduke Horatio Flynn,
Although he'd whiskers round his chin,
In a play took a part, and he touch'd ev'ry heart
As little Willie in 'East Lynne'.°   20
As the little dying child
Upon his snow-white bed he lay,
And amid their tears the people gave three cheers
When he said as he pass'd away,

CHORUS
Good–bye–ee! good–bye–ee! (etc.)

At a concert down at Kew°
Some convalescents dress'd in blue
Had to hear Lady Lee, who had turn'd eighty-three,°
Sing all the old, old songs she knew.
Then she made a speech and said,
'I look upon you boys with pride,   30
And for what you've done I'm going to kiss each one.'
Then they all grabb'd their sticks and cried,

CHORUS
Good–bye–ee! good–bye–ee! (etc.)

Little Private Patrick Shaw
He was a prisoner of war
Till a Hun with a gun called him 'pig-dog' for fun,°
Then Paddy punch'd him on the jaw.
Right across the barb-wire fence
The German dropp'd, then, dear, oh, dear!
All the wire gave way, and Paddy yell'd 'Hooray!'
As he ran for the Dutch frontier.°   40

CHORUS
Good–bye–ee! good–bye–ee! (etc.)

Oh! It's a Lovely War

Up to your waist in water, up to your eyes in slush,
using the kind of language that makes the sergeant blush;
who wouldn't join the army, that's what we all enquire,
don't we pity the poor civilians sitting beside the fire?

CHORUS
Oh! Oh! Oh! It's a lovely war,
who wouldn't be a soldier eh!

Oh! it's a shame to take the pay.
As soon as 'reveille' has gone, we feel just as heavy as lead,°
but we never get up till the sergeant brings our breakfast up to bed.
Oh! Oh! Oh! It's a lovely war,   10
what do we want with eggs and ham
when we've got plum and apple jam?°
Form fours! Right turn!°
How shall we spend the money we earn?
Oh! Oh! Oh! It's a lovely war.

When does a soldier grumble? When does he make a fuss?
No one is more contented in all the world than us:
Oh! it's a 'cushy' life, boys really we love it so,°
once a fellow was sent on leave and simply refus'd to go.

CHORUS
Oh! Oh! Oh! It's a lovely war, (etc.)

Come to the Cookhouse door boys, sniff at the lovely stew.°   20
Who is it says the Col'nel gets better grub than you?
Any complaints this morning? Do we complain? Not we,
what's the matter with lumps of onion floating around the tea?

CHORUS
Oh! Oh! Oh! It's a lovely war, (etc.)

EXPLANATORY NOTES

THOMAS HARDY

5 MEN WHO MARCH AWAY. *Date and Text*. 5 September 1914. Three days before, Hardy had been included in the gathering of eminent writers at Wellington House, London. The War Propaganda Bureau had wanted to encourage public statements of 'the strength of the British case and the principles for which the British troops and their allies are fighting' (Hardy, *The Later Years of Thomas Hardy*, 163). Copy text as published in *The Complete Poems*, ed. James Gibson (1976).

l. 8. *purblind*. Two meanings are relevant: having impaired vision; lacking in insight.

6 ENGLAND TO GERMANY IN 1914. *Date and Text*. Autumn 1914. Copy text as published in *The Complete Poems*, ed. James Gibson (1976).

l. 2. *Teuton*. The Teutons were an ancient Germanic tribe renowned for their courage, but the word was occasionally used to refer to modern-day Germans.

l. 6. *burgs*. Castles.

l. 7. *Rhine-stream*. The Rhine is the longest river in Germany, and one of the longest in Europe.

l. 8. *Your shining souls of deathless dowers*. The dower was a gift from the newly married husband to his wife, so that she would have provision in the event of her widowhood. The practice originated in medieval Germany. Cf. the final lines of Dante Gabriel Rossetti's 'Silent Noon', from his *House of Life* sonnet sequence: 'Oh! clasp we to our hearts, for deathless dower, | This close-companioned inarticulate hour | When twofold silence was the song of love' (ll. 12–14).

l. 12. *a flushed few whose blatant mood*. In his autobiography, Hardy remembered having been appalled by Guy Louis Busson Du Maurier's play *An Englishman's Home* (1909), which described an invasion of England by an unnamed power resembling Germany. Hardy believed that the play 'ought to have been suppressed as provocative, since it gave Germany, even if pacific in intention beforehand, a reason, or excuse, for directing her mind on a war with England' (Hardy, *The Later Years of Thomas Hardy*, 162).

ON THE BELGIAN EXPATRIATION. *Date and Text*. 18 October 1914. Expatriation is voluntary or enforced removal from a native land. More than one million Belgians fled their country as the Germans advanced in 1914; many thousands went to England. Copy text as published in *The Complete Poems*, ed. James Gibson (1976).

6 l. 1. *Land of Chimes*. Belgium: so called by Hardy because Belgium is famous for its carillons (see note to l. 12).

7 l. 5. *meted*. Allotted.

l. 11. *From Bruges they came, and Antwerp, and Ostend*. These three Belgian cities fell to the Germans early in the War.

l. 12. *carillons*. A carillon is a musical instrument that consists of a set of bells. It is often housed in a belfry.

l. 13. *gear*. Hardy uses the word in a way considered obsolete by *OED*: 'A material substance or stuff; in depreciatory sense, rubbish.'

THE PITY OF IT. *Date and Text*. April 1915. The poem provoked a hostile reaction in some quarters, to which Hardy responded privately: 'Fussy Jingoes, who were hoping for knighthoods, attacked H[ardy] for his assumption & asserted that we had no sort of blood relationship with Germany: But the Germans themselves, with far more commonsense, translated the poem, & approved of it, & remarked that when relations did fall out they fought more bitterly than any' (*The Personal Notebooks of Thomas Hardy*, ed. Richard H. Taylor (London: Macmillan, 1978), 291). The title alludes to *Othello*, IV.i.192: 'But yet the pity of it, Iago!' Copy text as published in *The Complete Poems*, ed. James Gibson (1976).

ll. 4–5. *'Thu bist', 'Er war', | 'Ich woll', 'Er sholl', and by-talk similar*. The old Dorset dialect forms that Hardy records are very close to German. They can be translated as: 'you are', 'he was', 'I will', 'he shall'. 'By-talk' is itself a dialect word, meaning small talk.

8 IN TIME OF 'THE BREAKING OF NATIONS'. *Date and Text*. 1915. According to Hardy's autobiography, the poem draws on a 45-year-old memory: 'On the day that the bloody battle of Gravelotte was fought [18 August 1870] they were reading Tennyson in the grounds of the rectory. It was at this time and spot that Hardy was struck by the incident of the old horse harrowing the arable field in the valley below, which, when in far later years it was recalled to him by a still bloodier war, he made into the little poem of three verses entitled "In Time of 'The Breaking of Nations'"' (Florence Hardy, *The Early Life of Thomas Hardy* (London: Macmillan, 1928), 104). Hardy's footnote to the poem directs the reader to Jeremiah 51: 20: 'Thou art my battle axe and weapons of war: for with thee will I break in pieces the nations, and with thee will I destroy kingdoms.' Copy text as published in *The Complete Poems*, ed. James Gibson (1976).

l. 6 *couch-grass*. A weed, destroyed by burning.

l. 8. *Dynasties*. Hardy had called his three-part epic drama of the Napoleonic campaigns *The Dynasts* (1904, 1906, 1908), because it depicted the war as a battle between rival dynasties.

l. 9. *wight*. An archaic word, here meaning 'man'.

BEFORE MARCHING AND AFTER. *Date and Text*. September 1915. The dedicatee ('F.W.G.') was Lieutenant Frank George, the son of

Hardy's second cousin. He had been killed in August 1915 at Gallipoli. Hardy made a note in his autobiography: 'Frank George, though so remotely related, is the first one of my family to be killed in battle for the last hundred years, so far as I know. He might say Militavi non sine gloria [I served as a soldier not without glory]—short as his career has been' (Hardy, *The Later Years of Thomas Hardy*, 169). Copy text as published in *The Complete Poems*, ed. James Gibson (1976).

l. 2. *Egdon*. A fictitious heath in Hardy's Wessex, mentioned many times throughout his works.

ll. 1–3. *Orion . . . The Pleiads*. Orion is a constellation named after a giant hunter from Greek mythology; the Pleiads (more commonly Pleiades) is a star cluster that takes its name from the seven heavenly daughters of the titan Atlas and the sea-nymph Pleione.

9 A NEW YEAR'S EVE IN WAR TIME. *Date and Text*. Hardy's date of 1915–16 may suggest a poem written across midnight on New Year's Eve 1915. However, he often assigned dates to poems for their dramatic value rather than their accuracy. The manuscript date is given as '1916'. The poem was first published in *The Sphere* on 6 January 1917. Copy text as published in *The Complete Poems*, ed. James Gibson (1976).

l. 9. *gable-cock*. Weather-cock.

l. 13. *Hand-hid*. At twelve o'clock, one hand of the clock 'hides' behind the other.

ll. 14–16. *I undo the lock, | And listen, and wait | For the Young Unknown*. This describes the custom of letting in the New Year, or 'Young Unknown'.

10 ll. 17–21. *In the dark there careers— | As if Death astride came | To numb all with his knock— | A horse at mad rate | Over rut and stone*. Tim Armstrong detects an allusion to Revelation 6: 8: 'And I looked, and behold a pale horse: and his name that sat on him was death, and Hell followed with him. And power was given unto them over the fourth part of the earth, to kill with sword, and with hunger, and with death, and with the beasts of the earth.' Hardy reported that he had indeed heard a horse galloping past at the stroke of midnight on New Year's Eve (quoted in *Thomas Hardy: Selected Poems*, ed. Tim Armstrong (London: Longman, 1993), 239–40).

I LOOKED UP FROM MY WRITING. *Date and Text*. Probably 1916. Copy text as published in *The Complete Poems*, ed. James Gibson (1976).

l. 3. *rapt in my inditing*. Absorbed in my writing.

11 l. 13. *tattle*. Chatter.

'ACCORDING TO THE MIGHTY WORKING'. *Date and Text*. 1917. The title comes from the Anglican burial service in the Book of Common Prayer of 1662: 'Christ . . . shall change our vile body, that it may be like unto his glorious body, according to the mighty working, whereby he is able to subdue all things to himself.' The poem first appeared in

The Athenæum on 4 April 1919, claiming a coincidental topicality from Hardy's public support for the reconstitution of Palestine as a Jewish nation. Copy text as published in *The Complete Poems*, ed. James Gibson (1976).

11 l. 1. *moiling*. Turmoil.

l. 8. *quick-cued mumming*. Mechanical acting.

12 'AND THERE WAS A GREAT CALM'. *Date and Text*. October or November 1920, but before 11 November, when it appeared in the Armistice supplement of *The Times*. The following account is given in Hardy's autobiography: 'The request to write this poem had been brought to him from London by one of the editorial staff. At first Hardy was disinclined, and all but refused, being generally unable to write to order. In the middle of the night, however, an idea seized him . . .' (Hardy, *The Later Years of Thomas Hardy*, 214–15). Copy text as published in *The Complete Poems*, ed. James Gibson (1976).

l. 5. *Spirit of Pity*. This spirit appears in Hardy's *The Dynasts*.

l. 17. *Sirius*. The brightest star in the night sky, colloquially known as the Dog Star.

13 l. 29. *flats*. Mud.

l. 34. *Spirit of Irony*. Another spirit from *The Dynasts*.

l. 35. *peradventures*. Chance occurrences.

l. 40. *weft-winged engines*. Aeroplanes.

l. 44. *Sinister Spirit*. Also from *The Dynasts*.

A. E. HOUSMAN

15 EPITAPH ON AN ARMY OF MERCENARIES. *Date and Text*. September 1917. Written in the tradition of Simonides' famous epitaph for the fallen Greeks at Thermopylae, the poem commemorates the small British army that helped to halt the German advance at the First Battle of Ypres in October and November 1914. Copy text as first published in *The Times*, 31 October 1917.

l. 3. *their mercenary calling*. The poem turns on competing definitions of 'mercenary', here privileging the neutral sense given by *OED* as 'Hired; serving for wages or hire.' Archie Burnett points out that other more negative definitions (for example, 'actuated by considerations of self-interest') would render the phrase 'mercenary calling' paradoxical (*The Poems of A. E. Housman*, 411). In Housman's hands, the soldiers' mercenary calling is the most reliable force for good, defending what even God has abandoned.

l. 4. *And took their wages and are dead*. Cf. Romans 6: 23: 'the wages of sin is death'.

l. 5. *Their shoulders . . . suspended*. The fate of Atlas was to bear the celestial spheres on his shoulders. Housman is truer to the classical myth than modern retellings, which often depict Atlas supporting the world.

MAY SINCLAIR

17   FIELD AMBULANCE IN RETREAT. *Date and Text.* October or November 1914. The subtitle refers to two roads: the Via Dolorosa (Way of Suffering) in Jerusalem, along which Christ is believed to have carried his cross to the site of crucifixion, and the Via Sacra (Sacred Way), which passed through the most important religious sites of ancient Rome. Copy text as first published in Hall Caine (ed.), *King Albert's Book: A Tribute to the Belgian King and People from Representative Men and Women throughout the World* (1914).

l. 6. *the great Flemish horses.* A particularly large breed from Flanders in northern Belgium, originally used to carry knights into battle. Flanders saw constant fighting from October 1914 until November 1918.

l. 16. *Red Cross Ambulance.* The Red Cross remained strictly neutral during the War as it provided medical and humanitarian support for soldiers and civilians of all nations.

18   l. 25. *the intolerable speed of an Ambulance in retreat.* In her *Journal of Impressions in Belgium* (1915), Sinclair comments on the retreat from the advancing German army: 'though we are not really going fast, the speed seems intolerable . . . The speed with its steady acceleration grows more intolerable with every mile. Your sense of safety grows intolerable' (248).

AFTER THE RETREAT. *Date and Text.* Between October 1914 and April 1915. Copy text as first published in *The Egoist* 5.2 (1 May 1915).

l. 2. *Flemish.* Of Flanders. See note to Sinclair, 'Field Ambulance in Retreat', l. 6 (above).

ll. 15–16. *Ostend, and Bruges, and Antwerp under her doom,* | *And the dear city of Ghent.* Sinclair saw all these Belgian cities, and visited Antwerp only days before it fell to the Germans.

19   DEDICATION. *Date and Text.* 8 March 1915. For Flanders, see note to Sinclair, 'Field Ambulance in Retreat', l. 6 (above). Copy text as first published in *A Journal of Impressions in Belgium* (1915).

l. 12. *lure.* A bait or apparatus that attracts animals so that they can be captured or killed.

20   ll. 32–3. *That is why I do not speak of you,* | *Calling you by your names.* Sinclair changed the names of the protagonists in her *Journal.*

l. 35. *Termonde and Antwerp, Dixmude and Ypres and Furnes.* Towns and cities in Flanders. Ypres saw some of the heaviest fighting at the Western Front, and was the site of three major battles. It was often pronounced 'Wipers' by British soldiers, hence the title of the trench newspaper, *The Wipers Times.*

W. B. YEATS

22 ON BEING ASKED FOR A WAR POEM. *Date and Text*. February 1915, with the title 'To a friend who has asked me to sign on his manifesto to the neutral nations'; revised during 1915 and 1916. When Henry James solicited Yeats in July 1915 for a contribution to Edith Wharton's *The Book of the Homeless* (1916), an anthology to raise money for Belgian refugees, Yeats submitted a revised version with a new (but still not final) title, 'A Reason for Keeping Silent', reporting that 'It is the only thing I have written of the war or will write' (*The Letters of W. B. Yeats*, 600). Copy text as in *The Wild Swans at Coole* (1919).

ll. 1–2. *I think it better that in times like these* | *A poet keep his mouth shut.* 'A Reason for Keeping Silent', published in Wharton's anthology, had begun: 'I think it better that at times like these | We poets keep our mouths shut'. Yeats would later revise these lines again for collected editions of his work: 'I think it better that in times like these | A poet's mouth be silent'.

AN IRISH AIRMAN FORESEES HIS DEATH. *Date and Text*. Probably June or July 1918. A draft of the poem, titled 'On the death of an Irish air-man who joined early in the War', was completed by 30 June 1918. Robert Gregory, son of Yeats's close friend Lady Gregory, had been shot down over Italy and killed on 23 January 1918. Copy text as in *The Wild Swans at Coole* (1919).

l. 5. *Kiltartan Cross*. Kiltartan was the barony in County Galway where Robert Gregory lived.

l. 10. *Nor public man, nor angry crowds*. Later revised in collected editions of Yeats's work to 'Nor public men, nor cheering crowds'.

RUDYARD KIPLING

25 'FOR ALL WE HAVE AND ARE'. *Date and Text*. Late August 1914. First published in *The Times*, 2 September 1914, with a note that irritated Kipling: 'At the request of Mr. Kipling we are sending £50 to the Belgian Relief Fund in his name.' After the War, Kipling wrote that the poem had been 'generally adjudged at the time it was written as "too serious for the needs of the case" but in 1915 it was realised that it was the truth and was generally used, for propaganda' (*The Letters of Rudyard Kipling*, iv. 541). Copy text as published in *The Years Between* (1919).

l. 4. *The Hun*. Kipling proudly claimed responsibility for popularizing the hostile term 'Hun' as a description of the Germans. He had called them 'the shameless Hun' in 'The Rowers' (1902), responding to this passage in a speech made by Kaiser Wilhelm II at the height of the Boxer Rebellion two years before: 'Just as the Huns a thousand years ago, under the leadership of [Attila], gained a reputation in virtue of which they still live in historical tradition, so may the name of Germany become known in such a manner in China that no Chinaman will ever again even dare to look askance at a German' (quoted in Gilbert Parker, *The World in the Crucible: An Account of the Origins & Conduct of the Great War* (New York: Dodd, Mead and Company, 1915), 45).

26 'TIN FISH'. *Date and Text.* Between 25 September and mid-November 1915. First published, untitled, in the *Daily Telegraph* on 27 November, prefacing an essay called 'Submarines', which was Kipling's fourth article (of six) on 'The Fringes of the Fleet'. Kipling had been commissioned by the Admiralty to celebrate the activities and successes of the navy. The phrase 'Tin Fish' is offered by Kipling as naval slang for submarines. Copy text as in *Sea Warfare* (1916), although the title '"Tin Fish"' was added much later for *Poems 1886–1929* (London: Macmillan, 1929).

27 THE CHILDREN. *Date and Text.* Between August 1914 and December 1916. Copy text as first published in *A Diversity of Creatures* (1917).

l. 4. *Alien.* Foreigner.

l. 23. *To be blanched or gay-painted by fumes.* Exposure to mustard gas— a sulphurous poison, first used by the Germans in 1917—causes the skin to redden, and later to blister and turn yellow.

28 l. 25. *take expiation.* Require and accept the amends made for sinful behaviour. This is crucially different from 'make expiation'—the guilt lies not only with the parents, but elsewhere.

'THE TRADE'. *Date and Text.* Probably between June and October 1916. Three articles about submarine warfare were published by Kipling in *The Times* between 21 and 28 June 1916. The first of them, 'Some Work in the Baltic', begins with the admission that 'No one knows how the title of "The Trade" came to be applied to the Submarine Service.' Collected in *Sea Warfare* six months later, the articles were prefaced by this poem. Copy text as published in *Sea Warfare* (1916).

ll. 1–2. *They bear, in place of classic names,* | *Letters and numbers on their skin.* Submarines were given a letter and a number, not names.

l. 5. *Sometimes they stalk the Zeppelin.* Zeppelins were rigid airships deployed by the Germans on bombing and reconnaissance missions. They were vulnerable to submarine attack because they patrolled the North Sea and Baltic Sea, advising the German navy of enemy shipping and mine-laying. Zeppelins were equipped to come down on the sea, if necessary.

l. 7. *Or where the Baltic ice is thin.* Kipling's 'Some Work in the Baltic', the prose piece that immediately follows this poem in *Sea Warfare*, describes the cooperation between a submarine and an ice-breaker in finding a path through the ice to sink a German destroyer.

l. 9. *prize-courts.* The Admiralty Prize Court evaluated the financial claims made by crews that had captured enemy ships. The implication here, and in the next line, is that submarines do not capture ships; they sink them.

28 l. 15. *the shearing of a pin*. Alistair Wilson states: ' "The shearing of a pin" refers to the act of firing a torpedo, when the discharge of the torpedo in its tube breaks a small pin, and this allows a valve to open to start the torpedo's engine' (http://www.kipling.org.uk/rg_seawarfare_trade_notes.htm).

l. 17. *The Scout's quadruple funnel flames*. The Scout was a type of four-funnelled warship, which sometimes showed flames at the top of the funnel when it was burning coal.

l. 18. *from Sweden to the Swin*. The Swin is a channel in the Thames Estuary. The area 'from Sweden to the Swin' roughly corresponds to the North Sea.

l. 19. *The Cruiser's thunderous screw*. A cruiser was larger than a destroyer. Its screw propeller was clearly audible.

ll. 21–3. *But only whiffs of paraffin | Or creamy rings that fizz and fade | Show where the one-eyed Death has been*. Kipling refers to the submarine's monocular attack periscope and to the traces left by the submarine after it has dived. 'In those days submarines of the earlier classes were still powered by "petrol" engines, and the "creamy rings" are from the last of the air in the ballast tanks being expelled through the vents in the tops of the tanks, as the submarine submerges' (Alistair Wilson, http://www. kipling.org.uk/rg_seawarfare_trade_notes.htm).

29 l. 29. *The Censor*. News during wartime was tightly regulated by official censors.

MY BOY JACK. *Date and Text*. Probably late August or September 1916. The poem was published, untitled, on 19 October 1916 in the *Daily Telegraph*, to accompany the first part of Kipling's prose account, 'Destroyers at Jutland'; it appeared with the same article in *Sea Warfare* (December 1916). Not until 1918 would it be given a title: 'My Boy Jack'. In recent times, this has been taken to refer to Kipling's son, John, who was killed at the Battle of Loos in September 1915. However, John was never known as Jack. The inspiration is the Battle of Jutland (31 May– 1 June 1916), after which the British Admiralty asked Kipling to write a number of morale-raising accounts of the naval attacks. 'Jack' was a generic name for a sailor: Jack Tar. Copy text as published in *The Years Between* (1919).

THE VERDICTS. *Date and Text*. Probably late August or September 1916; first published on 31 October 1916 in the *Daily Telegraph*, to accompany part four of Kipling's prose account, 'Destroyers at Jutland'. For the Battle of Jutland, see note to Kipling, 'My Boy Jack' (above). Copy text as published in *The Years Between* (1919).

30 MESOPOTAMIA. *Date and Text*. Between May and July 1917, but before 11 July when it was simultaneously published in the *New York Times* and the *Morning Post*. Mesopotamia (from the Greek for 'between rivers') comprises the vast region between the Tigris and the Euphrates, including parts of modern-day Iran, Syria, Turkey, and Iraq. In 1914 a mixed

British and Indian expeditionary force was sent to the area with priorities to capture Baghdad and stir up Arab rebellion against the Ottoman Empire. The campaign was initially a costly disaster, largely due to administrative incompetence and military blundering. In 1917 a commission of enquiry into the fiasco condemned politicians and generals for showing 'little desire to help and some desire actually to obstruct the energetic prosecution of the war' (quoted in David Lockwood, *The Indian Bourgeoisie: A Political History of the Indian Capitalist Class in the Early Twentieth Century* (New York: I. B. Tauris, 2012), 59). Copy text as published in *The Years Between* (1919).

31 ll. 15–16. *How softly but how swiftly they have sidled back to power | By the favour and contrivance of their kind?* The fate of Lord Hardinge, the Viceroy of India, was typical of those who had been severely criticized by the commission. At the end of his term, he was rewarded with a job as permanent under-secretary of state for foreign affairs, made a Knight of the Garter, and in 1920, appointed as British ambassador to France. Kipling noted in March 1919 that 'not one of the [implicated officials] has been punished or even permanently degraded for their share in the debacle' (*The Letters of Rudyard Kipling*, iv. 543).

GETHSEMANE. *Date and Text.* Between 1916 and 1918. Gethsemane is named in the gospels of Matthew and Mark as the garden at the foot of the Mount of Olives where Christ and his disciples prayed on the night before the Crucifixion. 'What makes war most poignant', Kipling wrote in 1919, 'is the presence of women with whom one can talk and make love, only an hour or so behind the line' (*The Letters of Rudyard Kipling*, iv. 544). Copy text as first published in *The Years Between* (1919).

l. 2. *Picardy.* A province in the north of France, which contains the battlefields of the Somme.

l. 12. *I prayed my cup might pass.* Kipling alludes to Christ's prayer at Matthew 26: 39: 'And he went a little farther, and fell on his face, and prayed, saying, O my Father, if it be possible, let this cup pass from me: nevertheless not as I will, but as thou wilt.' (The 'cup' Christ refers to is his suffering death by crucifixion.)

32 EPITAPHS. *Date and Text.* Probably 1915 to 1918. Kipling sent an early version of what became 'A Son' to C. R. L. Fletcher on 17 February 1918, describing it as one of a number of 'sepulchral unchristian epigrams' (*The Letters of Rudyard Kipling*, iv. 484). In 1919 Kipling told his American publisher, Frank Doubleday: 'The general point of these epitaphs is that England who was in the thick of the war had more experience than most of the different sorts of deaths that men *and* women died' (ibid., 544). The title was later extended to 'Epitaphs of the War', and new epitaphs were added. Copy text as first published in *The Years Between* (1919).

33 'Hindu Sepoy in France'. A sepoy is an Indian soldier serving a European power.

33 'A Grave Near Cairo'. Cairo, Egypt's capital city, was headquarters to the British garrison.

l. 1. *Nile*. The longest river in Africa, which enters the Mediterranean in Egypt.

'Pelicans in the Wilderness (A Grave Near Halfa)'. Halfa is a city in Northern Sudan.

34 'Native Water-Carrier (M. E. F.)'. The M.E.F. was the Mediterranean Expeditionary Force.

l. 1. *Prometheus brought down fire to men*. The Titan Prometheus stole fire from Zeus and gave it to humankind. He was punished by being bound to a rock; each day an eagle would feed on his liver, and each night the liver would grow back.

'Bombed in London'. London was the target of Zeppelin raids between May 1915 and September 1916.

'The Sleepy Sentinel'. A sentinel is a soldier whose job is to keep watch. During the War, sentinels could be executed for falling asleep.

36 'A Drifter Off Tarentum'. Tarentum is the ancient Roman name for the southern Italian coastal city of Taranto.

l. 2. *eggs of death spawned by invisible hulls*. Mines laid by submarines.

'Salonikan Grave'. Today known as Thessaloniki, in 1915 the Greek port of Salonika became the base for a Franco–British force established to help the Serbs in their struggle against the pro-German Bulgarians.

37 'V. A. D. (Mediterranean)'. VAD stands for Voluntary Aid Detachment. It consisted mainly of women, who served as nurses, cooks, and ambulance drivers.

l. 2. *Ægean*. The sea between the mainlands of Greece and Turkey is the Aegean Sea.

A DEATH-BED. *Date and Text*. 1918. It was rumoured that Kaiser Wilhelm II, the German Emperor, was suffering from throat cancer. Kipling imagines the death-bed, alternating the Kaiser's statements with those of his doctors. He positioned the poem directly after an elegy for Edward VII when he collected it in *The Years Between*. 'A Death-Bed' has been described by Kipling's biographer, Andrew Lycett, as 'sadistic and nasty' (*Rudyard Kipling*, 643). Copy text as published in *The Years Between* (1919).

ll. 1–2. *'This is the State above the Law | The State exists for the State alone.'* This comment, like all the later comments in quotation marks, is attributed to Kaiser Wilhelm.

38 l. 9. *'Regis suprema Voluntas lex'*. 'The King's Will is the supreme law' (Latin). One of the Kaiser's official pronouncements.

l. 31. *cots*. Beds.

39 JUSTICE. *Date and Text*. October 1918, but before 24 October, when it

appeared in *The Times*. Copy text as published in *The Years Between* (1919).

40   ll. 43–4. *A people with the heart of beasts | Made wise concerning men*. In a letter of 7 November 1918 to John Powell, Kipling explained that in these lines he was referring to 'a people with such an outlook on life as would be possessed by animals who had been laboriously instructed in the baser side of humanity and also the higher—a sort of were-wolf people in fact'. The same letter blamed 'a false education' for the 'whole gangrene' of German culture, and particularly accused 'the schools, the priests and the kings' (*The Letters of Rudyard Kipling*, iv. 519).

THE CHANGELINGS. *Date and Text*. Probably between November 1918 and December 1925. Andrew Lycett proposes 1915 as the date of composition, but see note to l. 18. The poem was first published in *Debits and Credits* (1926), a volume that, following Kipling's usual practice, interspersed poems among short stories. 'The Changelings' served as the preface to 'Sea Constables', a naval story of revenge against a war-profiteering neutral. A 'changeling' is a fairy child secretly substituted for a human child in infancy. Copy text as first published in *Debits and Credits* (1926).

l. 3. *Walworth*. A district in London, in the borough of Southwark.

ll. 1–4. *Or ever . . . a grocer's clerk*. Cf. an earlier poem, 'To W. A.', by Kipling's friend W. E. Henley: 'Or ever the Knightly years were gone | With the old world to the grave, | I was a King in Babylon | And you were a Christian slave.'

l. 5. *I was a dealer in stocks and shares*. A character in 'Sea Constables' is called 'Portson—of Portson, Peake and Ensell, Stock and Share Brokers'.

41   l. 18. *pied*. Having two or more colours. Probably a reference to dazzle camouflage—contrasting patterns of colours and geometric shapes—which the British navy deployed on its warships from 1917.

THE VINEYARD. *Date and Text*. Probably 1919, given the poem's similarity to a letter sent by Kipling to an American correspondent on 15 March 1919, criticizing the American President, Woodrow Wilson: 'At the present moment, he gives one rather the impression of the Labourer who entered the Vineyard at the Eleventh Hour and spent the time in a lecture on the Principles of Viticulture and the Horrors of Intemperance, instead of helping to clean up the winepress of the wrath of God' (*The Letters of Rudyard Kipling*, iv. 540). Kipling's allusion, here and in the poem, is to the parable of the labourers in the vineyard (Matthew 20). Christ teaches that any labourer who accepts the invitation to work in God's vineyard, however late in the day, will receive a reward equal to those of the other labourers. Kipling had been highly critical of American neutrality, and he privately welcomed the nation's joining the War in April 1917 with the satisfaction that the United States had 'at long last subscribed to the elementary decencies' (ibid., 436). Copy text as published in *Debits and Credits* (1926).

LAURENCE BINYON

43 FOR THE FALLEN. *Date and Text.* September 1914, before its publication in *The Times* on 21 September, but probably after the First Battle of the Marne (5–12 September). Copy text as published in *The Winnowing Fan: Poems on the Great War* (1914).

l. 14. *Age shall not weary them, nor the years condemn.* Cf. Enobarbus's description of Cleopatra in *Antony and Cleopatra*, II.ii.245–6: 'Age cannot wither her, nor custom stale | Her infinite variety.'

CHARLOTTE MEW

46 MAY, 1915. *Date and Text.* For this poem alone, Mew appended a date to her draft manuscript: 23 May 1915. Such precision suggests that she may have been reacting to the Quintinshill rail disaster, which took place the day before and remains the worst rail accident in British history. Of the 226 fatalities, most were soldiers travelling on a troop train. Copy text as published in *The Rambling Sailor* (1929).

JUNE, 1915. Probably June 1915. Copy text as first published in *The Rambling Sailor* (1929).

l. 1. *June's first rose.* In the context of the poem's shaken hope in seasonal renewal, and the spreading blindness of grief, this seems to allude to *Paradise Lost*, III.40–3: 'Thus with the year | Seasons return; but not to me returns | Day, or the sweet approach of even or morn, | Or sight of vernal bloom, or summer's rose.'

l. 4. *veiled lamps of town.* The first Zeppelin raids on London took place during the night of 31 May 1915. Subsequently, blackouts were imposed across the city.

THE CENOTAPH. *Date and Text.* July or August 1919. Copy text as first published in the *Westminster Gazette*, 7 September 1919.

47 l. 6. *Cenotaph.* Mew's description sounds nothing like the Whitehall monument from which her poem takes its title. Asked at two weeks' notice to design a 'catafalque' in time for the Allied Victory Parade on 19 July 1919, Sir Edwin Lutyens created a wood-and-plaster structure, which he called 'The Cenotaph', from the Greek meaning 'empty tomb'. It was replaced by a near-identical stone structure at the same spot in 1920. Mew may also have known Lutyens's plans for a more elaborate war memorial in Southampton, a city that she passed through regularly on family trips to the Isle of Wight. However, neither Cenotaph depicts 'Victory, winged, with Peace, winged too, at the column's head'. Mew's poem is an example of what John Hollander calls 'notional ekphrasis'—the verbal representation of an imaginary work of art (see Hollander, *The Gazer's Spirit: Poems Speaking to Silent Works of Art* (Chicago: University of Chicago Press, 1995), 7–23).

l. 18. *God is not mocked.* Cf. Galatians 6: 7–8: 'Be not deceived; God is not mocked: for whatsoever a man soweth, that shall he also reap. For he that soweth to his flesh shall of the flesh reap corruption; but he that soweth to the Spirit shall of the Spirit reap life everlasting.'

l. 23. *huckster's*. Two senses from *OED* are relevant: 'A retailer of small goods, in a petty shop or booth, or at a stall'; and 'A person ready to make his profit of anything in a mean or petty way.' Cf. the dedicatory poem of W. B. Yeats's *Responsibilities* (1913): 'Merchant and scholar who have left me blood | That has not passed through any huckster's loin, | Soldiers that gave, whatever die was cast' (ll. 7–9). G. K. Chesterton's 'For a War Memorial', collected in *The Ballad of St Barbara and Other Verses* (1922), begins: 'The hucksters haggle in the mart'. In the absence of evidence that Chesterton had published the poem previously, it appears that he was influenced by Mew, not vice versa.

ROBERT SERVICE

48 TIPPERARY DAYS. *Date and Text*. Between December 1915 and August 1916. Tipperary is a town in Ireland, best known (as here) for being mentioned in the popular song 'It's a Long Way to Tipperary' (1912). The chorus is repeated in various guises throughout the poem. Copy text as first published in *Rhymes of a Red Cross Man* (1916).

l. 5. *chaffing*. Teasing.

49 l. 7. *Strangers in a strange land*. Cf. Exodus 2: 21–2: 'And Moses was content to dwell with the man: and he gave Moses Zipporah his daughter. And she bare him a son, and he called his name Gershom: for he said, I have been a stranger in a strange land.'

ll. 9–16. *It's a long way to Tipperary . . . But my heart's right there*. The chorus of 'It's a long way to Tipperary' is quoted verbatim, except that Leicester Square (in London) is given as 'Lester Square'.

l. 23. *Marseillaise or Brabançon, anthem of that other land*. The Marseillaise is the French national anthem; the Brabançonne (not Brabançon) is the national anthem of Belgium.

ll. 25–32. *C'est un chemin long 'to Tepararee' . . . Mais mon coeur 'ees zaire.'* A rough translation of the song's chorus, in a mixture of French and English.

l. 33. *'Contemptibles!'* The Old Contemptibles were the regular British army of 1914, self-styled because of the belief that Kaiser Wilhelm II had referred to them as a 'contemptible little army'.

l. 35. *clabber*. Soured milk.

l. 35. *corby*. A variant of 'corbie', meaning raven.

l. 36. *Blighty*. England (from the Hindustani word *bilayati*, meaning 'foreign land').

50 ONLY A BOCHE. *Date and Text*. Between December 1915 and August 1916. 'Boche' was the French soldiers' term for a German, although it was

soon adopted by the English. It is an abbreviation of *alboche*, which is in turn a portmanteau word derived from *allemand* ('German') and *caboche* ('head'). Slightly more friendly than 'Hun', but more hostile than 'Fritz' or 'Jerry', the term implies obstinacy and obnoxiousness. Copy text as first published in *Rhymes of a Red Cross Man* (1916), with one alteration as noted below.

50   l. 2. *tyke*. 'A low-bred, lazy, mean, surly, or ill-mannered fellow' (*OED*). Given as '*type*' in the British and Canadian first editions.

l. 5. *Diable!* (French) Devil!

51   l. 17. *con*. Study attentively.

l. 19. *dummy hand*. In bridge, the dummy hand is displayed face up for all to see; the player who has the dummy for that round does not participate in the play.

l. 27. *Lying there in a coat grey-green instead of a coat grey-blue*. The German military uniform was 'grey-green', the French 'grey-blue'.

l. 37. *Zut!* (French) Blast!

52   l. 52. *Mon Dieu! Quelle vache de guerre!* (French) My God! What a cow the war is!

TRI-COLOUR. *Date and Text*. Between December 1915 and August 1916. The French flag is a tricolour of blue, white, and red—the colours of the three flowers named at the beginnings of the stanzas. Copy text as first published in *Rhymes of a Red Cross Man* (1916).

l. 4. *It dabbles the ferns and the clover*. Cf. the opening lines of Tennyson's *Maud*. 'I hate the dreadful hollow behind the little wood; | Its lips in the field above are dabbled with blood-red heath, | The red-ribb'd ledges drip with a silent horror of blood, | And Echo there, whatever is ask'd her, answers "Death"' (ll. 1–4).

l. 8. *a-welter*. A confused mass.

l. 12. *All in their dark-blue blouses*. A dark-blue shirt was worn by French soldiers.

EDWARD THOMAS

56   A PRIVATE. *Date and Text*. First draft during January 1915; revised in subsequent months. Copy text as published in *The Annotated Collected Poems*, ed. Edna Longley (2008).

l. 4. *Mrs Greenland's*. The name echoes William Blake's description of 'England's green and pleasant land' in his poem 'Jerusalem'. 'Mrs Greenland' personifies a natural force that presides over the nation.

l. 6. '*The Drover*'. Thomas names the inn after the old rural profession of droving—moving livestock by foot over large distances.

l. 7. *Wiltshire*. Thomas loved the county of Wiltshire and portrayed it several times in his poetry and prose as the centre of ancient and spiritual England.

THE OWL. *Date and Text.* 24 February 1915. Copy text as published in *The Annotated Collected Poems*, ed. Edna Longley (2008).

ll. 13–14. *And salted was my food, and my repose,* | *Salted and sobered, too, by the bird's voice.* Edna Longley quotes Vernon Scannell's explanation: 'the word salted certainly means flavoured or spiced, but at the same time less comfortable connotations are invoked: the harshness of salt, the salt in the wound, the taste of bitterness, and of tears' (*The Annoted Collected Poems*, 198).

57 IN MEMORIAM (EASTER, 1915). *Date and Text.* 6 April 1915. Copy text as published in *The Annotated Collected Poems*, ed. Edna Longley (2008).

THIS IS NO CASE OF PETTY RIGHT OR WRONG. *Date and Text.* November to December 1915. Thomas added a date of 26 December 1915 on the manuscript, but told Eleanor Farjeon that although the 'couplets' (ll. 19–26) had been written then, the rest had been done 'some weeks' earlier (Farjeon, *Edward Thomas: The Last Four Years* (Oxford: Oxford University Press, 1958), 180). One rough draft is dated 26 November 1915. Copy text as published in *The Annotated Collected Poems*, ed. Edna Longley (2008).

ll. 5–6. *Beside my hate for one fat patriot* | *My hatred of the Kaiser is love true.* The 'fat patriot' is possibly Horatio Bottomley—politician, swindler, founder of the jingoistic journal *John Bull*, and passionate advocate of the complete destruction of Germany. Bottomley was an effective public orator, who toured the country encouraging men to enlist. The poem expresses a preference even for Kaiser Wilhelm II, the German Emperor.

ll. 11–12. *Than in the storm smoking along the wind* | *Athwart the wood.* Edna Longley has pointed out the poem's indebtedness to Coleridge's 'Fears in Solitude', written in 1798 'during the alarm of an invasion' (*The Annotated Collected Poems*, 263). However, in these lines Thomas is also remembering a different poem by Coleridge: 'But oh! that deep romantic chasm which slanted | Down the green hill athwart a cedarn cover' ('Kubla Khan').

ll. 17–19. *something that historians* | *Can rake out of the ashes when perchance* | *The phoenix broods serene above their ken.* The phoenix is a legendary bird that perishes by fire, only for a newborn phoenix to arise out of the ashes.

l. 19. *ken.* Range of knowledge.

ll. 21–2. *lest* | *We lose what never slaves and cattle blessed.* The poem's drafts spell out Thomas's anxiety that a defeated England would become 'clothed and fed like animals'.

58 RAIN. *Date and Text.* 7 January 1916. The poem relates very closely to a passage in Thomas's travel book, *The Icknield Way* (1913): 'I lay awake listening to the rain, and at first it was as pleasant to my ear and my mind as it had long been desired; but before I fell asleep it had become a majestic and finally a terrible thing, instead of a sweet sound and symbol.

It was accusing and trying me and passing judgement.' Thomas goes on to describe the 'midnight rain', which 'buries' summer and eventually takes over: 'The truth is that the rain falls for ever and I am melting into it. Black and monotonously sounding is the midnight and solitude of the rain. In a little while or in an age—for it is all one—I shall know the full truth of the words I used to love, I knew not why, in my days of nature, in the days before the rain: "Blessed are the dead that the rain rains on"' (280–3). Copy text as published in *The Annotated Collected Poems*, ed. Edna Longley (2008).

58 l. 2. *this bleak hut.* From November 1915 until the following July, Thomas was stationed in a hut at Hare Hall camp, near Romford in Essex, where he taught map-reading skills to officer cadets.

l. 16. *the love of death.* Cf. John Keats, 'Ode to a Nightingale': 'I have been half in love with easeful Death' (l. 32).

ROADS. *Date and Text.* 22 January 1916. Copy text as published in *The Annotated Collected Poems*, ed. Edna Longley (2008).

59 ll. 33–6. *Helen of the roads,* | *The mountain ways of Wales* | *And the Mabinogion tales,* | *Is one of the true gods.* Writing to Eleanor Farjeon on 24 January 1916, Thomas explained: 'Helen is the lady in the Mabinogion, the Welsh lady who married Maxen the Emperor and gave her name to the great old mountain roads—Sarn Helen they are all marked on the maps . . . She is known to mythologists as one of the travelling goddesses of the dusk' (quoted by Farjeon, *Edward Thomas*, 182). The *Mabinogion* is a collection of stories from medieval Welsh manuscripts.

60 l. 48. *chanticleer.* The name commonly given to a cock or rooster in fables.

THE CHERRY TREES. *Date and Text.* 7 or 8 May 1916. Copy text as published in *The Annotated Collected Poems*, ed. Edna Longley (2008).

NO ONE CARES LESS THAN I. 25 or 26 May 1916. Copy text as published in *The Annotated Collected Poems*, ed. Edna Longley (2008).

61 AS THE TEAM'S HEAD-BRASS. *Date and Text.* 27 May 1916. Thomas wrote to his wife the following day that he had set out from Hare Hall camp on a walk, but 'sat down a good deal, both in the fields and at an inn, and passed or was passed by the same pair of lovers 3 or 4 times . . . I wrote some lines too and rewrote them' (quoted in *The Annotated Collected Poems*, 300). Copy text as published in *The Annotated Collected Poems*, ed. Edna Longley (2008).

l. 1. *As the team's head-brass flashed out on the turn.* The 'team' are the pair (or more) of horses pulling the plough, the 'head-brass' being the polished bridle, often embellished with brass ornaments. Thomas places 'turn' at the turn of a line, mimicking the plough's progress in the progress of his poem. The word 'verse' derives from the Latin *versus*, which has its own origins in the turn made by a ploughman.

l. 4. *fallow.* 'Ground that is well ploughed and harrowed, but left uncropped for a whole year or more' (*OED*).

l. 6. *charlock*. The popular name for field mustard.

l. 10 *share*. An abbreviation for 'ploughshare'.

ll. 20–2. *I could spare an arm. I shouldn't want to lose | A leg. If I should lose my head, why, so, | I should want nothing more.* Thomas wrote to his aunt on 15 November 1915: 'I really hope my turn will come and that I shall see what it really is and come out of it with my head and most of my limbs' (quoted by Longley, *The Annotated Collected Poems*, 302).

62 THE TRUMPET. *Date and Text*. Longley suggests 26–28 September 1916 as the dates of composition. Earlier that month, Thomas had moved to the Royal Artillery Barracks in Trowbridge, Wiltshire, from where he told Eleanor Farjeon that he had written some verses suggested by the trumpet calls: 'They are not well done and the trumpet is cracked, but the Reveillé pleases me' (Farjeon, *Edward Thomas: The Last Four Years*, 219). Copy text as published in *The Annotated Collected Poems*, ed. Edna Longley (2008).

WILFRID GIBSON

64 THE MESSAGES. *Date and Text*. Between August and October 1914, but before 17 October, when it was published in *The Nation*. Dominic Hibberd proposes that this may be 'the first poem of the war to imagine shellshock and mention trenches' (*Harold Monro and Wilfrid Gibson*, 15). Copy text as published in *Battle* (1915).

65 BREAKFAST. *Date and Text*. October 1914, but before 17 October, when it was published in *The Nation*. Roger Hogg has pointed out that, two weeks previously, *The Nation* had published an account of a Gordon Highlander: 'When I got my wound in the leg it was because I got too excited in arguing with Wee Geordie Ferris, of our company, about Queen's Park Rangers and their chances this season' (*Harold Monro and Wilfrid Gibson*, 15). Copy text as published in *Battle* (1915).

l. 4. *Hull United . . . Halifax*. Football teams from the north-east of England.

HIT. *Date and Text*. Between August 1914 and July 1915, probably before April 1915. Copy text as published in *Battle* (1915).

l. 5. *Falmouth*. A town on the south coast of Cornwall.

l. 10. *lucent*. Aglow; emitting light.

66 BETWEEN THE LINES. *Date and Text*. Probably between January and June 1915. Dominic Hibberd speculates that 'Between the Lines' was added to *Battle* at a late stage to bulk out what would otherwise have been a slender book (*Harold Monro and Wilfrid Gibson*, 20). The poem was also included in *Livelihood: Dramatic Reveries* (1917)—'restored to its place' according to Gibson's 'Prefatory Note'. Copy text as published in *Battle* (1915).

l. 7. *ascare*. Scared. Very rare—not in *OED*.

68 l. 79. *funk*. Fear; cowardice.

68 l. 84. *hunch*. Chunk (of bread).

70 STRAWBERRIES. *Date and Text*. Probably between January and September 1915. Copy text as published in *Livelihood: Dramatic Reveries* (1917).

71 l. 31. *mazed*. Amazed.

72 l. 59. *lad*. Young man, possibly also with the sense marked as Scottish by *OED*: 'sweetheart'.

73 OTTERBURN. *Date and Text*. Probably between January and August 1917. The village of Otterburn, which derives its name from the Otter Burn running nearby, is situated in Northumberland National Park, approximately twenty miles north of Gibson's home town of Hexham. Copy text as published in *Whin* (1918).

   l. 1. *Flanders*. See note to May Sinclair, 'Field Ambulance in Retreat', l. 6 (p. 237).

   AIR-RAID. *Date and Text*. Probably between May 1916 and April 1919. Copy text as published in *Neighbours* (1920).

   l. 8. *brake*. Thicket.

MARY BORDEN

76 AT THE SOMME. *Date and Text*. Probably between October 1916 and March 1917. The Somme, a river and department in Picardy, has become a byword for the slaughter of the Western Front. The Battle of the Somme, from 1 July to 18 November 1916, resulted in a six-mile advance for British and French forces at the cost of more than one million casualties. The authorial note referring to the French tricolour is an indication that Borden's field hospital was under French command. In October 1916 she was tasked with helping to run the French army's most important military hospital, near the village of Bray-sur-Somme. Copy text as first published in the *English Review* (August 1917).

   'Where is Jehovah?'
   l. 1. *Where is Jehovah, the God of Israel, with his Ark and his Tabernacle and his Pillars of Fire?* These accessories of God are all described in Exodus and elsewhere in the Old Testament: the Ark of the Covenant was the chest containing the tablets of stone on which the Ten Commandments were written (Exodus 31); the Tabernacle was a portable hut or tent, which housed the Ark during the Israelites' journey through the wilderness after their escape from slavery in Egypt (Exodus 25: 8–9); and the pillar of fire manifested God's presence, and guided them so that they could travel at night (Exodus 13: 21–2).

   l. 9. *Picardy*. See note to Rudyard Kipling, 'Gethsemane', l. 2 (p. 241).

77 l. 21. *Moses is dead—and Joshua, who led His people into the promised land, is dead*. According to the Old Testament, Moses and Joshua were leaders of the tribes of Israel. After Moses' death, Joshua led the Israelites into the land of Canaan, the 'promised land'.

l. 25. *creatures of wide metal wings.* Aeroplanes.

78 l. 48. *the Lord of Hosts.* A common biblical phrase. The 'Hosts' are the heavenly angels.

'The Song of the Mud'

l. 8. *poilu.* A French infantryman. Borden dedicated *The Forbidden Zone* to 'the poilus who came that way in 1914–1918'.

81 UNIDENTIFIED. *Date and Text.* Between August and December 1917. Borden wrote in a letter of 9 August 1917 that she was 'beginning a sort of poem' (Conway, *A Woman of Two Wars*, 77), and quoted the opening lines of what would eventually become 'Unidentified'. Copy text as first published in the *English Review* (December 1917).

SIEGFRIED SASSOON

88 THE REDEEMER. *Date and Text.* Drafted late November 1915; revised March 1916. Sassoon noted that it was his first front-line poem. Copy text as published in *Collected Poems, 1908–1956* (1961).

l. 13. *mirk.* An archaic spelling of 'murk'.

l. 19. *a woollen cap.* Steel hats, Sassoon later recalled, 'weren't the fashion until the spring of 1916' (quoted in *The War Poems*, 16).

l. 27. *Lancaster on Lune.* A pedantic way of referring to Lancaster, the county town of Lancashire, through which the River Lune flows. Sassoon's batman was a Lancastrian.

89 A WORKING PARTY. *Date and Text.* 30 March 1916. Sassoon stated that the poem was written 'while in the Front Line during [his] first tour of trenches' (quoted in *The War Poems*, 27). Copy text as published in *Collected Poems, 1908–1956* (1961).

l. 4. *bags of chalk.* These were often used to strengthen the trenches or to provide protection and shelter for front-line troops.

l. 7. *trench boards.* Wooden boards laid at the bottom of trenches.

l. 16. *A flare went up.* Flares were most often used for signalling, but at night they could also suddenly expose targets such as enemy soldiers.

90 l. 31. *a Midland town.* The Midlands is the area of central England.

l. 38. *parapet.* The front of the trench, normally lined with sandbags.

l. 43. *frowsty.* 'Fusty; having an unpleasant smell' (*OED*).

ll. 43–4. *the fumes | Of coke.* Coke was burnt on braziers for heat.

l. 47. *No Man's Land.* John Brophy and Eric Partridge describe no-man's-land as 'A strangely romantic name for the area between the front line trenches of either army, held by neither but patrolled, at night, by both' (*The Long Trail*, 154).

THE KISS. *Date and Text.* 25 April 1916, after Sassoon had attended a lecture, 'The Spirit of the Bayonet', by a Major Campbell, who had spoken with 'homicidal eloquence'. Among Campbell's memorable phrases was his observation that 'the bullet and the bayonet are brother and sister'. Writing to the anthologist Ian Parsons in the early 1960s, Sassoon was keen to emphasize that 'The Kiss' should not be understood as a 'fire-eating' poem: 'I originally wrote it as a sort of exercise—in Anglo-Saxon words, as far as I could manage it—after being disgusted by the barbarities of the famous bayonet-fighting lecture. To this day I don't know what made me write it, for I never felt that I could have stuck a bayonet into anyone, even in self-defence. The difficulty is that it doesn't show any sign of satire' (quoted in Parsons (ed.), *Men Who March Away*, 17). Copy text as published in *Collected Poems, 1908–1956* (1961).

91 A NIGHT ATTACK. *Date and Text.* July 1916. Unpublished during Sassoon's lifetime, the poem first appeared in 1970 under the title 'The rank stench of those bodies haunts me still'. Copy text as published in *The War Poems*, ed. Rupert Hart-Davis (1983).

l. 25. *Bosche.* Germans. See note to Robert Service, 'Only a Boche' (pp. 245–6). 'Bosche' is an alternative spelling, which does not affect pronunciation.

l. 31. *He was a Prussian.* Sassoon is here using the term 'Prussian' generically, to refer to all Germans, rather than in its strict sense, which would denote a native of the northern German state of Prussia.

92 ll. 35–6. *One night he yawned along a half-dug trench | Midnight.* Punctuation—probably a full stop—seems to be missing after 'trench', Sassoon never having submitted an edited version for publication.

ll. 37–8. *'hows' | Whistling to cut the wire with blinding din.* 'Hows' were howitzers—long-barrelled artillery pieces which fired shells. Their high trajectories gave a steep angle of descent, which was ideally suited for trench warfare.

CHRIST AND THE SOLDIER. *Date and Text.* 5 August 1916. Sassoon considered the poem to be an 'ambitious failure', and it was not published in his lifetime. He described the younger self who wrote it as 'a very incomplete and quite unpractising Christian', but denied that the poem gave any clue as to his own 'mental position': 'Like the soldier in the poem, all I could say was "O Jesus, make it stop!"' (quoted in *The War Poems*, 46–7). Copy text as published in *The War Poems*, ed. Rupert Hart-Davis (1983).

l. 9. *Blighty.* England. See note to Robert Service, 'Tipperary Days', l. 36 (p. 245).

93 l. 12. *Paraclete.* Helper or advocate. In Christianity, it refers specifically to the Holy Spirit.

l. 23. *shrives.* Gives absolution to penitents.

l. 29. *I have not died in vain between two thieves.* According to the gospels, Christ was crucified between two criminals: 'Then were there two thieves crucified with him, one on the right hand, and another on the left' (Matthew 27: 38).

l. 39. *Red Cross.* See note to May Sinclair, 'Field Ambulance in Retreat',
l. 16 (p. 237).

94 l. 44. *crown of thorns.* The gospels report that Roman soldiers mocked
Christ before his crucifixion: 'And when they had platted a crown of
thorns, they put it upon his head, and a reed in his right hand: and they
bowed the knee before him, and mocked him, saying, Hail, King of the
Jews!' (Matthew 27: 29).

'THEY'. *Date and Text.* 31 October or early November 1916. According to
his biographer, Max Egremont, Sassoon had heard his friend Robbie Ross
reading extracts from a sermon preached by the Bishop of London 'about
soldiers having their souls purged by the war' (*Siegfried Sassoon*, 116).
Sassoon later recalled that 'the thing just wrote itself' (quoted in *The War
Poems*, 57). His title may have come from Rudyard Kipling's famous
story, 'They' (1904), in which the narrator gradually realizes that the
stately house he is visiting is filled with the ghosts of children. Copy text
as published in *Collected Poems, 1908–1956* (1961), except that I have
removed opening quotation marks at the start of lines 2–6 and 9–11.

l. 10. *syphilitic.* Sassoon claimed that the word had never been used before
in poetry (Patrick Campbell, *Siegfried Sassoon: A Study of the War Poetry*
(Jefferson, NC: McFarland and Co., 1999), 125). Syphilis was rife among
troops of all nations during the War.

l. 12. *'The ways of God are strange!'* Cf. William Cowper's well-known
hymn: 'God moves in a mysterious way | His wonders to perform'.

THE POET AS HERO. *Date and Text.* November 1916. First published on
2 December 1916 in the *Cambridge Magazine*, but uncollected in Sassoon's
lifetime. Copy text as published in *The War Poems*, ed. Rupert Hart-
Davis (1983).

ll. 2–4. *you've asked me why . . . ugly cry.* 'The Hero', an earlier poem by
Sassoon, published in the *Cambridge Magazine*, attracted criticism from
the Liberal journalist Charles Geake, who had been 'disgusted' by it
(Egremont, *Siegfried Sassoon*, 118). Sassoon may have known about
Geake's letter and written 'The Poet as Hero' in reply. The letter and the
new poem were published together on the same page.

95 ll. 5–9. *once I sought the Grail . . . now I've said good-bye to Galahad.* The
Holy Grail, a legendary dish or cup with magical properties, is supposed
to have been used by Christ at the Last Supper. The quest for the Grail
runs throughout Arthurian romance: in many retellings, Galahad is the
knight destined to discover it. Several of Sassoon's early poems dwelt on
this medieval world of courts and chivalry.

l. 13. *Wound for red wound I burn to smite their wrongs.* Cf. Exodus 21: 23–5:
'And if any mischief follow, then thou shalt give life for life, eye for eye,
tooth for tooth, hand for hand, foot for foot, burning for burning, wound
for wound, stripe for stripe.'

l. 14. *absolution.* A state in which forgiveness for sins has been given by
God.

95 'BLIGHTERS'. *Date and Text.* 4 February 1917. Sassoon had been appalled by a jingoistic revue that he saw at the Liverpool Hippodrome. 'Blighters' are rascals or scoundrels. Copy text as published in *Collected Poems, 1908–1956* (1961).

l. 1. *The House.* The theatre (as in 'a full house').

l. 4. *'We're sure the Kaiser loves our dear old Tanks!'* The German Emperor, Kaiser Wilhelm II, may not have loved the enemy's tanks, but he would certainly have been surprised by them: they were introduced into battle during 1916. *OED* dates the first recorded use of the word 'tank' (in the sense of an armoured military vehicle) as occurring on 18 September 1916.

l. 6. *rag-time tunes, or 'Home, sweet Home'.* *OED* describes ragtime as 'a musical rhythm characterized by a syncopated melodic line and regularly-accented accompaniment'. 'Home, Sweet Home' is a popular song from the early nineteenth century.

l. 7. *Music-halls.* Theatres that hosted variety entertainments, such as performances of popular songs and comedy acts.

l. 8. *the riddled corpses round Bapaume.* Bapaume, ten miles south of Arras, was held by the Germans under fierce attack during the Battle of the Somme (1916). The 'corpses' may be Allied or German, and 'riddled' with bullets or with maggots.

BASE DETAILS. *Date and Text.* 4 March 1917. Copy text as published in *Collected Poems, 1908–1956* (1961).

l. 6. *the Roll of Honour.* The list of fallen soldiers.

96 THE REAR-GUARD. *Date and Text.* 22 April 1917, 'at Denmark Hill Hospital about ten days after I was wounded. [Edmund] Gosse, after seeing me there, wrote to Uncle Hamo that he thought I was suffering from severe shock. But if so, could I have written such a strong poem?' (Quoted in *The War Poems*, 76.) At the time, Sassoon considered 'The Rear-Guard' 'the best "horrible" poem [he] should ever do' (Egremont, *Siegfried Sassoon*, 134). The job of the rearguard is to protect an army from attack from the rear. The setting for the poem is a part of the Hindenburg Line, a complex system of defences that the Germans had built in the winter of 1916–17. Copy text as published in *Collected Poems, 1908–1956* (1961).

ll. 11–13. *'I'm looking for headquarters.' No reply . . . through this stinking place.* On one occasion earlier in April 1917, Sassoon's company commander had mistakenly shaken a dead German's shoulder to ask for directions. Max Egremont notes that in his *Memoirs of an Infantry Officer* it is Sassoon who shakes the corpse (*Siegfried Sassoon*, 129).

l. 15. *livid face.* Sassoon draws on two meanings of 'livid'. The face is of a bluish-black colour, as if bruised; and it displays the passion of rage.

THE GENERAL. *Date and Text.* April 1917. Copy text as published in *Collected Poems, 1908–1956* (1961).

97 l. 6. *Arras*. The city in the north of France near which the Battle of Arras took place in April and May 1917.

REPRESSION OF WAR EXPERIENCE. *Date and Text*. June or July 1917. Written at Sassoon's family home in Weirleigh, Kent, where the guns were audible from across the Channel. The sound, Sassoon reported, 'nearly drives me dotty sometimes' (Egremont, *Siegfried Sassoon*, 149). The poem's title came late, and was taken from a lecture and paper by Sassoon's psychiatrist, W. H. R. Rivers. Copy text as published in *Collected Poems, 1908–1956* (1961).

98 COUNTER-ATTACK. *Date and Text*. First draft, July 1916; substantially revised between August and November 1917. Copy text as published in *Collected Poems, 1908–1956* (1961).

l. 5. *Lewis guns*. Light machine-guns used by the British during the War.

l. 16. *Allemands*. Germans (from the French word for Germans, but probably with English pronunciation).

l. 17. *five-nines*. 5.9-calibre German artillery shells.

l. 18. *dud*. An explosive that fails to detonate.

99 l. 26. *fire-step*. A step cut into the side of the trench, approximately three feet above the floor (and therefore almost halfway up). It allowed soldiers to peer or climb over the side of the trench.

l. 29. *sap*. A narrow trench dug into no-man's-land at ninety degrees to existing lines.

HOW TO DIE. *Date and Text*. Between August and October 1917, but before 6 October, when the poem appeared in the *Cambridge Magazine*. Copy text as published in *Collected Poems, 1908–1956* (1961).

l. 2. *craters*. That is, shell craters.

l. 10. *go West*. Die. According to *OED*, this euphemism became common during the War. The West is the land of death in many cultures, because the sun sets in the west.

100 GLORY OF WOMEN. *Date and Text*. Between August and November 1917. First published in the *Cambridge Magazine* in December 1917. Copy text as published in *Collected Poems, 1908–1956* (1961).

l. 5. *You make us shells*. The phrase combines a double accusation: the women hollow men out, and they make the explosives that men use to kill each other in war.

l. 6. *By tales of dirt and danger fondly thrilled*. In his diaries around this time, Sassoon speculated about the sexual pleasure that women derived from accounts of male courage and injury.

EVERYONE SANG. *Date and Text*. April 1919. Sassoon reported that the poem had come to him whole, in a few minutes, with the force of a religious revelation (Egremont, *Siegfried Sassoon*, 235). Copy text as published in *Collected Poems, 1908–1956* (1961).

101   ON PASSING THE NEW MENIN GATE. *Date and Text*. Between 25 July 1927 and January 1928. The Menin Gate Memorial to the Missing, in Ypres, Belgium, was unveiled on 24 July 1927. Designed by the British architect Reginald Blomfield and built under the auspices of the British government, it lists the names of over 54,000 Commonwealth soldiers who died in the Ypres Salient and whose bodies were never recovered. Copy text as published in *Collected Poems, 1908–1956* (1961).

l. 5. *the Salient*. A salient is a spur of land that projects into enemy territory. As such, it is vulnerable to attack on three sides. The Ypres Salient, around the town of Ypres, was the location of fierce trench fighting throughout the War.

l. 10. *'Their name liveth for ever,' the Gateway claims*. The exact phrase is 'Their name liveth for evermore', a quotation from Ecclesiasticus 44: 14, which Rudyard Kipling chose, on behalf of the Commonwealth War Graves Commission, to be added to stones of remembrance.

l. 11. *immolation*. Sacrifice.

RUPERT BROOKE

104   1914. *Date and Text*. From 19 October to 25 December 1914. The sonnets were probably written in the following order: 'Safety'; 'Peace'; 'The Dead' ('Blow out, you bugles'); 'The Dead' ('These hearts were woven'); 'The Soldier'. They were first published in an issue of *New Numbers*, which, although dated December 1914, in fact appeared in February 1915. Dominic Hibberd and John Onions suggest that these were 'perhaps the first poems by a volunteer who had been in action' (*The Winter of the World*, 41). Brooke described writing the sonnets as 'rather like developing photographs', and was not altogether convinced of their merits: 'God they're in the rough, these five camp children . . . 4 and 5 are good, though, and there are phrases in the rest' (quoted in *The Collected Poems of Rupert Brooke* (London: Sidgwick and Jackson, 1918), p. cxxxvi). Copy text as published in *1914 and Other Poems* (1915).

I. Peace
l. 1. *Now, God be thanked*. Cf. 'Now thank we all our God', a seventeenth-century German hymn written by Martin Rinkart and translated by Catherine Winkworth in 1856. The hymn calls on God to be thanked 'with hearts and hands and voices'; Brooke's sonnet mentions 'hand' and 'hearts' in its first six lines.

ll. 8–9. *And all the little emptiness of love! | Oh! we, who have known shame*. Cf. Shakespeare's Sonnet 129, ll. 1–2: 'Th'expense of spirit in a waste of shame | Is lust in action'.

II. Safety
l. 1. *Dear!* Although unidentified by the poem, the addressee is Brooke's lover, Cathleen Nesbitt.

l. 4. *'Who is so safe as we?'* Brooke takes the phrase from John Donne's

'The Anniversarie': 'Here upon earth, we'are Kings, and none but we | Can be such Kings, nor of such subjects be. | Who is so safe as we?' (ll. 23–5). Cathleen Nesbitt had read Donne's poem to Brooke when he visited her at Great Yarmouth in October 1914 (Jones, *Rupert Brooke*, 387–8).

105 III. The Dead ('Blow out, you bugles')

l. 2. *There's none of these so lonely and poor of old.* Nigel Jones detects an allusion to Shakespeare's *Henry V*, specifically King Henry's promise before Agincourt that any man who fights alongside him—'be he ne'er so vile'—will be his brother (*Henry V*, IV.iii.60–2; Jones, *Rupert Brooke*, 393). Brooke's emphasis on youth, on honour, and on 'a king' who has 'Paid his subjects with a royal wage', makes the entire sonnet indebted to Henry's speech.

106 V. The Soldier

This sonnet engages throughout with Thomas Hardy's 'Drummer Hodge', a Boer War poem about death and burial in a distant land: 'foreign' and 'home' are crucial words in both poems, as is 'eternal' ('eternally' in 'Drummer Hodge') and 'dust' ('dusty'). But whereas Hodge's body is forced to 'Grow to some Southern tree', Brooke's soldier remains untransformed in his Englishness; and whereas Hodge must endure eternity under 'strange-eyed constellations', Brooke's soldier lies 'under an English heaven'.

[FRAGMENT]. *Date and Text.* Between 11 and 19 April 1915. Written aboard the *Grantully Castle* as it sailed to Gallipoli. The title has been added by later editors. Copy text as published in *The Collected Poems of Rupert Brooke* (1931).

107 l. 15. *phosphorus.* The chemical phosphorus takes its name from the Greek for 'light-giving'. Brooke describes the glow emitted as the wave breaks.

JULIAN GRENFELL

108 PRAYER FOR THOSE ON THE STAFF. February or March 1915. Staff officers helped military command with strategic planning and communication. They were frequently the objects of scorn, perceived as leading a cushy and privileged life. Copy text based on a transcription by Elizabeth Vandiver of the holograph manuscript at Hertford Archives and Local Records, except that I have changed an ampersand to 'and' in line 4.

109 l. 7. *Upper Ten.* The top stratum in a hierarchy of servants.

l. 12. *General French.* General John French was commander-in-chief of the British Expeditionary Force until December 1915, when he was replaced by Douglas Haig.

l. 19. *A.D.C.* An abbreviation for 'aide-de-camp'—assistant to a senior military officer or head of state.

l. 28. *costive.* Constipated; slow or unforthcoming.

110 INTO BATTLE. *Date and Text.* 29 April 1915. Copy text as published in Elizabeth Vandiver, *Stand in the Trench, Achilles* (2010).

110   ll. 17–18. *The Dog-star, and the Sisters Seven,* | *Orion's Belt and sworded hip.* The Dog Star is Sirius, the brightest star in the night sky. The Seven Sisters, better known as the Pleiades, is a constellation, as is Orion, the stars of which make the shape of a belt and sword.

T. P. CAMERON WILSON

113   MAGPIES IN PICARDY. *Date and Text.* Between March and August 1916, but before 16 August, when it was published in the *Westminster Gazette.* It was collected as the title poem to Wilson's posthumous volume in 1919, but with the final two stanzas missing. For Picardy, see note to Rudyard Kipling, 'Gethsemane', l. 2 (p. 241). Copy text as published in *Waste Paper Philosophy, to which has been added Magpies in Picardy and Other Poems* (1920).

ll. 28–30. *These dusty highways . . . Through Picardy to war.* Picardy was one of the battlegrounds of the Hundred Years War (1337–1453).

114   SONG OF AMIENS. *Date and Text.* Probably July or August 1916. Amiens is a city in Picardy through which the Somme flows. Copy text as published in *Waste Paper Philosophy, to which has been added Magpies in Picardy and Other Poems* (1920).

115   l. 24. *Delville Wood.* The Battle of Delville Wood took place between 14 July and 3 September 1916, in an area north-east of the town of Longueval in northern France. It was a victory for the Allied forces, albeit with heavy losses on both sides.

PATRICK SHAW STEWART

117   [I SAW A MAN THIS MORNING]. *Date and Text.* Internal evidence dates the poem to 13 July 1915, when Shaw Stewart was unexpectedly recalled from leave, having enjoyed just 'three days' peace' on the island of Imbros. The title has been added by later editors. Copy text as found in Shaw Stewart's copy of A. E. Housman's *A Shropshire Lad.*

l. 6. *Dardanelles.* A narrow strait in north-west Turkey, connecting the Aegean Sea to the Sea of Marmara. Troy was situated near its western entrance. The Dardanelles was known in ancient times as the Hellespont (literally, 'sea of Helle'), a fact that prepares for the poem's wordplay on Helen–hell–shell.

ll. 13–16. *O hell of ships and cities . . . Fatal second Helen . . . thee?* Helen was the immediate cause of the Trojan Wars, having abandoned her husband for the Trojan prince Paris. In Greek, *helein* means to destroy. Elizabeth Vandiver argues that this stanza alludes to Aeschylus' *Agamemnon*, lines 681–90, especially its punning catalogue of 'helanas, helandros, heleptolis' (ship-destroyer, man-destroyer, city-destroyer) (*Stand in the Trench, Achilles* (2010), 274).

l. 18. *Chersonese.* The Thracian Chersonese was the ancient name given to what is now the Gallipoli Peninsula.

l. 19. *He turned from wrath to battle*. Enraged at the death of his close friend Patroclus, the Greek hero Achilles took up arms and devastated the Trojan defenders.

l. 26. *Imbros*. The island in the Aegean Sea on which Shaw Stewart spent his brief leave before sailing to Gallipoli.

ll. 27–8. *Stand in the trench, Achilles, | Flame-capped, and shout for me*. These lines are usually understood to allude to the fact that Achilles' helmet was made by the god of fire, Hephaestus. However, Vandiver proposes a source in Homer's *Iliad* 18.203–29, in which Athena sets a golden cloud around the head of Achilles and kindles a fire from it: 'He stood there and he shouted . . . and he raised immense confusion among the Trojans' (*Stand in the Trench, Achilles*, 276).

IVOR GURNEY

120 PAIN. *Date and Text*. February 1917. Gurney sent an early version to his friend, the musicologist and critic Marion Scott, on 7 February 1917, explaining that 'Pain' would be 'the first of Sonnetts [*sic*] 1917, five of them, for admirers of Rupert Brooke'. This sequence, Gurney promised, would amount to 'the protest of the physical against the exalted spiritual; of the cumulative weight of small facts against the one large' (*Collected Letters*, 210). In the event, 'Pain' appeared in Gurney's first volume, *Severn & Somme*, as the *second* in a sequence of five 'Sonnets 1917' dedicated 'To the Memory of Rupert Brooke'. Copy text as first published in *Severn & Somme* (1917).

l. 9. *foredone*. *OED* offers 'Exhausted, overcome, tired out'. This does not seem quite bleak enough. Gurney's usage also remembers a sense of 'foredo' that *OED* considers obsolete or archaic: 'To put (a living being) out of existence, to kill; to put an end to (life).'

121 TO THE PRUSSIANS OF ENGLAND. *Date and Text*. Early October 1917, but before 12 October, when Gurney sent the poem to Marion Scott. Prussia was the dominant state of the German Empire; it became strongly associated with conservatism and aggressive militarism. Detecting the same characteristics in England, the revolutionary language of Gurney's poem alarmed Marion Scott, who required reassurance that she was not among its intended targets. Copy text as published in *Collected Letters*, ed. R. K. R. Thornton (1991).

l. 2. *Ypres pools*. For Ypres, see note to May Sinclair, 'Dedication', l. 35 (p. 237). The 'pools' were shell craters that had filled with water.

l. 3. *blither*. 'Nonsense' (*OED*).

l. 4. *lying at length*. Lying prostrate.

l. 10. *Brotherhood of man*. Gurney's source may have been Mark Twain, who spoke often to the effect that: 'The universal brotherhood of man is our most precious possession' (*Mark Twain's Notebook*, ed. Albert Bigelow Paine (New York: Harper & Brothers, 1935), 347).

121 ll. 11-14. *An armed Mistress . . . Will cut the cancer threatens England's life.* Gurney often personified England as female. Here he may also be thinking of Britannia (who 'rules the waves' in James Thomson's famous poem 'Rule Britannia'). Proud of her achievements across the sea, she will also be empowered to cut out the disease of Prussian 'mastery' at home.

TO HIS LOVE. *Date and Text.* January 1918. Sending the poem to Marion Scott on 20 January, Gurney wrote at the end of the manuscript: 'Seaton Delaval | Northumberland | Jan 1917'. R. K. R. Thornton has noted that this 'is obviously a slip for 1918': Gurney did not arrive at the Seaton Delaval camp until November 1917 (*Collected Letters*, 398). The title may echo Christopher Marlowe's 'The Passionate Shepherd to His Love'; line 4 of Gurney's poem refers to 'sheep'. Although often thought to be an elegy for Gurney's friend and fellow poet, F. W. Harvey, who had been reported missing, presumed dead, in August 1916, 'To His Love' seems to have been written after Gurney had heard that Harvey had been captured alive. Copy text as first published in *War's Embers* (1919).

l. 1. *He's gone.* In correspondence, Philip Lancaster has pointed out the debt to Wilfrid Gibson's dedicatory poem, 'To the Memory of Rupert Brooke', in *Friends* (1916): 'He's gone. | I do not understand' (ll. 1-2).

ll. 3-4. *Cotswold | Where the sheep feed.* The Cotswolds are a range of hills mostly located within Gloucestershire and Oxfordshire. The name Cotswold was wrongly thought to mean 'the sheep enclosure in the hills'.

l. 8. *Severn river.* Britain's longest river, the Severn flows through Gurney's native city of Gloucester.

122 l. 16. *Cover him, cover him soon!* Stallworthy and Potter hear an allusion to John Webster's *The White Devil* (V.iv.102-6): 'Call for the robin-redbreast and the wren, | Since o'er shady groves they hover | And with leaves and flowers do cover | The friendless bodies of unburied men' (*Three Poets*, 119). Gurney praised Webster's play in a letter of February 1916.

l. 18. *memoried.* 'Full of or fraught with memories' (*OED*).

THE BUGLE. *Date and Text.* January or February 1919. Gurney wrote a longer poem titled 'Bugle of Victory' several months later, using many of the lines from 'The Bugle'. This shorter version was first published in *The Guardian*, 13 November 2010. Copy text is a manuscript in Gurney's hand, D10500/1/P/2/7/24 in the Gloucestershire Archives.

l. 5. *embronze.* Embody in bronze, or colour as bronze.

l. 17. *Ypres or the Somme.* For Ypres, see note to May Sinclair, 'Dedication', l. 35 (p. 237). For the Somme, see note to Mary Borden, 'At the Somme' (p. 250).

123 BILLET. *Date and Text.* 1921 or 1922, revised 1924. A billet is a place of rest for soldiers. Copy text as in the 'Rewards of Wonder' typescript held at Gloucestershire Archives.

l. 9. *Brewery.* Probably the Frome Brewery, based in Stroud.

l. 10. *Stroud.* A market town in Gurney's home county of Gloucestershire.

l. 12. *Horsepool's turning.* Horsepools [*sic*] is a tiny hamlet where roads meet, several miles north of Stroud.

FIRST TIME IN. *Date and Text.* Mid-1922. This is one of two poems by Gurney titled 'First Time In'. He described his first experience of a front-line trench as 'one of the most notable evenings of [his] life': the Welsh soldiers whom he met talked of 'Welsh Folksong, or George Borrow, of Burns, of the RCM [Royal College of Music]; of—yes— of Oscar Wilde, Omar Khayyam, Shakespeare and of the war'. They also sang with 'delightful' voices (*Collected Letters*, 86, 91). So excited was Gurney by this new intellectual companionship that he scarcely slept for two days. Copy text is a transcription by Marion Scott, D10500/1/P/6/3/1/23 in the Gloucestershire Archives.

l. 1. *red yarns of the Line.* John Lucas reads the reference to 'red yarns' politically, assuming that they are stories of 'mutiny' and 'socialist defiance' (Lucas, *Ivor Gurney* (Tavistock: Northcote House, 2001), 47, 91); more likely, especially in the context of 'dread tales', they are accounts of war's horrors. Gurney wrote to Herbert Howells that 'Unlike some men out here, [the Welsh] didn't try to frighten us with norrible [*sic*] details' (*Collected Letters*, 94–5). The 'Line' is the front line.

l. 6. *slitten.* The past participle of 'slit'.

l. 14. *Ulysses.* Ulysses, otherwise known as Odysseus, was the hero of Homer's *Odyssey.*

124 l. 15. *'David of the White Rock', the 'Slumber Song'.* Gurney wrote in an undated letter of early June 1916 that among the Welsh regiment he had 'met four of the nicest young men you could meet, possibly. They knew folksong. And one of them sang "David of the White Rock" and "A Slumber Song", both of which Somervell has arranged, and both beauties' (*Collected Letters*, 89). The composer Sir Arthur Somervell (1863–1937) was known to Gurney as a teacher at the Royal College of Music.

ll. 15–17. *that | Beautiful tune to which roguish words by Welsh pit boys | Are sung.* Gurney's letters do not identify the particular tune, but it was common practice among soldiers to add bawdy or obscene lyrics to traditional melodies. 'Pit boys' were children who worked in mines. An Act of 1911 had raised the age limit for mineworkers to 14 years.

STRANGE HELLS. *Date and Text.* Mid-1922. Copy text is a transcription by Marion Scott, D10500/1/P/6/3/1/23 in the Gloucestershire Archives. I have made one alteration, correcting the French in line 9 to 'la guerre' from 'le guerre'.

l. 8. *tin and stretched-wire.* Barbed-wire.

l. 8. *tinkle.* Jingle; light song.

l. 8 *blither.* 'Nonsense' (*OED*). Cf. Gurney, 'To the Prussians of England', l. 3: 'Then read the blither written by knaves for fools' (p. 121).

l. 9. *'Après la guerre fini'.* For this popular trench song, see p. 226. The title—pidgin French for 'After the war is over'—is a catchphrase implying 'never' or, at best, some time in the distant future.

124 l. 10. *12 inch—6 inch and 18 pounders.* Abbreviated descriptions of ordnance.

l. 11. *State-doles.* Welfare support from government; the demobilized soldiers have not been given jobs.

l. 12. *tatterns.* Rags.

FAREWELL. *Date and Text.* July 1924. Copy text is a manuscript in Gurney's hand, D10500/1/P/4/13 in the Gloucestershire Archives. I have corrected the spelling where Gurney wrote 'Hancocks' at l. 5 and 'Battallion' at ll. 21 and 26.

ll. 1–2. *to have had gas . . . and to get Blighty.* 'Blighty' was England (see note to Robert Service, 'Tipperary Days', l. 36 (p. 245)), so to 'get Blighty' or 'get a Blighty one' was to be wounded badly enough to be shipped home. Gurney was exposed to gas on or not long before 12 September 1917, but initially regretted that his case was not more severe: 'Being gassed (mildly) with the new gas is no worse than catarrh or a bad cold' (*Collected Letters*, 326). Having written to Marion Scott just a few days earlier with the hope that he might 'get a Blighty'—'and O if it were but a small hole in the leg!' (*Collected Letters*, 321)—he was delighted to learn that his wish had been granted, even if the nature of the 'Blighty' had been unforeseen.

ll. 3–4. *not anyway exact— | To Ypres, or bad St Julien or Somme Farm.* For Ypres, see note to May Sinclair, 'Dedication', l. 35 (p. 237). Gurney fought at Saint-Julien (where he inhaled gas) and Somme Farm, east of Ypres, in late August and early September 1917, as part of the Third Battle of Ypres. Given the brutality of the fighting, in these lines he notes his surprise that such a relatively minor ailment should have been adjudged a 'Blighty'.

l. 5. *Don Hancox.* See the headnote to the poem. Lance Corporal Leonard Dodd Hancox was killed at Ypres on 23 August 1917.

l. 5. *frore.* Frozen; ice-cold.

l. 7. *Monger.* Lance Corporal John Edgar Monger of the Gloucestershire Regiment was killed on 9 February 1918.

125 ll. 12–15. *Gloucester with Stroud debating . . . Nor to hear Cheltenham hurling at Cotswold demands | Of civilization; nor West Severn joking at East Severn?* Gurney describes the banter between men from different towns and regions of Gloucestershire.

l. 19. *Somme or Aubers.* For the Somme, see note to Mary Borden, 'At the Somme' (p. 250). The Gloucesters spent many months stationed near the French village of Aubers, close to the Belgian border and fifteen miles west of Lille. It had been the site of a disastrous offensive by the British on 9 May 1915.

l. 24. *Northlands.* This seems to refer to Northumberland. After being gassed, Gurney recovered at Edinburgh War Hospital in September 1917. He was discharged in early November, and sent to Seaton

Delaval in Northumberland on a signalling course. The final stanza of 'De Profundis' (written in October 1918) complains of 'the Northland grey-drear'.

l. 25. *And after to meet evil not fit for the thought one touch to dwell on.* Gurney suffered a nervous breakdown during 1918, and was finally incarcerated in September 1922.

l. 31. *They bruise my head and torture with their own past-hate | Sins of the past, and lie so as earth moves at it.* Gurney complained of being tortured with electricity when first committed to the asylum. So egregious are the lies told by his persecutors, he suggests in these lines, that they cause tremors in the earth.

l. 32. *unbroken wires.* Although artillery fire was intended to have destroyed barbed-wire defences before infantry assaults, advancing soldiers often encountered 'unbroken wires'. Cf. Gurney, 'The Retreat', ll. 140–1: 'no holes at all in the wire. | So much for artillery fire . . .' (p. 131); and Gurney, 'The Silent One', l. 4.: 'Yet faced unbroken wires' (p. 134).

LA RIME. *Date and Text.* March 1925. 'La Rime' is French for 'The Rhyme'. Gurney reported in a letter to Marion Scott on 13 September 1916: 'I read a great deal of Kipling's *Fringes of the Fleet* in a shell hole, during one of the most annoying times we have had. It was during heavy fatigue, and the Bosches spotted us and let fly with heavy shrapnel and 5.9s' (*Collected Letters*, 146). Copy text as in the 'Memories of Honour' typescript held at Gloucestershire Archives, with the following alterations: I have changed 'Fritzy' to 'Fritz' throughout (the typist having misread the extravagant downward tail on Gurney's 'z' in this and other poems), and I have corrected the title from 'Le Rime' to 'La Rime'.

1. 1. *Fritz.* According to Brophy and Partridge: 'Diminutive of *Friedrich*. German soldiers, singly or collectively' (*The Long Trail*, 124), Fritz is a relatively affectionate name for the German soldier, making him the counterpart of the British Tommy.

l. 1. *fatigue party.* A group of soldiers carrying out fatigue duties. Fatigues were the 'extra-professional duties of a soldier' (*OED*), such as cleaning accommodation, preparing food, or transporting materials.

l. 4. *powder, cordite or T.N.T.* Three kinds of explosive used during the War.

l. 9. *ragtime.* See note to Siegfried Sassoon, 'Blighters', l. 6 (p. 254).

126 l. 13. *Red House.* The battalion headquarters at Laventie, near where Gurney was posted with the 2/5 Gloucesters in June 1916.

l. 14. *home-critics.* Journalists who criticized the war effort but showed no inclination to enlist were a common target of abuse. However, Gurney may be referring particularly to critics, editors, and reviewers of verse. Gurney's attitude towards them can be gauged from a letter written to Marion Scott with a postmark of 23 August 1917, after one of his poems was rejected: 'The poem on Gloucester has been returned, but with request for more. My feelings are too seriously hurt for that, though, at present. How dare he?' (*Collected Letters*, 307).

126   SERENADE. *Date and Text.* March 1925. Copy text as in the 'Memories of Honour' typescript held at Gloucestershire Archives.

l. 1. *Somme.* See note to Mary Borden, 'At the Somme' (p. 250).

l. 5. *The tune of Schubert which belonged to days mathematical.* The Austrian composer Franz Schubert (1797–1828). Gurney draws an implicit contrast between 'days mathematical' (that is, ordered, controlled, precise) and the chaos of war.

l. 8. *"Heldenleben".* *Ein Heldenleben* ('A hero's life') is a tone poem by Richard Strauss (1864–1949), which received its premiere in 1899. In a letter dated 17 July 1916, Gurney's 'horrid imagination' was at work: 'Supposing instead of a strafe, [the Germans] played Heldenleben at us . . .' (*Collected Letters*, 120).

l. 9. *Gloucesters.* The Gloucestershire Regiment, to which Gurney belonged.

ll. 9–10. *'Strauss is our favourite wir haben | Sich geliebt'.* The German is awkwardly expressed, but means something like 'Strauss is our favourite[;] we have enjoyed [his work]'.

l. 10. *Aubers.* See note to Gurney, 'Farewell', l. 19 (p. 262).

JOYEUSE ET DURANDAL. *Date and Text.* March 1925. The title names wartime bayonets after two famous swords: the Joyeuse ('Joyful') belonged to the Emperor Charlemagne, and the Durandal (often called Durendal) was the sword of Charlemagne's paladin, Roland. This poem is previously unpublished. Copy text as in the 'Memories of Honour' typescript held at Gloucestershire Archives.

l. 1. *Old Army.* Those parts of the army that pre-dated the War.

l. 7. *War Office.* The department of the British government which had responsibility for the management of the army.

l. 7. *green envelopes.* 'A form of envelope not subject to the ordinary regimental censorship. The writer signed a declaration on the outside that the contents gave no military information. Green envelopes were issued sparsely and infrequently, but some could be obtained by bribery or by barter' (Brophy and Partridge (eds.), *The Long Trail*, 129).

l. 8. *do worrying fatigues on Rest for a day.* For fatigues, see note to Gurney, 'La Rime', l. 1 (p. 263). Any soldier who volunteered to carry out fatigues while 'on Rest'—out of the front line—was making a notable sacrifice, especially as fatigue parties were sniped at or came under bombardment sometimes.

127   THE STOKES GUNNERS. *Date and Text.* Early March 1925. The Stokes Mortar, invented by Wilfred Stokes (1860–1927), was used extensively by British and Commonwealth armies in the second half of the War. It was simple in design, portable, and could fire more than twenty mortars

per minute. Gurney's hostility to the gunners can be explained by reference to Charles Sorley's comments to his mother in a letter of 10 July 1915: 'For either side to bomb the other would be a useless violation of the unwritten laws that govern the relations of combatants permanently within a hundred yards of distance of each other, who have found out that to provide discomfort for the other is but a roundabout way of providing it for themselves' (*The Letters of Charles Sorley*, 283). 'The Stokes Gunners' is previously unpublished. Copy text as in the 'Memories of Honour' typescript held at Gloucestershire Archives.

l. 1. *Fritz.* See note to Gurney, 'La Rime', l. 1 (p. 263).

l. 4. *stove-pipe.* Literally, the chimney of a wood- or coal-burning stove; here used to describe the metal tube through which mortar bombs were fired.

l. 5. *Ticklers jams.* Tickler's jam, usually—and notoriously—plum and apple, was standard issue in the trenches. 'Is it plum and apple?' 'No, it's apple and plum' was a common exchange. The empty tins were often redeployed as containers for bombs, hence the phrase 'Tickler's Artillery'.

l. 11. *Gloucesters.* The Gloucestershire Regiment.

l. 12. *Montreal and Seattle.* Aside from their considerable distance from the front, it is unclear why these cities, of Canada and the United States respectively, should have been singled out.

THE BOHEMIANS. *Date and Text.* March 1925. Copy text as in the 'Memories of Honour' typescript held at Gloucestershire Archives.

l. 3. *putties.* Putties, or puttees, were strips of cloth which were wound round the leg from ankle to knee to provide support.

l. 15. *'Lights out'.* The bugle call at night to signal lights out.

l. 17. *Artois or Picardy.* The province of Artois in northern France was the site for much of the fighting on the Western Front. For Picardy, see note to Rudyard Kipling, 'Gethsemane', l. 2 (p. 241).

128 THE RETREAT. *Date and Text.* 23 April 1925. The poem describes the events leading up to Gurney's injury at Vermand on Good Friday, 6 April 1917. He also wrote a prose account titled 'The Move Forward' on 3 May 1926. 'The Retreat' has been published only in an appendix to *Collected Poems* (rev. edn. 2004), where it is accompanied by a note from the editor, P. J. Kavanagh: 'This long autobiographical poem, one of many, is included because Gurney begins to describe his front-line experiences— even the shooting at people—in comic terms. This is typical of a certain vein in Gurney (perhaps typical of certain aspects of war) and he would not be fully represented were it to be left out.' Copy text as in D10500/1/P/4/141 held at Gloucestershire Archives. I have corrected the spelling of 'billetts' (ll. 4 and 19) and of 'Omiecourt' (l. 19, where Gurney wrote 'Amiecourt'); added an apostrophe to 'Sommes Land' (l. 53); changed 'spinnies' to 'spinneys' (l. 64); changed 'of' to 'off' (l. 111); added an extra closing parenthesis (l. 115); added a comma after 'Wurtemburg' (l. 155); and added a closing quotation mark (l. 158).

128 l. 2. *Chaulnes*. A village in the Somme department of Picardy, completely destroyed during the War.

l. 11. *Fritz*. See note to Gurney, 'La Rime', l. 1 (p. 263).

l. 16. *No mans land*. See note to Siegfried Sassoon, 'A Working Party', l. 47 (p. 251).

l. 19. *Omiecourt*. A hamlet in Picardy which consisted of a château and a few nearby farms.

l. 30. *Somme*. See note to Mary Borden, 'At the Somme' (p. 250).

l. 34. *Y*. A hamlet in the Somme department of Picardy. Gurney wrote a poem—'To Y'—about what he called 'the shortest village of all Europe'.

l. 35. *Caulaincourt*. A hamlet in Picardy. Its château was destroyed in the War.

129 ll. 36–7. *Home of the dead men of Napoleon's man | Lay in the Mausoleum*. The Marquis de Caulaincourt (1773–1827) was a French general who served under Napoleon, as did his two sons. His body rests in the Panthéon in Paris, but his heart is in the Mausoleum at Caulaincourt.

ll. 38–9. *Gloucesters guarding a place . . . the old rule Rousseau or Le Sage knew*. Jean-Jacques Rousseau (1712–1778), the Genevan philosopher, spent much of his life in France and was buried in the Panthéon. There are several possible Le Sages, but in this context the most likely candidate is the French novelist and playwright Alain-René Lesage (often written Le Sage; 1668–1747). Both Rousseau and Lesage knew and lived through 'the old rule'—the *ancien régime*, feudal in nature, which prevailed in France until the Revolution. Gurney points out that common soldiers like the Gloucesters are now sole guardians of aristocratic architecture.

l. 43. *Artois*. See note to Gurney, 'The Bohemians', l. 17 (p. 265).

l. 44. *'Lights Out'*. See note to Gurney, 'The Bohemians', l. 15 (p. 265).

l. 48. *Vermand*. A small town in Picardy, about which Gurney wrote several poems.

l. 64. *spinneys*. A spinney is a thicket of trees and bushes.

l. 67. *fortissimo*. Very loudly. From the Italian, the term is commonly used as a description or direction in music.

130 l. 88. *Platoon*. A military unit comprising approximately fifty men and usually led by a lieutenant.

l. 95. *Verey lights of Laventie*. Named after their American inventor, Edward Very, 'very' or 'verey' lights were flares fired at night in order to detect and expose enemy movement. Laventie, about which Gurney wrote several poems, is a French town close to the Belgian border, which saw heavy fighting during the War.

l. 104. *Burghers*. Wealthy townfolk.

ll. 107–8. *Newspapers Anglais, Français Papers daily,* | *What have you told us of hungry or cowed Bavaria, Saxony?* English and French newspapers eagerly reported rumours of food shortages in German states such as Bavaria and Saxony.

131 ll. 112–14. *O Wurtemburgherie,* | *Is this the population you fake your figures on?* | *Is this the beaten horde of conscripts, beginners?* Gurney is probably referring to the Württembergische Armee—the army of the former state of Württemberg, which was also part of the Imperial German Army. It was based on the Western Front for most of the War. Gurney closely followed the news of German conscription, and took heart when he heard that the lower age limit had been reduced: 'I see by the French papers that Prussia is about to call the boys of sixteen to military service. Surely this is the last straw; the women will hardly stand that' (to Marion Scott, 13 September 1916, *Collected Letters*, 145).

132 ll. 153–4. *the double* | *Treachery of Fritz to Europe and to English music.* Shot in the shoulder, Gurney fears that his plans for a post-war career as a composer and pianist are in jeopardy.

ll. 155–7. *Pomerania, Saxony, Wurtemburg, Bavaria,* | *Prussia, Rheinland, Mecklenburg . . . Franconia, Swabia.* German states.

l. 160. *a Blighty.* A wound serious enough to require treatment in England. See note to Ivor Gurney, 'Farewell', ll. 1–2 (p. 262).

l. 163. *Oxfords.* Soldiers from the Oxfordshire Regiment.

SIGNALLERS. *Date and Text.* June 1925. The job of the signaller was to provide signals communications from the front line back to headquarters. This was done by telephone where possible, but often required visual signalling by flags, mirrors, or lamps. Copy text as in the 'Pictures and Memories' manuscript held at Gloucestershire Archives.

l. 3. *estaminet.* A small café.

l. 8. *on tick.* On credit.

133 l. 11. *skilly.* A thin soup or gruel.

ll. 14–17. *Signallers gentlemen all away from the vulgar* | *Infantry . . . that they were dead.* Gurney wrote to Marion Scott in June 1916: 'lately, I have had a very soft time, being newly made (6 weeks?) a signaller . . . Give me signalling, first last and all the time. Had I but known before, O the drudgery I should have escaped!' (*Collected Letters*, 100).

l. 19. *Company fours.* During the War, British soldiers marched in fours. A company was a military unit comprising four platoons; approximately 200 soldiers made up a company.

IT IS NEAR TOUSSAINTS. *Date and Text.* September or October 1925. La Toussaint is 1 November, All Saints' Day. Gurney writes more often about La Toussaint than any other day, always misspelling it as 'Toussaints'. Copy text as in D10500/1/P/4/246/8 held at Gloucestershire Archives.

133   ll. 6–7. *When I spoke of my breaking . . . in London.* Gurney had suffered
a mental collapse in the spring of 1913 while studying in London at the
Royal College of Music.

l. 11. *Hilaire Belloc was all our Master.* Hilaire Belloc (1870–1953) was a
novelist, satirist, journalist, travel writer, poet, and politician. During
the War he became the military correspondent of a new periodical, *Land
and Water.* Gurney described *The Path to Rome* (1902), Belloc's account
of a walking pilgrimage from central France to Rome, as his 'trench com-
panion' (*Collected Letters*, 112). Belloc's name headed a list of literary
figures whom Gurney would most have liked to meet.

l. 13. *Pray Michael, Nicholas, Maries.* Churches in Gloucester, namely
St Michael's Church, St Nicholas's Church, and the three churches
collected together by Gurney as the 'Maries': St Mary de Lode, St Mary
Magdalene, and St Mary Crypt.

l. 14. *the old City of our dear love.* Gurney's native city, Gloucester.

l. 16. *'Madame—no bon!'* Pidgin French: 'Madame—no good!'

134   THE SILENT ONE. *Date and Text.* October 1925. Copy text as in the 'Best
Poems' manuscript held at Gloucestershire Archives.

l. 3. *Bucks.* Buckinghamshire.

l. 5. *stripes.* The visible indicators of rank worn on the uniform.

l. 9. *finicking.* Excessively refined.

l. 17. *screen.* A cover at the front of the trench to disguise movement or
protect soldiers from the debris of an explosion.

ISAAC ROSENBERG

137   [A WORM FED ON THE HEART OF CORINTH]. *Date and Text.* Probably
late May 1916. The title has been added by later editors. The ancient city-
state of Corinth was situated roughly halfway between Athens and Sparta.
Copy text as published in *The Poems and Plays of Isaac Rosenberg*, ed.
Vivien Noakes (2004).

ll. 1–2. *Corinth,* | *Babylon and Rome.* Rosenberg lists three great civiliza-
tions which are often said to have fallen as a consequence of corruption
and decadence.

l. 3. *Not Paris raped tall Helen.* Paris was the son of Priam, King of Troy.
His abduction of Helen, wife of Menelaus, King of Sparta, caused the
siege of Troy.

l. 6. *amorphous.* Shapeless.

l. 10. *Solomon.* According to the Old Testament (1 Kings 11: 3), Solomon,
King of Israel, had 700 wives and 300 concubines.

BREAK OF DAY IN THE TRENCHES. *Date and Text.* June or July 1916.
The title alludes to John Donne's aubade, 'Break of Day'. Rosenberg also
incorporates several lines from 'In the Trenches', a shorter poem which

he was writing contemporaneously. Copy text as published in *The Poems and Plays of Isaac Rosenberg*, ed. Vivien Noakes (2004).

l. 2. *Druid.* 'One of an order of men among the ancient Celts of Gaul and Britain, who, according to Caesar were priests or religious ministers or teachers, but who figure in native Irish and Welsh legend as magicians, sorcerers, soothsayers, and the like' (*OED*). In a letter to Edward Marsh dated 4 August 1916, Rosenberg explained that the line was his attempt to convey the 'sanctity sense of dawn' (quoted in *The Poems and Plays*, 359).

l. 5. *parapet's.* See note to Siegfried Sassoon, 'A Working Party', l. 38 (p. 251).

ll. 9–10. *Now you have touched this English hand | You will do the same to a German.* Vivien Noakes identifies an allusion to John Donne's 'The Flea' (l. 3): 'It suck'd me first, and now sucks thee.'

138 ll. 23–4. *Poppies whose roots are in man's veins | Drop, and are ever dropping.* Cf. George Herbert, 'Virtue': 'Sweet rose, whose hue angry and brave | Bids the rash gazer wipe his eye: | Thy root is ever in its grave, | And thou must die' (ll. 5–8).

AUGUST 1914. *Date and Text.* Summer 1916. Britain had entered the war on 4 August 1914. Copy text as published in *The Poems and Plays of Isaac Rosenberg*, ed. Vivien Noakes (2004).

LOUSE HUNTING. *Date and Text.* Between Summer 1916 and February 1917. Copy text as published in *The Poems and Plays of Isaac Rosenberg*, ed. Vivien Noakes (2004).

l. 8. *Godhead.* The divine essence.

139 l. 20. *smutch.* Smear.

FROM FRANCE. *Date and Text.* Probably 1916. Copy text as published in *The Poems and Plays of Isaac Rosenberg*, ed. Vivien Noakes (2004).

ll. 9–10. *Heaped stones . . . and dead folk under.* It is a Jewish custom to place a stone on a grave as a mark of respect.

l. 11. *And some birds sing.* Cf. John Keats, 'La belle dame sans merci' (l. 4): 'And no birds sing.'

RETURNING, WE HEAR THE LARKS. *Date and Text.* 1917. Copy text as published in *The Poems and Plays of Isaac Rosenberg*, ed. Vivien Noakes (2004).

140 ll. 7–8. *But hark! joy—joy—strange joy. | Lo! heights of night ringing with unseen larks.* Cf. *Cymbeline*, II.ii.22: 'Hark! Hark! The lark, at heaven's gate sings.'

ll. 10–12. *Death could drop from the dark | As easily as song— | But song only dropped.* Vivien Noakes detects an allusion to Percy Shelley's 'To a Skylark': 'From rainbow clouds there flow not | Drops so bright to see | As from thy presence showers a rain of melody' (ll. 33–5).

DEAD MAN'S DUMP. *Date and Text.* April or early May 1917. Rosenberg wrote to Edward Marsh on 8 May: 'Ive [*sic*] written some lines suggested by going out wiring, or rather carrying the wire up the line on limbers & running over dead bodies lying about' (quoted in *Issac Rosenberg*, ed. Vivien Noakes, 331). Copy text as published in *The Poems and Plays of Isaac Rosenberg*, ed. Vivien Noakes (2004).

140   l. 1. *limbers*. A limber is the two-wheeled wooden portion of a gun-carriage which can be detached and used for transporting other materials.

l. 3. *crowns of thorns*. A crown woven of thorn twigs was placed on Christ's head before his crucifixion. See note to Siegfried Sassoon, 'Christ and the Soldier', l. 44 (p. 253).

ll. 4–5. *And the rusty stakes like sceptres old | To stay the flood of brutish men*. Stallworthy and Potter note: 'In Matthew's account of the crucifixion, the soldiers put a reed (as sceptre) in Christ's right hand; but Rosenberg's principal allusion is to the legend of Canute the Great, eleventh-century king of Denmark and England, seated at the sea's edge, ordering the tide to obey his rule (represented by his sceptre) and retire' (*Three Poets*, 146).

l. 11. *Man born of man, and born of woman*. Cf. Job 14: 1: 'Man that is born of a woman is of few days, and full of trouble.'

141   l. 27. *None saw their spirits' shadow shake the grass*. Cf. Psalm 103: 15–16: 'As for man, his days are as grass: as a flower of the field, so he flourisheth. For the wind passeth over it, and it is gone; and the place thereof shall know it no more.'

l. 34. *ichor*. According to Greek mythology, the fluid that flows in the gods' veins.

142   ll. 63–79. *His dark hearing . . . grazed his dead face*. Vivien Noakes notices Rosenberg's indebtedness to Wilfrid Gibson's 'Wheels', from his pre-war collection, *Thoroughfares* (1914). Gibson's poem describes a road accident in which a traffic policeman is knocked down: 'He tumbled heavily, but all unheard, | Among the scurry of wheels that crashed and whirred | About his senseless head' (ll. 3–5); 'and as he lay | He heard again the wheels he'd heard all day' (ll. 7–8); 'And still within a hair's breadth of his ear | The crunch and gride of wheels rings sharp and clear— | Huge lumbering wagons' (ll. 35–7).

DAUGHTERS OF WAR. *Date and Text*. Between October 1916 and June 1917. Rosenberg considered it to be 'a much finer poem' (*The Poems and Plays*, 372) than 'Dead Man's Dump', possibly even his finest poem of all. Copy text as published in *The Poems and Plays of Isaac Rosenberg*, ed. Vivien Noakes (2004).

143   l. 22. *Amazons*. In Greek mythology, a race of female warriors, renowned for their size and courage.

l. 38. *terrene*. Earthly.

l. 42. *thewed*. Muscular.

144   [THROUGH THESE PALE COLD DAYS]. *Date and Text*. March 1918. Rosenberg sent the poem to Edward Marsh, calling it a 'slight thing' (*The Poems and Plays*, 375), in a letter four days before his death. The title

has been added by later editors. Copy text as published in *The Poems and Plays of Isaac Rosenberg*, ed. Vivien Noakes (2004).

l. 3. *Out of three thousand years*. Moses died around 1400 BCE. He is often credited as the founder of Judaism for having received the Ten Commandments from God and written the Torah. Stallworthy and Potter suggest that the poem may, instead, be referring to Saul, who became the first King of Israel around 1020 BCE (*Three Poets*, 151).

l. 7. *the pools of Hebron*. Hebron is a city in the West Bank, holy for both Jews and Muslims. Between Hebron and Bethlehem lie the three ancient reservoirs commonly known as King Solomon's Pools.

l. 8. *Lebanon's summer slope*. Rosenberg probably has in mind the slope of Mount Hermon, close to the border between Syria and Lebanon. The mountain is mentioned several times in the Bible.

ARTHUR GRAEME WEST

146 THE NIGHT PATROL. *Date and Text*. March 1916. West had described the experiences which inspired the poem in a letter of 12 February: 'I had rather an exciting time myself with two other men on a patrol in the "no man's land" between the lines. A dangerous business, and most repulsive on account of the smells and appearance of the heaps of dead men that lie unburied there as they fell, on some attack or other, about four months ago. I found myself much as I had expected in the face of these happenings: more interested than afraid, but more careful for my own life than anxious to approve any new martial ardour' (*The Diary of a Dead Officer*, 11). Copy text as published in *The Diary of a Dead Officer* (n.d. [1919]).

l. 16. *bandoliers*. Belts for storing ammunition, usually slung over the shoulder.

147 ll. 30–1. *crossed | His legs Crusader-wise*. Tomb effigies of knights with crossed legs are believed by some historians to indicate that they took part in the Crusades.

l. 32. *Elia and his Temple Church*. Charles Lamb (1775–1834), English essayist and poet, wrote under the pseudonym Elia after 1820. He had grown up at the Inner Temple in London; its Temple Church is famous for its nine effigy tombs of knights.

l. 37. *archipelago*. A group of islands.

GOD! HOW I HATE YOU, YOU YOUNG CHEERFUL MEN! *Date and Text*. Probably August 1916. The headnote misspells H. Rex Freston's name. Freston had been killed by a shell in January 1916, and his volume of poems, *The Quest of Truth*, appeared within months of his death. The note also slightly misquotes Freston's 'To the Atheists', altering some punctuation and omitting the stanza break after line 8. Copy text as published in *The Diary of a Dead Officer* (n.d. [1919]).

148 ll. 4–8. *the tears | Of mothers . . . sentimental elegies*. Although West describes the paraphernalia of memorial volumes in general, Freston's

The Quest of Truth may still be uppermost in his mind: it contains a photograph, a consolatory note from the rector of his Oxford college, and a sentimental elegy titled 'To H. Rex Freston' by Russell Markland.

148 l. 11. *ductile.* Pliable; capable of changing form without breaking.

l. 14. *'Oh happy to have lived these epic days'.* This is the opening line of Freston's poem, 'O Fortunati!'

l. 15. *And he'd been to France.* West may be wrong in his assumption. Freston's poems are likely to have preceded his posting to France in December 1915. He was in the trenches for only ten days before his death.

l. 17. *periscope.* Periscopes were used to view no-man's-land safely from the trench.

l. 23. *firing-step.* Fire-step. See note to Siegfried Sassoon, 'Counter-Attack', l. 26 (p. 255).

149 l. 27. *parados.* The back or rear of the trench.

ll. 30–31. *Yet still God's in His heaven, all is right* | *In the best possible of worlds.* These lines merge two well-known quotations: 'God's in His heaven— | All's right with the world' (Robert Browning, 'Pippa Passes'), and 'all is for the best in the best of all possible worlds' (the mantra of the Leibnizian philosopher Pangloss in Voltaire's *Candide*).

ll. 36–9. *We do not die . . . Because a grass-blade dies.* Another allusion to Freston's 'To the Atheists': 'I know that God will never let me die. | He is too passionate and intense for that' (ll. 1–2); 'God, Who sorrows all a summer's day | Because a blade of grass has died' (ll. 10–11).

l. 43. *Huns.* A derogatory term for Germans. See note to Rudyard Kipling, ' "For All We Have and Are" ', l. 4 (pp. 238–9).

ll. 47–8. *what a faith is ours (almost, it seems,* | *Large as a mustard-seed).* Ironic, because mustard seeds are tiny. Christ's parable of the mustard seed appears in three of the gospels. 'Then said he, Unto what is the kingdom of God like? and whereunto shall I resemble it? It is like a grain of mustard seed, which a man took, and cast into his garden; and it grew, and waxed a great tree; and the fowls of the air lodged in the branches of it' (Luke 13: 18–19).

l. 51. *slake.* Satisfy; quench (a thirst).

l. 53. *Flanders.* See note to May Sinclair, 'Field Ambulance in Retreat', l. 6 (p. 237).

WILFRED OWEN

153 ANTHEM FOR DOOMED YOUTH. *Date and Text.* September or October 1917. Owen reported that Siegfried Sassoon had 'supplied the title' (*Collected Letters*, 496). Copy text as published in *The Complete Poems and Fragments*, ed. Jon Stallworthy (1983).

l. 1. *passing-bells.* Cf. the 'Prefatory Note' in the anonymously edited *Poems of To-Day* (1916), of which Owen owned a copy. The note explained that the themes of the anthology would 'mingle and inter-penetrate throughout, to the music of Pan's flute, and of Love's viol, and the bugle-call of Endeavour, and the passing-bell of Death'.

l. 4. *orisons*. Prayers.

l. 7. *The shrill, demented choirs of wailing shells*. Cf. John Keats, 'To Autumn': 'Then in a wailful choir the small gnats mourn' (l. 27).

l. 12. *pall*. The cover for a coffin, often white.

l. 14. *And each slow dusk a drawing-down of blinds*. Dominic Hibberd points out that this referred to the custom of drawing the blinds when a death had occurred in the house, or when a funeral procession was pass-ing (*Wilfred Owen: War Poems and Others* (London: Chatto & Windus, 1973), 147).

THE SENTRY. *Date and Text*. Between August and October 1917; revised 1918. In January 1917, under heavy bombardment, a sentry posted by Owen was blown down a flight of stairs and blinded. Copy text as pub-lished in *The Complete Poems and Fragments*, ed. Jon Stallworthy (1983).

l. 1. *Boche*. German. See note to Robert Service, 'Only a Boche' (pp. 245–6).

154 l. 8. *whizz-bangs*. Shells from 77 mm German field guns, so called (and feared) because the 'whizz' of the shell through the air and the 'bang' of the explosion were nearly simultaneous.

l. 28. *And one who would have drowned himself for good*. Describing the blinding of his sentry, Owen wrote to his mother in January 1917: 'I nearly broke down and let myself drown in the water that was now slowly rising over my knees' (*Collected Letters*, 480).

DULCE ET DECORUM EST. *Date and Text*. October 1917; revised early 1918. The title can be translated as 'It is sweet and decorous', and alludes to Horace's *Odes*, III.ii.13: 'It is sweet and decorous to die for one's coun-try.' Several poems of the First World War made reference to Horace's motto. Reporting on the Soudan campaign in the *Morning Post* on 6 October 1898, Winston Churchill had already argued against the phrase because it was inappropriate to the squalid reality of death in battle: 'I have tried to gild war, and to solace myself for the loss of dear and gal-lant friends, with the thought that a soldier's death for a cause he believes in will count for much, whatever may be beyond this world. When the soldier of a civilised power is killed in action his limbs are composed and his body is borne by friendly arms reverently to the grave . . . But there was nothing *dulce et decorum* about the Dervish dead . . . The conviction was borne in on me that their claim beyond the grave in respect of a vali-ant death was as good as that which any of our countrymen could make.' Copy text as published in *The Complete Poems and Fragments*, ed. Jon Stallworthy (1983).

155 l. 8. *Five-Nines*. German 5.9 inch artillery shells.

l. 25. *My friend*. Earlier drafts dedicated the poem 'To Jessie Pope' and 'To a Certain Poetess'. Jessie Pope (1868–1941) was a novelist, poet, and journalist, who wrote patriotic verse in aid of the war effort. By removing the dedication, Owen makes his address universal.

155 ll. 27–8. *Dulce et decorum est | Pro patria mori.* See the headnote to the poem, above.

INSENSIBILITY. *Date and Text.* Between October 1917 and January 1918. As Stallworthy has noted, the title is taken from a passage in Percy Shelley's *A Defence of Poetry*, with which the poem engages ironically throughout: '[Poetry] is as it were the interpenetration of a diviner nature through our own; but its footsteps are like those of a wind over a sea, which the coming calm erases, and those traces remain only, as on the wrinkled sand which paves it. These and corresponding conditions of being are experienced principally by those of the most delicate sensibility and the most enlarged imagination; and the state of mind produced by them is at war with every base desire.' Copy text as published in *The Complete Poems and Fragments*, ed. Jon Stallworthy (1983).

l. 1. *Happy are men.* The first of three stanzas in the poem that begin with the word 'happy'. There may be an allusion to William Wordsworth's 'Character of the Happy Warrior', which begins: 'Who is the happy warrior?'

l. 3. *fleers.* Laughs contemptuously.

156 l. 9. *gaps for filling.* Owen refers to the recruiting slogan, 'Fill up the ranks!'

l. 17. *shilling.* To take the King's (or Queen's) shilling was to enlist in the army or navy.

l. 18 *decimation.* Literally, to decimate is to kill one in ten—a better rate of survival than British soldiers could hope for in the War.

l. 28. *cautery.* 'A heated metallic instrument used for burning or searing organic tissue; also a caustic drug or medicine for the same purpose' (*OED*). Wounds can be staunched by cauterizing, hence the reference in the next line to their having been 'ironed'.

157 GREATER LOVE. *Date and Text.* Between October 1917 and January 1918; revised July 1918. Stallworthy notes that the poem is a response to Swinburne's 'Before the Mirror': 'White rose in red rose-garden | Is not so white; | Snowdrops that plead for pardon | And pine for fright | Because the hard East blows | Over their maiden rows || Grow not as this face grows from pale to bright' (ll. 1–7). The title alludes to John 15: 13: 'Greater love hath no man than this, that a man lay down his life for his friends.' The sentiment was commonplace, but if Owen needed a contemporary source, it may have been Alice Meynell's 'Summer in England, 1914': 'Who said "No man hath greater love than this, | To die to serve his friend"? | So these have loved us all unto the end' (ll. 25–7). Copy text as published in *The Complete Poems and Fragments*, ed. Jon Stallworthy (1983).

l. 5. *lure.* Enticement. See note to May Sinclair, 'Dedication', l. 12 (p. 237).

158 l. 24. *Weep, you may weep, for you may touch them not.* Cf. John 20: 15–17: 'Jesus saith unto [Mary Magdalene], Woman, why weepest thou? . . . Touch me not; for I am not yet ascended to my Father: but go to my brethren, and say unto them, I ascend unto my Father, and your Father; and to my God, and your God.'

DISABLED. *Date and Text.* October 1917; revised July 1918. Copy text as published in *The Complete Poems and Fragments*, ed. Jon Stallworthy (1983).

l. 1. *wheeled chair.* Wheelchair. *OED* gives the first recorded use of 'wheel-chair' as 1700, and the word is found in Austen and Thackeray, so Owen's 'wheeled chair' seems formal, even fustian.

159 l. 22. *After the matches, carried shoulder-high.* Cf. A. E. Housman's 'To an Athlete Dying Young': 'The time you won your town the race | We chaired you through the market-place; | Man and boy stood cheering by, | And home we brought you shoulder-high' (ll. 1–4).

l. 23. *peg.* A measure of liquor.

l. 27. *jilts.* A contemptuous Scottish term for girls or young women.

l. 29. *Smiling they wrote his lie.* Owen implies that the recruitment office may have connived in the deception, knowing that the boy was younger than he claimed.

l. 35. *Esprit de corps.* The loyalty and morale within a group.

160 ll. 45–6. *Why don't they come | And put him into bed? Why don't they come?* Dominic Hibberd has heard in this refrain 'a mocking echo of the slogan on a recruiting poster . . . which shows soldiers in action and in need of reinforcements. The slogan reads, "Will they never come?"' (*Notes and Queries*, xxvi (1979), 333).

APOLOGIA PRO POEMATE MEO. *Date and Text.* The manuscript is dated November 1917. Robert Graves wrote to Owen on 22 December 1917: 'For God's sake cheer up and write more optimistically—The war's not ended yet but a poet should have a spirit above wars' (Owen, *Collected Letters*, 596). As Stallworthy notes, 'Graves may have said much the same to [Owen] earlier.' Owen's title, its faulty Latin ('apologia pro poema mea') having been corrected by Siegfried Sassoon, means 'a defence of my poem'; he had previously given a fuller title ('Apologia lectorem pro Poema Disconsolatia Mea', meaning 'A Defence to the reader of My Disconsolate Poem'). On one draft Owen has written, 'If there be a bright side to war, it is a crime to exhibit it,' thereby translating Henri Barbusse's comment in *Le Feu*: 'Ce serait un crime de montrer les beaux côtés de la guerre, même s'il y en avait!' (see Hibberd, *Wilfred Owen*, 405). Copy text as published in *The Complete Poems and Fragments*, ed. Jon Stallworthy (1983).

l. 1. *I, too, saw God through mud.* Dennis Welland suggests that the line responds to Robert Graves's 'Two Fusiliers' (p. 197), in which the fusiliers are bound 'By friendship blossoming from mud' (l. 15) (Welland,

Wilfred Owen: A Critical Study, rev. edn. (London: Chatto & Windus, 1978), 67–8).

160 l. 10. *Behind the barrage.* A barrage is a coordinated artillery bombardment, often with the purpose (as here) of allowing infantry to advance behind it.

l. 15. *oblation.* A sacrifice or offering to God.

ll. 19–20. *For love is not the binding of fair lips | With the soft silk of eyes that look and long.* Cf. 'L'Amour', by Owen's cousin Leslie Gunston, published in *The Nymph and Other Poems* (1917): 'Love is the binding of souls together, | The binding of lips, the binding of eyes.'

ll. 22–3. *But wound with war's hard wire whose stakes are strong; | Bound with the bandage of the arm that drips.* The allusion to Graves's 'Two Fusiliers' is more certain here: 'there's no need of pledge or oath | To bind our lovely friendship fast . . . By wire and wood and stake we're bound' (ll. 3–4, 7).

161 THE SHOW. *Date and Text.* November 1917; revised May 1918. Originally titled 'Vision', alluding to the first chapter ('The Vision') of Henri Barbusse's *Le Feu*, which Owen had read in translation during 1917: 'The man at the end of the rank cries, "I can see crawling things down there"—"Yes, as though they were alive"—"Some sort of plant perhaps"—"Some kind of men"—' (quoted in *The Poems of Wilfred Owen*, ed. Jon Stallworthy (London: Hogarth Press, 1985), 133). A 'show' was euphemistic slang for a battle. The epigraph from Yeats's play *The Shadowy Waters* is slightly misquoted: 'tarnished' should read 'burnished'. Copy text as published in *The Complete Poems and Fragments*, ed. Jon Stallworthy (1983).

162 l. 17. *Brown strings, towards strings of grey, with bristling spines.* The uniforms of the British and Germans were respectively khaki and grey. The bristling spines of the caterpillars are files of soldiers.

l. 20. *Ramped.* Reared up threateningly.

ll. 26–7. *And He, picking a manner of worm, which half had hid | Its bruises in the earth, but crawled no further.* Cf. Owen's description of going over the top in a letter to his brother Colin on 14 May 1917: 'When I looked back and saw the ground all crawling and wormy with wounded bodies, I felt no horror at all but only an immense exultation at having got through the Barrage' (*Collected Letters*, 458).

[I SAW HIS ROUND MOUTH'S CRIMSON]. *Date and Text.* November or December 1917. The title has been added by subsequent editors; it is unclear from the state of Owen's manuscript whether this is a fragment or a complete poem. Copy text as published in *The Complete Poems and Fragments*, ed. Jon Stallworthy (1983).

163 A TERRE. *Date and Text.* December 1917; final revisions in July 1918. The title comes from the French meaning 'To earth', which may allude to the burial service: 'earth to earth, ashes to ashes, dust to dust'. Copy text as

published in *The Complete Poems and Fragments*, ed. Jon Stallworthy (1983).

l. 5. *peg out*. A slang euphemism for 'die'.

l. 7. *pennies on my eyes*. Ancient Greeks put coins on the eyes of the dead so that their souls could pay the ferryman on the journey across the Styx to Hades. Putting pennies on a corpse's eyes is also a way of keeping them shut.

l. 9. *ribbons*. Military ribbons are awarded for duty in particular campaigns and for bravery.

ll. 13–14. *puffy, bald,* | *And patriotic.* Cf. Siegfried Sassoon, 'Base Details' (p. 95):

> If I were fierce, and bald, and short of breath,
> I'd live with scarlet Majors at the Base,
> And speed glum heroes up the line to death.
> You'd see me with my puffy petulant face . . . (ll. 1–4)

l. 28. *How well I might have swept his floors for ever.* Cf. Ivor Gurney, 'Servitude': 'To keep a brothel, sweep and wash the floor | Of filthiest hovels were noble to compare | With this brass-cleaning life' (ll. 3–5).

164 ll. 44–5. *'I shall be one with nature, herb, and stone,'* | *Shelley would tell me. Shelley would be stunned.* Percy Shelley was possibly, after Keats, Owen's favourite poet. The allusion is to 'Adonais'—Shelley's elegy for Keats:

> He is made one with Nature: there is heard
> His voice in all her music, from the moan
> Of thunder, to the song of night's sweet bird;
> He is a presence to be felt and known
> In darkness and in light, from herb and stone,
> Spreading itself where'er that Power may move
> Which has withdrawn his being to its own,
> Which wields the world with never-wearying love,
> Sustains it from beneath, and kindles it above. (ll. 370–8)

l. 47. *'Pushing up daisies'.* Dead—another slang euphemism.

ll. 48–50. *To grain, then, go my fat, to buds my sap,* | *For all the usefulness there is in soap.* | *D'you think the Boche will ever stew man-soup?* For Boche, see note to Robert Service, 'Only a Boche' (pp. 245–6). Rumours of atrocities committed by the Germans included the belief that they boiled corpses down for fat.

l. 59. *fronds*. The leaves of ferns. Cf. 'Miners' (p. 166): 'I listened for a tale of leaves | And smothered ferns, | Frond-forests, and the low sly lives | Before the fauns' (ll. 5–8).

165 EXPOSURE. *Date and Text.* Probably between December 1917 and February 1918; revised September 1918, when Owen changed the title

from 'Nothing Happens'. Copy text as published in *The Complete Poems and Fragments*, ed. Jon Stallworthy (1983).

165 l. 1. *Our brains ache, in the merciless iced east winds that knive us.* Cf. the opening of John Keats's 'Ode to a Nightingale': 'My heart aches, and a drowsy numbness pains | My sense' (ll. 1–2).

l. 3. *salient.* A spur of land projecting into enemy territory. See note to Siegfried Sassoon, 'On Passing the New Menin Gate', l. 5 (p. 256).

ll. 13–14. *Dawn massing in the east her melancholy army | Attacks once more in ranks on shivering ranks of grey.* The German army wore grey, and was massed in the east.

l. 26. *glozed.* Jon Stallworthy suggests a conflation of 'glowing' and 'glazed'. To gloze, according to *OED*, is to make a marginal note, to palliate, or to flatter. All three meanings may be possible here: the 'jewels' are a marginal embellishment to the fires.

166 MINERS. *Date and Text.* 13 or 14 January 1918. The Minnie pit disaster on 12 January at Halmer End in Staffordshire had killed 155 miners. Owen reported: 'Wrote a poem on the Colliery Disaster: but I get mixed up with the War at the end. It is short, but oh! sour' (*The Poems of Wilfred Owen*, ed. Edmund Blunden (London: Chatto & Windus, 1931), 125). 'Miners' appeared in *The Nation* later that month—one of only five poems published by Owen during his lifetime. Copy text as published in *The Complete Poems and Fragments*, ed. Jon Stallworthy (1983).

l. 7. *Frond.* The leaf of a fern. Cf. 'A Terre' (p. 164): 'Soldiers may grow a soul when turned to fronds' (l. 59).

l. 8. *fauns.* Rustic male spirits, with goat-like horns and hooves.

167 l. 26. *amber.* A golden-yellow fossilized resin.

THE LAST LAUGH. *Date and Text.* February or March 1918; revised mid-1918. Owen sent an early draft to his mother on 18 February, stating that: 'There is a point where prayer is indistinguishable from blasphemy. There is also a point where blasphemy is indistinguishable from prayer' (*Collected Letters*, 534). Copy text as published in *The Complete Poems and Fragments*, ed. Jon Stallworthy (1983).

168 STRANGE MEETING. *Date and Text.* Between January and March 1918. Harold Monro had published a volume of poems titled *Strange Meetings* in 1917. However, the largest debt is to a passage in Percy Shelley's *The Revolt of Islam*: ' "Ye stabbed as they did sleep—but they forgive ye now" ' (l. 1809); 'When I awoke, I lay mid friends and foes' (l. 1824); 'And one whose spear had pierced me, leaned beside | With quivering lips and humid eyes;—and all | Seemed like some brothers on a journey wide | Gone forth, whom now strange meeting did befall | In a strange land' (ll. 1828–32); 'Through many a cavern which the eternal flood | Had scooped' (ll. 2914–15). Copy text as published in *The Complete Poems and Fragments*, ed. Jon Stallworthy (1983).

ll. 3–4. *Through granites which titanic wars had groined . . . encumbered sleepers.*

Noting that the 'hell' described is a 'sullen hall', its architecture more classical than Christian, Elizabeth Vandiver has shown that Owen is here remembering the imprisonment of the Titans in Tartarus after their defeat in the war against the Olympians (*Stand in the Trench, Achilles* (2010), 303–4). They are 'encumbered' because enchained. A 'groin' is 'the edge formed by the intersection of two vaults' (*OED*), its verb form meaning 'to build with groins'.

l. 13. *flues*. Ducts; outlets for heat or gas.

l. 25. *The pity of war*. See Owen's draft preface to a collection of his poems that remained unpublished at his death: 'My subject is War, and the pity of War.'

169   l. 40. *I am the enemy you killed, my friend*. Cf. Oscar Wilde, 'The Ballad of Reading Gaol': 'Yet each man kills the thing he loves' (l. 37).

FUTILITY. *Date and Text*. May 1918. Owen had written to his mother on 4 February 1917 to report on a tour of the 'advanced Front Line': 'The marvel is that we did not all die of cold. As a matter of fact, only one of my party actually froze to death' (*Collected Letters*, 430). Copy text as published in *The Complete Poems and Fragments*, ed. Jon Stallworthy (1983).

ll. 8–9. *Think how it wakes the seeds— | Woke once the clays of a cold star*. Cf. John Davidson, 'Thirty Bob a Week': 'A little sleeping seed, I woke— I did, indeed— | A million years before the blooming sun' (ll. 71–2).

l. 12. *Was it for this the clay grew tall?* Cf. Wordsworth's *Prelude*: 'Was it for this | That one, the fairest of all rivers, loved | To blend his murmurs with my nurse's song . . . ?' (I. 269–71).

THE SEND-OFF. *Date and Text*. April or May 1918; revised July 1918. Owen changed the title from 'The Draft' at a late stage. Copy text as published in *The Complete Poems and Fragments*, ed. Jon Stallworthy (1983).

170   MENTAL CASES. *Date and Text*. May 1918; revised July 1918, when its title was changed from 'The Deranged'. Mark Sinfield has pointed out the poem's debt to Revelation 7: 13–17, each stanza opening with an ironic echo of its diction and structure: 'And one of the elders answered, saying unto me, What are these which are arrayed in white robes? and whence came they? And I said unto him, Sir, thou knowest. And he said to me, These are they which came out of great tribulation, and have washed their robes, and made them white in the blood of the Lamb. Therefore are they before the throne of God, and serve him day and night in his temple: and he that sitteth on the throne shall dwell among them. They shall hunger no more, neither thirst any more; neither shall the sun light on them, nor any heat. For the Lamb which is in the midst of the throne shall feed them, and shall lead them unto living fountains of waters: and God shall wipe away all tears from their eyes' (quoted in *The Poems of Wilfred Owen*, ed. Stallworthy, 147). Copy text as published in *The Complete Poems and Fragments*, ed. Jon Stallworthy (1983).

171 ll. 12–14. *Multitudinous murders . . . Wading sloughs of flesh these helpless wander,* | *Treading blood.* Occurring in a context of killing and madness, the passage conflates two passages from *Macbeth* in which Macbeth expresses the impossibility of forgiveness or repentance: 'Will all great Neptune's ocean wash this blood | Clean from my hand? No, this my hand will rather | The multitudinous seas incarnadine' (II.ii.63–5); 'I am in blood | Stepped in so far that should I wade no more, | Returning were as tedious as go o'er' (III.iv.136–8).

l. 18. *Rucked.* Tightly packed.

THE PARABLE OF THE OLD MAN AND THE YOUNG. *Date and Text.* July 1918. Lines 1–14, with the exception of line 8, parallel Genesis 22: 7–13: 'And Isaac spake unto Abraham his father, and said, My father: and he said, Here am I, my son. And he said, Behold the fire and the wood: but where is the lamb for a burnt offering? And Abraham said, My son, God will provide himself a lamb for a burnt offering: so they went both of them together. And they came to the place which God had told him of; and Abraham built an altar there, and laid the wood in order, and bound Isaac his son, and laid him on the altar upon the wood. And Abraham stretched forth his hand, and took the knife to slay his son. And the angel of the LORD called unto him out of heaven, and said, Abraham, Abraham: and he said, Here am I. And he said, Lay not thine hand upon the lad, neither do thou any thing unto him: for now I know that thou fearest God, seeing thou hast not withheld thy son, thine only son from me. And Abraham lifted up his eyes, and looked, and behold behind him a ram caught in a thicket by his horns: and Abraham went and took the ram, and offered him up for a burnt offering in the stead of his son.' Copy text as published in *The Complete Poems and Fragments*, ed. Jon Stallworthy (1983).

l. 8. *parapets.* See note to Siegfried Sassoon, 'A Working Party', l. 38 (p. 251).

172 SPRING OFFENSIVE. *Date and Text.* July 1918; revised September 1918. Owen was unsure of the poem's merits. Sending the first seventeen lines to Sassoon in September 1918, he asked: 'Is this worth going on with? I don't want to write anything to which a soldier would say No Compris!' (quoted in *The Poems of Wilfred Owen*, ed. Stallworthy, 170). Copy text as published in *The Complete Poems and Fragments*, ed. Jon Stallworthy (1983).

l. 20. *begird.* Embrace; encompass.

173 SMILE, SMILE, SMILE. *Date and Text.* September 1918. Jon Stallworthy explains that Owen had been vexed by articles in *The Times* and *Daily Mail*, and in a letter of 22 September to Siegfried Sassoon underlined objectionable words and phrases: 'Did you see what the Minister of Labour said in the *Mail* the other day? "The first instincts of the men after the cessation of hostilities will be to return home." And again—"All classes acknowledge their indebtedness to the soldiers & sailors..." About the same day, Clemenceau [the French prime minister] is reported by

the *Times* as saying: "<u>All</u> are worthy . . . yet we should be untrue to our-selves if we forgot that the <u>greatest</u> glory will be to the splended poilus [French infantrymen], who, etc."' (*Collected Letters*, 578). The poem's title alludes to the popular marching song by George Asaf and Felix Powell: 'Pack up your troubles in your old kit bag, | And smile, smile, smile' (see pp. 223–4). Copy text as published in *The Complete Poems and Fragments*, ed. Jon Stallworthy (1983).

ll. 2–3. *Yesterday's Mail; the casualties (typed small)* | *And (large) Vast Booty from our Latest Haul.* Under its proprietor, Lord Northcliffe, the *Daily Mail* before the War had advocated an increased defence budget to protect the country from a German plot to destroy the British Empire. After the outbreak of War, it positioned itself as friend of the common soldier and scourge of government incompetence.

l. 12. *indemnified.* Compensated.

MARGARET POSTGATE COLE

176 PRÆMATURI. *Date and Text.* Between 1915 and 1918. The title means 'the untimely ones' or 'the premature ones', being the nominative mascu-line plural form of the Latin adjective *præmaturus.* Copy text as first published in *Margaret Postgate's Poems* (1918).

THE FALLING LEAVES. *Date and Text.* November 1915. Copy text as first published in *Margaret Postgate's Poems* (1918).

l. 12. *Flemish.* Of Flanders. See note to May Sinclair, 'Field Ambulance in Retreat', l. 6 (p. 237).

177 AFTERWARDS. *Date and Text.* 1918. Copy text as first published in *Margaret Postgate's Poems* (1918).

l. 5. *Sheer.* Although this seems to be a place name, no such place exists. In correspondence, Clare Griffiths has suggested that it is a misprint for 'Shere', a village in Surrey near Guildford.

l. 8. *O cakes, O cakes, O cakes, from Fuller's!* The line may be an advertising jingle. Fuller's was a company that made cakes and other confectionery.

l. 13. *pit-props.* Wooden supports used to prop up the roofs of mine-tunnels.

MAY WEDDERBURN CANNAN

179 AUGUST 1914. *Date and Text.* March 1915. The title names the month in which war was declared. Copy text as published in *In War Time: Poems* (1917).

l. 11. *parapet.* See note to Siegfried Sassoon, 'A Working Party', l. 38 (p. 251).

180 ROUEN. *Date and Text.* November 1915. Cannan records the dates of her stay in Rouen, Normandy, where she worked for four weeks at the railhead in a canteen serving soldiers. Many of the details are also recalled

in her autobiography, particularly the circumstances of the men's departure: 'When the whistle blew they stood to save the King and the roof came off the sheds. Two thousand men, maybe, singing—it was the most moving thing I knew. Then there'd be the thunder of seats pushed back, the stamp of army boots on the pavé, and as the train went out they sang Tipperary . . . Going up the Line to Railhead in that early Spring the drafts always sang it and it still brings back to me rain and blurred lanterns and men's voices dying away in the dark' (*Grey Ghosts and Voices*, 92). Copy text as published in *In War Time: Poems* (1917).

180   l. 12. *tatties*. A tatty is 'a screen or mat, usually made of the roots of the fragrant cuscus grass, which is placed in a frame so as to fill up the opening of a door or window, and kept wet, in order to cool and freshen the air of a room' (*OED*).

l. 15. *woodbines*. A brand of cigarette.

l. 22. *the khaki Red Cross train*. See note to May Sinclair, 'Field Ambulance in Retreat', l. 16 (p. 237).

182   LAMPLIGHT. *Date and Text*. December 1916. Copy text as first published in *In War Time: Poems* (1917).

ll. 9–10. *crossed swords in the Army List,* | *My Dear, against your name*. The Army List is the official register of army officers. The names of those killed in battle are marked with crossed swords.

l. 19. *A scarlet cross on my breast*. Nurses during the War wore a long white apron with a red cross in the middle—the symbol of the International Red Cross.

l. 27. *You set your feet upon the Western ways*. A euphemistic expression for dying. To 'go west' is, according to one sense given in *OED*, 'to die, perish, disappear'.

183   'AFTER THE WAR'. *Date and Text*. February 1917. Copy text as published in *In War Time: Poems* (1917).

THE ARMISTICE. *Date and Text*. Between November 1918 and August 1919. Cannan's autobiography describes her own role in conveying the news:

'On the morning of November 11th I was called into the Colonel's room [in Paris] "to take some notes from the telephone." They were all there and got up and made room for me at the table . . . A voice, very clear, thank God, said "Ready?" and began to dictate the Terms of the Armistice. They muttered a bit crowding round me and I said fiercely "Oh shut up, I can't *hear*" and the skies didn't fall.

I wrote in my private short-long-hand and half my mind was in a prayer that I should be able to read it back. I could feel my heart thumping and hear the silence in the room round me. When the voice stopped I said mechanically "understood" and got up.

I made four copies of what I had written and took them in and went back to my little office staff and told them' (*Grey Ghosts and Voices*, 135).

Copy text as published in *The Splendid Days: Poems* (1919).

ll. 17–18. *'It's awf'lly like Recessional,* | *Now when the tumult has all died away'*. Cf. Rudyard Kipling's 'Recessional': 'The tumult and the shouting dies—' (l. 7).

184   l. 28. *Ypres.* See note to May Sinclair, 'Dedication', l. 35 (p. 237).

FOR A GIRL. *Date and Text.* Between November 1918 and August 1919. The subtitle gives the date of the Armistice. Cannan writes of her reaction in her autobiography: 'I can only remember being so cold, and crying, and trying not to let the others see . . . That night it was all over Paris. There were sounds of cheering and rejoicing down the Boulevards as I walked home' (*Grey Ghosts and Voices*, 135–6). Copy text as published in *The Splendid Days: Poems* (1919).

185   PERFECT EPILOGUE. *Date and Text.* Despite the authorial date given after the poem, Cannan's handwritten copy of this elegy for Bevil Quiller-Couch is dated 1930. Copy text as first published in *The Tears of War: The Love Story of a Young Poet and a War Hero*, ed. Charlotte Fyfe (2000).

l. 10. *great host.* Great crowd. Particularly relevant is a definition now considered archaic and poetical by *OED*: 'An armed company or multitude of men; an army.'

CHARLES SORLEY

187   [ALL THE HILLS AND VALES ALONG]. *Date and Text.* A note added to the fourth edition by Sorley's father, William Ritchie Sorley, states that 'There is external evidence, though it is not quite conclusive, for dating this poem in August 1914' (*Marlborough and Other Poems*, 4th edn. (Cambridge: Cambridge University Press, 1919), 131). The title has been added by later editors. Copy text as first published in *Marlborough and Other Poems* (1916).

l. 12. *Jesus Christ and Barabbas.* According to the gospels, at Passover it was customary for the governor of Judaea to commute the death penalty for one prisoner. Following the wishes of the crowd, Pontius Pilate released the notorious criminal, Barabbas, rather than Jesus.

l. 22. *Hemlock for Socrates.* Hemlock is a highly poisonous plant. Condemned for polluting the minds of the youth and denying the state's gods, the ancient Athenian philosopher Socrates died by drinking an infusion of hemlock.

188   TO GERMANY. *Date and Text.* See the headnote to Sorley's '[All the hills and vales along]'. According to Sorley's father, 'There is the same evidence for dating this poem also in August 1914' (*Marlborough and Other Poems*, 4th edn., 131). Copy text as first published in *Marlborough and Other Poems* (1916).

189   [A HUNDRED THOUSAND MILLION MITES WE GO]. *Date and Text.* September 1914. The title has been added by later editors. Copy text as first published in *Marlborough and Other Poems* (1916).

189 l. 11. *Vicissitude.* 'A change or alteration in condition or fortune; an instance of mutability in human affairs' (*OED*). Capitalized, Vicissitude becomes a malign deity in Sorley's poem.

190 TWO SONNETS. *Date and Text.* Sorley gives a date of 12 June 1915. His father added a note to the fourth edition: 'A copy of the former of these two sonnets was sent to a friend with the title "Death—and the Downs"' (*Marlborough and Other Poems*, 4th edn., 131). Copy text as first published in *Marlborough and Other Poems* (1916).

II Such, such is Death.

l. 4. *effete.* Exhausted, weak.

191 [WHEN YOU SEE MILLIONS OF THE MOUTHLESS DEAD]. *Date and Text.* Sorley's father reported that the sonnet 'was found in the author's kit sent home from France after his death' (*Marlborough and Other Poems*, 4th edn., 131). This suggests a date of composition not long before Sorley's death on 13 October 1915. Copy text as first published in *Marlborough and Other Poems* (1916), where it is listed on the contents page as 'A Sonnet'.

ll. 3–4. *Say not soft things as other men have said,* | *That you'll remember.* The 'other men' probably include Rupert Brooke, whose poem 'The Soldier' (p. 106) is concerned with dictating the terms by which the war-dead should be remembered.

l. 10. *'Yet many a better one has died before.'* An allusion to Achilles' response in Homer's *Iliad* 21.107 when the Trojan prince Lycaon begs him for mercy: 'Even Patroclus died, a far, far better man than you' (trans. Robert Fagles (1990)). In a letter of 28 November 1914, Sorley proposed that the line 'should be read at the grave of every corpse in addition to the burial service', and went on to argue that 'no saner and splendider comment on death has been made, especially, as here, where it seemed a cruel waste' (*The Letters of Charles Sorley*, 245).

l. 13. *spook.* Ghost. 'Spook' is an American word. Noting that it is often colloquial or jocular, *OED* gives the first recorded usage as 1801.

ROBERT GRAVES

193 IT'S A QUEER TIME. *Date and Text.* Probably March or April 1915. Graves later recalled: 'One of the realistic war poems for which I was best known [during the War], "It's a Queer Time", was written at my regimental depot in Wales some weeks before I had a chance of verifying my facts' ('The Poets of World War II', in *The Common Asphodel: Collected Essays on Poetry, 1922–1949* (London: Hamish Hamilton, 1949), 308). Copy text as published in *Complete Poems*, i, ed. Beryl Graves and Dunstan Ward (1995).

l. 7. *Treasure Island.* Robert Louis Stevenson's adventure novel, *Treasure Island* (1883), which Graves's poem associates with childhood.

l. 9. *Red West.* The sun sets in the west, which represents the land of death in many cultures.

l. 11. *You're charging madly at them yelling 'Fag!'* In the idiom of Charterhouse, Graves's public school, a 'fag' was a younger boy assigned to act as a servant to a more senior pupil.

l. 17. *back in the old sailor suit again.* Very young boys were often dressed in sailor suits. A family photograph survives of Graves, aged five, in a sailor suit.

194   l. 23. *lyddite.* A high explosive made from picric acid and used by the British during the War.

l. 28. *Bosches.* Germans. See note to Robert Service, 'Only a Boche' (pp. 245–6). Graves used both spellings, but explained in a letter of 1918 that 'Bosche' is more expressive: 'it has all the ugliness & nastiness in it which the term implies' (quoted in *Complete Poems*, i. 340).

l. 31. *Tipperary or their Hymn of Hate.* For 'Tipperary', see note to Robert Service, 'Tipperary Days' (p. 245). In 1914 the German poet Ernst Lissauer wrote 'Haßgesang gegen England', translated as 'Hymn of Hate against England' when it appeared in the *New York Times* during October 1914. The poem was well enough known in England to inspire a music-hall parody by Tom Clare in 1916.

A DEAD BOCHE. *Date and Text.* July 1916. Graves described the scene in *Good-bye to All That* (1929): 'For the next two days we were in bivouacs outside the wood. We were in fighting kit and the nights were wet and cold. I went into the wood to find German overcoats to use as blankets. Mametz Wood was full of dead of the Prussian Guards Reserve, big men, and of Royal Welch and South Wales Borderers of the new-army battalions, little men. There was not a single tree in the wood unbroken. I got my greatcoats and came away as quickly as I could, climbing over the wreckage of green branches. Going and coming, by the only possible route, I had to pass by the corpse of a German with his back propped against a tree. He had a green face, spectacles, close shaven hair; black blood was dripping from his nose and beard. He had been there for some days and was bloated and stinking' (263–4). For 'Boche', see note to Robert Service, 'Only a Boche' (pp. 245–6). Copy text as published in *Complete Poems*, i, ed. Beryl Graves and Dunstan Ward (1995).

ll. 3–4. *(you've heard it said before)* | *'War's Hell!'* The saying 'War is hell' is attributed to William Sherman (1820–1891), a Union general of the American Civil War.

l. 5. *Mametz Wood.* The Battle of Mametz Wood began on 7 July 1916. The wood was captured by the 38th (Welsh) Division—with huge loss of life on both sides—after five days of fighting.

CORPORAL STARE. *Date and Text.* 1916 or 1917. Graves wrote in *Good-bye to All That* (1929): 'I saw a ghost at Béthune. He was a man called Private Challoner who had been at Lancaster with me and again in F Company at Wrexham. When he went out with a draft to join the First Battalion he shook my hand and said: "I'll meet you again in France, sir." He had been killed at Festubert in May and in June he passed by our

C Company billet where we were just having a special dinner to celebrate our safe return from Cuinchy. There was fish, new potatoes, green peas, asparagus, mutton chops, strawberries and cream, and three bottles of Pommard. Challoner looked in at the window, saluted and passed on. There was no mistaking him or the cap-badge he was wearing. There was no Royal Welch battalion billeted within miles of Béthune at the time. I jumped up and looked out of the window, but saw nothing except a fag-end smoking on the pavement. Ghosts were numerous in France at the time' (161). Copy text as published in *Complete Poems*, Vol. 1, ed. Beryl Graves and Dunstan Ward.

194 l. 2. *Béthune*. A city in northern France, twenty miles west of Lille. It was held by the Allies throughout the War, but suffered a devastating bombardment in the early part of 1918.

195 l. 4. *batman*. A soldier who acts as servant to an officer.

l. 11. *in choro*. In chorus.

l. 12. *Bethlehem and Hermon snow*. According to the gospels of Matthew and Luke, the city of Bethlehem was the birthplace of Jesus. Mount Hermon, between Syria and Lebanon, is often snow-capped; the gospels of Matthew and Mark report that Jesus visited the city of Caesarea Philippi at its base.

l. 14. *Pommard*. A French wine produced in the village of the same name, in the Côte d'Or.

l. 16. *La Bassée*. A French town near the Belgian border. It formed the southern point of what has been called 'the forgotten front' running from Armentières in the north.

l. 22. *Festubert*. A commune in the north of France, not far south of Neuve Chapelle. It was captured by the British—and largely destroyed—during the Battle of Festubert, 15–25 May 1915.

A CHILD'S NIGHTMARE. *Date and Text*. Between July 1916 and November 1917. The poem, according to Graves's biographer Miranda Seymour, 'evokes the memory of a monstrous phantom who preyed on him when he lay wounded in High Wood' (Seymour, *Robert Graves: Life on the Edge* (London: Doubleday, 1995), 64). Copy text as published in *Complete Poems*, i, ed. Beryl Graves and Dunstan Ward (1995).

196 l. 25. *Morphia*. Morphia, or morphine, is an opiate which takes its name from Morpheus, the Greek god of dreams.

l. 26. *High Wood*. The site of particularly bitter fighting during the Battle of the Somme, the wood was of supreme strategic importance because of its elevation. It came under assault on 14 July 1916, but was not captured by the Allies until two months later. Graves was severely wounded there by an exploding shell on 20 July, and presumed dead.

197 TWO FUSILIERS. *Date and Text*. Probably 1917, but before November, when the poem was published in *Fairies and Fusiliers*. The two fusiliers are Graves and Sassoon. Copy text as published in *Complete Poems*, i, ed. Beryl Graves and Dunstan Ward (1995).

l. 8. *By Fricourt and by Festubert*. Fricourt is a commune in Picardy, less than a mile from Mametz Wood. For Festubert, see note to Graves, 'Corporal Stare', l. 22 (p. 286). Both Fricourt and Festubert were close to the front line throughout the War.

l. 12. *Picard*. Of Picardy. See note to Rudyard Kipling, 'Gethsemane', l. 2 (p. 241).

SERGEANT-MAJOR MONEY. *Date and Text*. 1917. Graves's account of the incident in *Good-bye to All That* caused public controversy. The revised description appeared in the 1957 edition: 'Two young miners, in another company, disliked their sergeant, who had a down on them and gave them all the most dirty and dangerous jobs. When they were in billets he crimed them for things they hadn't done; so they decided to kill him' (Graves, *Goodbye to All That*, rev. edn. (London: Cassell, 1957), 96–7). The two men mistakenly killed their sergeant-major instead, and having reported their deed, were executed by firing squad. Copy text as published in *Complete Poems*, i, ed. Beryl Graves and Dunstan Ward (1995).

l. 3. *Arras*. See note to Siegfried Sassoon, 'The General', l. 6 (p. 255).

l. 8. *swaddies*. Military slang for low-ranking soldiers, now superseded by the word 'squaddies'.

198 l. 9. *Old Army*. See note to Ivor Gurney, 'Joyeuse et Durandal', l. 1 (p. 264).

l. 11. *rest-billets*. Sleeping quarters.

l. 15. *butties from the Rhondda*. 'Butties' is Welsh slang for 'friends'. The Rhondda is a region in south Wales, renowned for coal-mining.

l. 20. *New . . . Army*. The New Army, or Kitchener's Army, was established after the outbreak of the War, and consisted of volunteers, until conscription was introduced in 1916.

RECALLING WAR. *Date and Text*. February or early March 1935. According to Graves's journal, on 6 March 1935 he and Laura Riding looked over this poem and four others. 'Recalling War' had 'already been seen by her and recast according to her suggestions. She now passed them all with only two amendments' (quoted in *Complete Poems*, ii. 315). Copy text as published in *Complete Poems*, ii, ed. Beryl Graves and Dunstan Ward (1997).

DAVID JONES

201 from IN PARENTHESIS. *Date and Text*. Between 1927 and 1936. Section headings are mine, and line breaks are observed even in the prose sections. Jones states in his 'Preface': 'I frequently rely on a pause at the end of a line to aid the sense and form. A new line, which the typography would not otherwise demand, is used to indicate some change, inflexion, or emphasis.' Copy text as first published in *In Parenthesis* (1937).

[The march from training camp to the embarcation port, from Part 1]
l. 7. *Kipt'*. Keep to.

201   l. 9. *Keept' y'r siction o'four—can't fall out.* That is, 'Keep to your section of four'; during the War, the army marched in fours. To fall out is to break the military formation.

ll. 12–14. *It's a proper massacre of the innocents in a manner of speaking, no so-called seven ages o' man only this bastard military age.* The original 'massacre of the innocents' was Herod's killing of first-born male children in Bethlehem, as reported in the gospel of Matthew. The 'so-called seven ages o' man' refers to the monologue by Jaques beginning 'All the world's a stage' in *As You Like It*, II.vii.139–66. The fourth age of man, according to Jaques, is the 'soldier'.

202   ll. 19–20. *armoury-rack.* A contraption on which to store weapons.

l. 24. *Of Hector and Lysander and such great names as these.* Hector and Lysander were great soldiers, both killed in battle. According to Homer's *Iliad*, Hector was the Trojan prince who led the armies of the besieged city. Lysander (died 395 BC) was the general whose military victories ensured the dominance of Sparta over Greece.

l. 25. *march proper to them. The British Grenadiers* is the ceremonial march of all Grenadier and Fusilier Regiments. [Author's note.]

[A nocturnal march, from Part 3]
l. 12. *china.* Mate (by the logic of rhyming slang: china plate).

ll. 13–14. *mind | the wire here.* Field-telephone wires, which were a frequent impediment in trench or on roads by night. They ran in the most unexpected fashion and at any height; and, when broken, trailed and caught on any jutting thing, to the great misery of hurrying men. [Author's note.]

ll. 18–19. *it may well be | you'll sweat on its unbrokenness.* The caution against breaking one's own barbed wire serves as a reminder that unbroken wire was a powerful defence against assault.

[What the sentry hears at night, from Part 3]
l. 2. *no-man's-land.* See note to Siegfried Sassoon, 'A Working Party', l. 47 (p. 251).

203   ll. 13–22. *Those broad-pinioned . . . white-tailed eagle.* Cf. the Anglo-Saxon poem, *The Battle of Brunanburh.* [Author's note.] Jones describes the metamorphosis of battlefield predators from the raptors of Anglo-Saxon poetry into the rats of the present.

l. 23. *where the sea wars against the river.* Cf. Dafydd Benfras (thirteenth century), *Elegy to the Sons of Llywelyn the Great*: 'God has caused them to be hidden from us, where the troughs of the sea race, where the sea wars against the great river' (trans. J. Glyn Davies, Cymm. Soc. Transtns., 1912–13). [Author's note.]

l. 24. *the speckled kite of Maldon.* There is no mention of a kite in *The Battle of Maldon.* Jones did not provide a footnote for this reference.

l. 29. *furrit.* Unknown to *OED*, but meaning something like 'furred'; that usage occurs in (for example) 'The Garmond of Fair Ladies' by the fifteenth-century poet Robert Henryson.

l. 37. *cushy*. 'Soft; comfortable; luxurious. Especially, safe where danger was the general rule. Other people were always getting cushy jobs' (Brophy and Partridge (eds.), *The Long Trail*, 107). The word was new enough for Ivor Gurney to need to explain in a letter to Marion Scott, on 1 August 1916, that ' "Cushy rhymes with bushy, not rushy" ' (Gurney, *Collected Letters*, 128).

[Distribution of rations, from Part 4]

l. 3. *traverse*. A recess that protects the trench from enfilading gunfire by breaking it into sections or compartments.

l. 4. *lance-jack*. A nickname for a lance corporal.

204 l. 15. *Field Service*. The label given to the various services that support soldiers in the field, such as food preparation, sanitation, and (as here) postal services.

l. 20. *Tickler's plum and apple*. Jam. See note to Ivor Gurney, 'The Stokes Gunners', l. 5 (p. 265).

l. 21. *Trumpeter*. A common brand of cigarette, distributed as standard issue.

[The moments before going over the top, from Part 7]

l. 2. *O blow fall out the officers*. To hear the bugle sound 'Fall out the Officers' was welcome to men on a wet day doing field exercises. It connoted the break off of operations. [Author's note.]

l. 2. *cantcher*. That is, 'can't you'.

l. 3. *King's Birthday*. A holiday for H.M. Forces—after the ceremonial parade. [Author's note.]

l. 7. *show*. See note to Wilfred Owen, 'The Show' (p. 276).

ll. 4–8. *Or you read it . . . in the Garden*. Cf. the Gospels (narrative of the Agony and of the Betrayal). [Author's note.] Jones may also have in mind Kipling's 'Gethsemane' (pp. 31–2), which refers to the same passage at Matthew 26: 39: 'And he went a little farther, and fell on his face, and prayed, saying, O my Father, if it be possible, let this cup pass from me: nevertheless not as I will, but as thou wilt.'

l. 9. *forbid the banns*. The banns are the public announcement of a forthcoming marriage; an objection to the marriage on legal grounds is an attempt to 'forbid the banns'.

l. 11. *family*. Used in this context to refer to a military Company.

[Encountering the enemy, from Part 7]

l. 1. *Acid Copse*. Acid Drop Copse was a small copse adjacent to Mametz Wood, from which enemy machine-gun fire—together with friendly fire from British 'heavies'— devastated the advancing soldiers.

l. 2. *heavies*. Heavy artillery.

l. 2. *phut*. Broken down.

205 l. 8. *interstices*. Small openings or spaces between objects.

l. 11. *stick-bomb*. A grenade attached to a handle (or 'stick'). The fuse lit automatically when the grenade became detached from its stick.

l. 16. *flange*. The grenade's protruding rim.

l. 21. *filigree*. Intricate ornamentation made from fine twisted wire.

l. 30. *Burkersdorf in Saxe Altenburg*. Burkersdorf is a hamlet a mile south-west of the town of Altenburg, previously in the duchy of Saxe-Altenburg but now in Thuringia.

l. 33. *the coloured label on the handle*. I cannot recall what it was, either stamped or labelled on the handle of a German stick-bomb, but I know the sight of it gave me some kind of pleasure—just as one likes any foreign manufacture, I suppose. [Author's note.]

[Digging in after an assault, from Part 7]

206 l. 4. *Jerry picks*. That is, German pick-axes. Jerry was a nickname for Germans, far less common in the First World War than the Second.

ll. 11–12. *The First Field Dressing is futile as frantic seaman's shift bunged to stoved bulwark*. Jones compares the doomed attempt to staunch the wound to a seaman's attempt to close up a hole in the side of a ship.

l. 18. *halsing*. Two meanings are relevant: entreating; embracing.

l. 19. *clip green wounds*. Close fresh wounds—although this context in which seasonal rebirth is denied gives the word 'green' a natural force.

l. 20. *weeping Maries bringing anointments*. A reference to Mark 16: 1, after Christ's crucifixion: 'And when the sabbath was past, Mary Magdalene, and Mary the mother of James, and Salome, had bought sweet spices, that they might come and anoint him.'

l. 24. *renascent*. Showing renewed growth or vigour.

ll. 26–7. *nor shaving of the head nor ritual incising for these viriles under each tree*. The virile young men, killed in their prime, are denied traditional burial rites and appropriate rituals of mourning.

ll. 28–9. *No one sings. Lully lully | for the mate whose blood runs down*. Cf. poem:

> 'Lully lulley; lully lulley!
> The falcon hath borne my mate away!' [Author's note.]

EDMUND BLUNDEN

208 FESTUBERT: THE OLD GERMAN LINE. *Date and Text*. May 1916. For Festubert, see note to Robert Graves, 'Corporal Stare', l. 22 (p. 286). Blunden crossed the 'old German line' in 1916 on his way to the new Front. Copy text as first published in *The Poems of Edmund Blunden, 1914–30* (1930).

l. 6. *malison*. Malediction (archaic).

l. 9. *gray rags*. The German military uniform was grey.

209 THIEPVAL WOOD. *Date and Text*. September 1916. Capture of the village of Thiepval in Picardy, and surrounding countryside, was a key British objective during the Battle of the Somme. In *Undertones of War*, Blunden remembered seeing Thiepval Wood 'alive with tossing flares, which made it seem a monstrous height, and with echo after echo in stammering mad pursuit the guns threshed that area' (68). Copy text as first published in *The Poems of Edmund Blunden, 1914–30* (1930).

l. 1. *heavies*. Heavy artillery.

l. 3. *chalkdown*. Chalk downland.

l. 5. *gibbet trees*. Trees from which the bodies of executed criminals were hanged. The reference here is figurative.

1916 SEEN FROM 1921. *Date and Text*. Probably 1920; first published as 'Festubert, 1916' in December 1920. Copy text as published in *The Poems of Edmund Blunden, 1914–30* (1930).

210 l. 21. *redoubt*. Military fortification.

l. 25. *Sweet Mary's shrine between the sycamores!* At Festubert there was a chapel dedicated to the Virgin Mary.

ILLUSIONS. *Date and Text*. Between April 1924 and July 1927. Copy text as published in *The Poems of Edmund Blunden, 1914–30* (1930).

l. 8. *gloze*. Make excuses. See note to Wilfred Owen, 'Exposure', l. 26 (p. 278). Here, 'gloze' means 'gloss over'.

l. 13. *malkins*. *OED* gives the relevant sense of 'malkin': 'A scarecrow . . . a ragged puppet or grotesque effigy; a "guy".' The word is obsolete except in dialect usage.

CONCERT PARTY: BUSSEBOOM. *Date and Text*. Between April 1924 and July 1927, although Blunden remembered that the poem had been 'composed in [his] mind' almost as soon as the concert ended—during an early spring evening in 1917 (quoted in *The Deceitful Calm*, 119). Busseboom is a tiny hamlet in the west of Flanders, about eight miles west of Ypres. Copy text as published in *The Poems of Edmund Blunden, 1914–30* (1930).

211 l. 17. *Saint Eloi*. A village south of Ypres, heavily mined by both sides during the War.

l. 23. *Larch Wood*. The location of British tunnels three miles south-east of Ypres. When they were discovered by the Germans, the miners had to fight unarmed.

VLAMERTINGHE: PASSING THE CHATEAU, JULY 1917. *Date and Text*. Between April 1924 and July 1927. The village of Vlamertinghe in Flanders is five miles west of Ypres. Copy text as published in *The Poems of Edmund Blunden, 1914–30* (1930).

ll. 1–2. *'And all her silken flanks with garlands drest'*— | *But we are coming to the sacrifice*. Cf. John Keats, 'Ode on a Grecian Urn': 'Who are these coming to the sacrifice? | To what green altar, O mysterious priest, | Lead'st thou that heifer lowing at the skies, | And all her silken flanks with garlands drest?' (ll. 31–4).

212 LA QUINQUE RUE. *Date and Text.* Between April 1924 and July 1927. La Quinque Rue is a road north of Festubert. Copy text as published in *The Poems of Edmund Blunden, 1914–30* (1930).

213 'TRENCH NOMENCLATURE'. *Date and Text.* Between April 1924 and July 1927. Copy text as published in *The Poems of Edmund Blunden, 1914–30* (1930).

l. 3. *Jacob's Ladder.* Those who named the trench had in mind Jacob's dream in Genesis 28: 12: 'And he dreamed, and behold a ladder set up on the earth, and the top of it reached to heaven: and behold the angels of God ascending and descending on it.'

l. 4. *Angles.* The Germanic tribe after which England is named.

l. 5. *Brock's Benefit commanded endless fireworks.* Brocks was a well-known manufacturer of fireworks, and their Benefits were free public displays.

l. 6. *coruscations.* Flashes of light.

l. 7. *Picturedome.* Cinema.

l. 7. *Turner.* J. M. W. Turner (1775–1851), one of the greatest British landscape painters.

l. 8. *morass.* Boggy ground; but also with a secondary sense of confusion or complication.

l. 11. *breastwork.* A temporary fortification built up to breast height.

l. 14. *quean.* Prostitute or impudent woman.

l. 15. *Yser.* The river which acted as a crucial border in attempts to halt the German advance through Belgium. It was deliberately flooded to become impassable.

l. 17. *what's in a name?* Cf. *Romeo and Juliet*, II.ii.43–4: 'What's in a name? That which we call a rose | By any other word would smell as sweet'.

l. 18. *From the fabled vase the genie in his shattering horror came.* A reference to the Middle Eastern folktale of Aladdin, in which a genie must fulfil the wishes of anyone who summons him from his magic lamp. This power becomes destructive when the lamp temporarily falls into the hands of a wicked sorcerer.

'CAN YOU REMEMBER?' *Date and Text.* January 1936. Copy text as published in *An Elegy and Other Poems* (1937).

l. 8. *fosse.* A ditch or moat.

214 ANCRE SUNSHINE. *Date and Text.* 3 September 1966. The River Ancre meets the Somme near the town of Corbie in Picardy. The Battle of Ancre—the final phase of the Battle of the Somme—took place in November 1916, almost fifty years before Blunden wrote his poem. 'Ancre Sunshine' is quite possibly (as Rennie Parker and Margi Blunden have claimed) 'the last poem about the war published by any surviving soldier poet'. Copy text as published in *The Deceitful Calm*, ed. Rennie Parker and Margi Blunden (2006).

l. 11. *Claire*. Blunden's wife.

l. 12. *Miraumont*. A village at the source of the Ancre in Picardy.

l. 12. *lea*. Field.

215 l. 15. *Arras*. See note to Siegfried Sassoon, 'The General', l. 6 (p. 255).

l. 20. *mill*. Blunden had written of the same 'burnt unraftered mill' in 'The Ancre at Hamel: Afterwards', published in 1924.

EDGELL RICKWORD

217 WINTER WARFARE. *Date and Text*. Probably November or December 1918. Rickword variously described the poem as having been written 'at the end of the war' and (in common with all his other war poems) 'after the end of hostilities' (Hobday, *Edgell Rickword*, 41). It was first published in the magazine *Land and Water* on 10 July 1919. The most commonly anthologized of Rickword's poems, it became disliked as a 'juvenile trifle' by its author (ibid., 275). Copy text as published in *Collected Poems*, ed. Charles Hobday (1991).

l. 15. *Hauptmann Kälte*. Strictly, this German phrase means 'Captain Cold' rather than 'Colonel Cold'.

THE SOLDIER ADDRESSES HIS BODY. *Date and Text*. Between November 1918 and its first publication in March 1920. Copy text as published in *Collected Poems*, ed. Charles Hobday (1991).

218 l. 13. *Hippogriff*. A legendary beast, the offspring of a griffin and a mare.

l. 14. *agate*. An ornamental banded gemstone.

l. 16. *Wyvern*. According to *OED*, 'a chimerical animal imagined as a winged dragon with two feet like those of an eagle, and a serpent-like, barbed tail'.

l. 17. *kvass*. A fermented Russian drink, made from rye flour or bread, and often flavoured with fruit.

ADVICE TO A GIRL FROM THE WAR. *Date and Text*. Between November 1918 and June 1920. Rickword omitted the poem from his first volume, *Behind the Eyes* (1921), but a decade later he included it in his third with a companion piece later collected as 'Advice to a Girl after the War'. Copy text as published in *Collected Poems*, ed. Charles Hobday (1991).

219 TRENCH POETS. *Date and Text*. Between November 1918 and November 1921. His biographer, Charles Hobday, reports that like the soldier in 'Trench Poets', Rickword read John Donne's poetry at the Western Front, having taken the two-volume Muses' Library edition to France in September 1918 (*Edgell Rickword*, 33). Copy text as published in *Collected Poems*, ed. Charles Hobday (1991).

ll. 5–7. *I used to read,* | *to rouse him, random things from Donne—* | *like 'Get with child a mandrake-root.'* The second line of John Donne's 'Song' takes to absurdity the belief that the root of a mandrake sometimes resembles a human figure, by suggesting that it may be made pregnant.

219 l. 12. '*I long to talk with some old lover's ghost.*' The opening line of Donne's poem, 'Love's Deity'.

ll. 13–15. *I tried the Elegies one day* . . . '*What needst thou have more covering than a man?*' The forty-eighth and final line of Donne's Elegy XIX, 'To his Mistress Going to Bed'. The line is addressed by the naked speaker to his lover, encouraging her to undress. There is also a *double entendre*: the speaker is offering to 'cover' her.

l. 20. *Maud.* Alfred Tennyson's *Maud* (1855) is a long narrative poem about a doomed love affair. At the end of the poem, the main protagonist goes to fight in the Crimean War.

WAR AND PEACE. *Date and Text.* Between November 1918 and November 1921. Copy text as published in *Collected Poems*, ed. Charles Hobday (1991).

220 MOONRISE OVER BATTLEFIELD. *Date and Text.* Probably 1923 or 1924. Charles Hobday speculates that the poem refers to a moonlit night attack beyond Epéhy by the Berkshires on 21–22 September 1918, in which fifty Germans were killed. Copy text as published in *Collected Poems*, ed. Charles Hobday (1991).

l. 6. *fard.* 'Paint (*esp.* white paint) for the face' (*OED*).

l. 9. *punk.* In this context, the obsolete or archaic form suggested by *OED* is evidently intended: 'prostitute, strumpet, harlot'.

l. 14. *Boche.* Germans. See note to Robert Service, 'Only a Boche' (pp. 245–6).

MUSIC-HALL AND TRENCH SONGS

222 NEVER MIND. *Date and Text.* 1914. This parodies the chorus of a sentimental song of 1913 by Harry Dent and Tom Goldburn: 'Though your heart may ache awhile, never mind! | Though your face may lose its smile, never mind! | For there's sunshine after rain, and then gladness follows pain. | You'll be happy once again, never mind!' Copy text as published in Roy Palmer (ed.), '*What a Lovely War!' British Soldiers' Songs from the Boer War to the Present Day* (1990).

l. 5. *Jerry.* A nickname for Germans.

MADEMOISELLE FROM ARMENTEERS. *Date and Text.* 1914 or 1915. Perhaps the most famous of all trench songs, it exists in countless versions, and can be as obscene or chaste as the audience requires. One notorious offshoot is 'Skiboo', otherwise known as 'Three German Officers Crossed the Rhine'. The tune dates from the early nineteenth century. 'Armenteers' is Armentières, a French town on the Belgian border. Copy text as published in Max Arthur (ed.), *When this Bloody War Is Over: Soldiers' Songs of the First World War* (2001).

l. 1. *parlay-voo.* From the French 'parlez-vous'—'do you speak'.

l. 6. *top kick.* A nickname given by lower ranks to the first sergeant.

223 l. 16. *Paree.* Paris—the English spelling of the French pronunciation.

l. 19. '*Je t'adore*'. (French) 'I adore you'.

PACK UP YOUR TROUBLES IN YOUR OLD KIT-BAG. *Date and Text.*
1915. Written by George Asaf and Felix Powell. The chorus became
ubiquitous—the title of Wilfred Owen's 'Smile, Smile, Smile' alludes
to it—while the rest of the song was soon forgotten. Copy text as first
published in *Pack up your troubles in your old kit-bag* (1915).

l. 1. *codger.* Normally, an eccentric old man. In this context, the eccentri-
city seems to dominate, and the age of Private Perks is less relevant.

l. 3. *artful little dodger.* Named after Dickens's character in *Oliver Twist,*
an artful dodger is a mischief maker who cunningly evades responsibility
for his actions.

l. 5. *Flush or broke.* Affluent or penniless.

l. 11. *a lucifer to light your fag.* A match to light your cigarette.

224 l. 17. *Flanders.* See note to May Sinclair, 'After the Retreat', l. 2 (p. 237).

l. 25. *Bosche.* Germans. See note to Robert Service, 'Only a Boche' (p. 245).
Bosche is an alternative spelling which does not affect pronunciation.

FRED KARNO'S ARMY. *Date and Text.* Between 1914 and 1916. Fred
Karno was a theatre impresario who toured his troupe of comedians—
'Fred Karno's Army'—in music halls across Britain and the United
States. The 'Army' specialized in knockabout imbecility. Each regiment
would adapt the words to its own situation. Copy text as published in
Max Arthur (ed.), *When this Bloody War Is Over: Soldiers' Songs of the
First World War* (2001), with several small changes to punctuation. See
note to l. 18 below.

l. 6. *Kaiser.* Kaiser Wilhelm II, the German Emperor.

l. 7. *'Hoch! Hoch! Mein Gott'.* (German) 'Hoch! hoch!' is used here as an
exclamation of surprise. 'Mein Gott'—'My God'.

l. 9. *ragtime.* See note to Siegfried Sassoon, 'Blighters', l. 6 (p. 254).

225 l. 13. *Charlie Chaplin our O.C.* Charlie Chaplin was the most famous
actor–comedian of the war years. Earlier in his career he had been part of
the Fred Karno troupe. In *Tommy's Tunes,* F. T. Nettleingham annotates
a footnote to another song that mentions the comedian: 'It will be noted
that Mr. Chaplin is a frequently mentioned individual, in one case attain-
ing the dignity of a C.Q. [Charge of Quarters]' (47).

l. 18. *Are the ragtime infantry.* Each company or regiment would tailor this
line for its own purposes. Max Arthur's version offers: 'Are the boys of
Company C!'

I WANT TO GO HOME. *Date and Text.* Between 1914 and mid-1916. Ivor
Gurney reports in a letter of 22 June 1916 that the Gloucesters sang it
when 'the last strafe was at its hottest—a very popular song about here;
but not military'. Gurney goes on to note: 'Not a brave song, but brave
men sing it' (Gurney, *Collected Letters,* 106). Copy text as published in
Roy Palmer (ed.), *'What a Lovely War!' British Soldiers' Songs from the
Boer War to the Present Day* (1990).

225 l. 3. *whizzbangs*. See note to Wilfred Owen, 'The Sentry', l. 8 (p. 273).

l. 4. *Alleyman*. Germans (from the French, *allemands*).

l. 8. *Jack Johnsons*. The burst of a heavy artillery German shell, named after the heavyweight boxing champion.

THE BELLS OF HELL. *Date and Text*. Between 1914 and 1916. Paul Fussell has observed that the song is inspired by a passage from an anonymous lyric in Arthur Quiller-Couch's *Oxford Book of English Verse* (1900): 'Hey nonny no! | Men are fools that wish to die! | Is't not fine to dance and sing | When the bells of hell do ring?' Copy text as published in John Brophy and Eric Partridge (eds.), *The Long Trail: What the British Soldier Sang and Said in The Great War of 1914–1918* (rev. edn., 1965).

ll. 5–6. *O Death, where is thy sting-a-ling-a-ling,* | *O Grave, thy victor-ee?* Cf. 1 Corinthians 15: 55: 'O Death, where is thy sting? O grave, where is thy victory?'

226 IF IT'S A GERMAN—GUNS UP! *Date and Text*. Between 1914 and 1917. George Simmers notes: 'The shooting of prisoners by British soldiers was a taboo subject in fiction during wartime (though it features in several texts of the early twenties, such as [Wilfrid] Ewart's *Way of Revelation*). The Hunnish mistreatment of prisoners and civilians by Germans, on the other hand, was a fictional commonplace' (Great War Fiction website). Copy text as published in F. T. Nettleingham (ed.), *Tommy's Tunes: A Comprehensive Collection of Soldiers' Songs, Marching Melodies, Rude Rhymes, and Popular Parodies* (1917).

l. 8. *Kamerad*. (German) Comrade.

APRÈS LA GUERRE FINI. *Date and Text*. Between 1914 and 1917. F. T. Nettleingham gives a version of this song in *Tommy's Tunes* (1917), and adds a caustic footnote: 'The pidgin French is typical of the way Tommy and the natives converse. I blush to say that Tommy sings this at his best when passing through a small village, where, unhappily, its truth is only too apparent, though, naturally, it is not necessary or possible to wait for the end of the war, as the words indicate. The curious and pathetic part in most cases is that mothers are not always certain whether these war babies are French, English, or even German. Time is inexorable, but blood will out—*on verra*'. 'Après la guerre', or 'après la guerre fini' (pidgin French for 'after the war is over') became a stock expression to refer to impossibly distant future events. Copy text as published in Max Arthur (ed.), *When this Bloody War Is Over: Soldiers' Songs of the First World War* (2001) with small changes to punctuation.

l. 2. *Soldat Anglais parti*. (Pidgin French) 'the English soldier will leave'.

l. 3. *Mam'selle Fransay boko pleuray*. (Pidgin French) 'the French mam'selle will cry a lot'. 'Boko' is *beaucoup*, 'a lot'; and 'pleuray' is a comically wayward attempt at the future tense of the verb *pleurer*, 'to cry'.

l. 7. *in the family way*. Pregnant.

THE OLD BARBED WIRE. *Date and Text*. Between 1915 and 1918.

This song could be—and did often threaten to be—expanded indefinitely. It is sometimes known as 'Hanging on the Old Barbed Wire'. Paul Fussell quotes J. B. Priestley's comment that there is 'a flash of genius, entirely English, in that "old," for it means that even that devilish enemy, that death-trap, the wire, has somehow been accepted, recognized and acknowledged almost with affection, by the deep rueful charity of this verse' (*The Great War and Modern Memory*, 179–80). Copy text as published in John Brophy and Eric Partridge (eds.), *The Long Trail: What the British Soldier Sang and Said in The Great War of 1914–1918* (rev. edn., 1965).

227   l. 10. *quarter-bloke*. An informal word for the quartermaster: the officer who is responsible for the battalion's supplies.

l. 28. *C.O.* The commanding officer.

228   HUSH! HERE COMES A WHIZZ-BANG. *Date and Text*. Between 1915 and 1918. For 'whizz-bang', see note to Wilfred Owen, 'The Sentry', l. 8 (p. 273). Copy text as published in Max Arthur (ed.), *When this Bloody War Is Over: Soldiers' Songs of the First World War* (2001).

THAT SHIT SHUTE. *Date and Text*. 1916 or 1917. Written by A. P. Herbert (1890–1971), a poet in the Royal Naval Division before achieving greater post-war acclaim as a novelist, librettist, humorist, and politician. His target was Cameron Shute, an unpopular British general who was highly critical of the RND's standards of hygiene. Copy text as published in Max Arthur (ed.), *When this Bloody War Is Over: Soldiers' Songs of the First World War* (2001).

229   BOMBED LAST NIGHT. *Date and Text*. Between 1916 and 1918. Mustard gas was used for the first time in 1916. Copy text as published in Max Arthur (ed.), *When this Bloody War Is Over: Soldiers' Songs of the First World War* (2001).

l. 4. *Higher Germany*. High Germany (rarely known as Higher Germany) is an archaic phrase referring to the mountainous region in the south of Germany.

l. 12. *Phosgene and Mustard Gas*. Chemical weapons used during the War.

I WORE A TUNIC. *Date and Text*. 1917. John Brophy and Eric Partridge argue that the song 'displays resentment against those who evaded military service' (*The Long Trail*, 47). Max Arthur, more persuasively, believes that the song is sung by 'the veterans of Kitchener's army' to the conscripts who came out in 1917 (*When this Bloody War Is Over*, 75). Copy text as published in John Brophy and Eric Partridge (eds.), *The Long Trail: What the British Soldier Sang and Said in The Great War of 1914–1918* (rev. edn., 1965).

l. 4. *Loos*. The Battle of Loos took place between 25 September and 14 October 1915. After initial promise of a breakthrough, the British assault was repelled, with more than 60,000 casualties.

230 l. 12. *Menin Road*. The road running south-eastwards from Ypres was exposed to heavy shelling from both sides at the First and Third Battles of Ypres (1914 and 1917).

GOOD-BYE-EE! *Date and Text*. 1917. Written by R. P. Weston and Bert Lee. Copy text as first published in *Good-bye-ee!* (1917).

l. 2. *do his bit*. Do his share.

l. 3. *lieutenant 'pips'*. A lieutenant in the British army wore two stars (or 'pips') on his shoulder epaulettes.

l. 6. *all the 'Birds!* All the women. The description of women as 'birds' dates back to Chaucer. The punctuation suggests that ''Birds' is an abbreviation, possibly of 'Dolly Birds'—attractive and made-up young women—although the phrase was barely current during the War.

ll. 15–16. *Bonsoir, old thing! cheerio! chin-chin! | Nahpoo! Toodle-oo!* A collection of informal tags, mostly from other languages: 'Bonsoir' is French for 'good evening'; 'chin-chin' is a drinking toast originally from the Chinese, meaning 'salutations'; 'Nahpoo' (more often 'Napoo'), meaning 'finished' or 'gone', is a corruption of the French *il n'y en a plus*, 'there is no more'; 'Toodle-oo!' comes from the French *à tout à l'heure* and means 'see you later'.

l. 20. *little Willie in 'East Lynne'*. *East Lynne* was a novel of 1861 by Ellen Wood, later adapted for the stage. The first film version was released in 1913. As the song suggests, Willie is a young boy who dies in the course of the novel.

231 l. 25. *Kew*. Kew is in the London borough of Richmond.

l. 27. *Lady Lee, who had turn'd eighty-three*. This seems to be a fictional character. There was a Lady Lee in 1917, but she was considerably younger.

l. 35. *Hun*. A derogatory term for Germans. See note to Rudyard Kipling, 'For All We Have and Are', l. 4 (p. 238).

l. 40. *the Dutch frontier*. The Netherlands remained neutral during the War.

OH! IT'S A LOVELY WAR. *Date and Text*. 1917. Written by J. P. Long and Maurice Scott. The song is mentioned (anachronistically) in David Jones's *In Parenthesis*, and gives its title to the stage play and film, *Oh! What a Lovely War!* (1963, 1969). Its own ironies seem to have preserved the song from trench parodies. Copy text as first published in *Oh! It's a Lovely War* (1917) with small changes to punctuation.

232 l. 8. *'reveille'*. The bugle or trumpet call to rouse soldiers at sunrise. Although deriving from the French verb *réveiller*, 'to wake', it is pronounced 'revalley'.

l. 12. *plum and apple jam*. See note to Ivor Gurney, 'The Stokes Gunners', l. 5 (p. 265).

l. 13. *Form fours!* During the War, the British army marched in fours.

l. 18. *'cushy'*. Soft; comfortable; luxurious. See note to David Jones, '[What the sentry hears at night, from Part 3]', l. 37 (p. 289).

l. 20. *Come to the Cookhouse door boys*. This phrase was familiar as a mnemonic for the bugler's call to dinner: 'Come to the cookhouse door, boys, come to the cookhouse door.'

ACKNOWLEDGEMENTS

ANTHOLOGIES are collaborative by nature. This project would not have been possible without assistance from the following: Clara Abrahams, Jacqueline Baker, Fran Brearton, Jane Conway, Jenni Crosskey, Santanu Das, Charlotte Fyfe, Peter Gibbs, Judy Greenway, Clare Griffiths, Carl Hahn, Hazel Hutchison, Philip Lancaster, Peter McDonald, Roy Palmer, Jane Potter, Rosemary Roberts, Suzanne Steele, and Elizabeth Vandiver. I am grateful to the University of Exeter, which provided me with research leave, and to my editor, Judith Luna, for her advice and expertise. My family has been supportive throughout. This anthology is dedicated to Jon Stallworthy—tutor, mentor and friend.

Acknowledgement is made to the following copyright holders for permission to include poems in the anthology:

Laurence Binyon: 'For the Fallen' reprinted by permission of The Society of Authors as the Literary Representative of the Estate of Laurence Binyon.

Edmund Blunden: from *Selected Poems* (Carcanet, 1982). Reprinted by permission of David Higham Associates Ltd.

Mary Borden: 'At the Somme' from *English Review* (August 1917); 'Unidentified' from *English Review* (December 1917). Copyright © Patrick Aylmer. Reprinted by permission of Patrick Aylmer.

May Wedderburn Cannan: 'August 1914', 'Rouen', 'Lamplight', 'After the War' from *In War Time: Poems* (Blackwell, 1917); 'The Armistice', 'For a Girl' from *The Splendid Days: Poems* (Blackwell, 1919); 'Perfect Epilogue' from *The Tears of War: The Love Story of a Young Poet and a War Hero*, ed. Charlotte Fyfe (Cavalier, 2000). Reprinted by permission of Mrs C. M. Abrahams.

Margaret Postgate Cole: 'Præmaturi', 'The Falling Leaves', 'Afterwards', reprinted by permission of David Higham Associates Ltd.

Wilfrid Gibson: from *Collected Poems, 1904–1925* (Macmillan, 1933), copyright © Wilfrid Gibson 1933, reprinted by permission of Pan Macmillan, London.

Robert Graves: from *The Complete Poems in One Volume* (Carcanet, 2000). Reprinted by permission of Carcanet Press Limited and A. P. Watt on behalf of the Trustees of the Robert Graves Copyright Trust.

Ivor Gurney: 'Pain', 'To the Prussians of England', 'To His Love', 'The Bugle', 'Billet', 'First Time In', 'Strange Hells', 'Farewell', 'La Rime', 'Serenade', 'Joyeuse et Durandal', 'The Stokes Gunners', 'The Bohemians', 'The Retreat', 'Signallers', 'It is Near Toussaints', 'The Silent One', reprinted by permission of the Ivor Gurney Trust.

David Jones: from *In Parenthesis* (Faber, 1937). Reprinted by permission of Faber & Faber Ltd., and the Trustees of W. D. Jones.

Rudyard Kipling: 'The Changelings', 'The Vineyard', reproduced courtesy of the National Trust for Places of Historic Interest or Natural Beauty.

Edgell Rickword: from *Collected Poems* (Carcanet, 1991). Reprinted by permission of Carcanet Press Limited.

Siegfried Sassoon: 'The Redeemer', 'A Working Party', 'The Kiss', ' "They" ', ' "Blighters" ', 'Base Details', 'The Rear-Guard', 'The General', 'Repression of

War Experience', 'Counter-Attack', 'How to Die', 'Glory of Women', 'Everyone Sang', 'On Passing the New Menin Gate', from *Collected Poems, 1908–1956* (Faber, 1961); 'A Night Attack', 'Christ and the Soldier', 'The Poet as Hero', from *The War Poems*, ed. Rupert Hart-Davis (Faber, 1983). Copyright Siegfried Sassoon by kind permission of the Estate of George Sassoon.

Robert Service: from *Rhymes of a Red Cross Man* (Barse & Hopkins, 1916). Reprinted by permission of the Krasilovsky Copyright Agency.

May Sinclair: 'Field Ambulance in Retreat' from *King Albert's Book: A Tribute to the Belgian King and People from Representative Men and Women throughout the World*, ed. Hall Caine (The Daily Telegraph in conjunction with The Daily Sketch, The Glasgow Herald, and Hodder and Stoughton, 1914), copyright © May Sinclair 1914; 'After the Retreat' from *The Egoist* 5.2 (1 May 1915), copyright © May Sinclair 1915; 'Dedication' from May Sinclair, *A Journal of Impressions in Belgium* (Macmillan, 1915), copyright © May Sinclair 1915. All reproduced with permission of Curtis Brown Group Ltd., London, on behalf of the Estate of May Sinclair.

INDEX OF TITLES AND FIRST LINES

American Literature

British and Irish Literature

Children's Literature

Classics and Ancient Literature

Colonial Literature

Eastern Literature

European Literature

Gothic Literature

History

Medieval Literature

Oxford English Drama

Philosophy

Poetry

Politics

Religion

The Oxford Shakespeare

A complete list of Oxford World's Classics, including Authors in Context, Oxford English Drama, and the Oxford Shakespeare, is available in the UK from the Marketing Services Department, Oxford University Press, Great Clarendon Street, Oxford OX2 6DP, or visit the website at www.oup.com/uk/worldsclassics.

In the USA, visit www.oup.com/us/owc for a complete title list.

Oxford World's Classics are available from all good bookshops. In case of difficulty, customers in the UK should contact Oxford University Press Bookshop, 116 High Street, Oxford OX1 4BR.

	Late Victorian Gothic Tales
JANE AUSTEN	**Emma** **Mansfield Park** **Persuasion** **Pride and Prejudice** **Selected Letters** **Sense and Sensibility**
MRS BEETON	**Book of Household Management**
MARY ELIZABETH BRADDON	**Lady Audley's Secret**
ANNE BRONTË	**The Tenant of Wildfell Hall**
CHARLOTTE BRONTË	**Jane Eyre** **Shirley** **Villette**
EMILY BRONTË	**Wuthering Heights**
ROBERT BROWNING	**The Major Works**
JOHN CLARE	**The Major Works**
SAMUEL TAYLOR COLERIDGE	**The Major Works**
WILKIE COLLINS	**The Moonstone** **No Name** **The Woman in White**
CHARLES DARWIN	**The Origin of Species**
THOMAS DE QUINCEY	**The Confessions of an English Opium-Eater** **On Murder**
CHARLES DICKENS	**The Adventures of Oliver Twist** **Barnaby Rudge** **Bleak House** **David Copperfield** **Great Expectations** **Nicholas Nickleby** **The Old Curiosity Shop** **Our Mutual Friend** **The Pickwick Papers**

CHARLES DICKENS	**A Tale of Two Cities**
GEORGE DU MAURIER	**Trilby**
MARIA EDGEWORTH	**Castle Rackrent**
GEORGE ELIOT	**Daniel Deronda**
	The Lifted Veil and Brother Jacob
	Middlemarch
	The Mill on the Floss
	Silas Marner
SUSAN FERRIER	**Marriage**
ELIZABETH GASKELL	**Cranford**
	The Life of Charlotte Brontë
	Mary Barton
	North and South
	Wives and Daughters
GEORGE GISSING	**New Grub Street**
	The Odd Women
EDMUND GOSSE	**Father and Son**
THOMAS HARDY	**Far from the Madding Crowd**
	Jude the Obscure
	The Mayor of Casterbridge
	The Return of the Native
	Tess of the d'Urbervilles
	The Woodlanders
WILLIAM HAZLITT	**Selected Writings**
JAMES HOGG	**The Private Memoirs and Confessions of a Justified Sinner**
JOHN KEATS	**The Major Works**
	Selected Letters
CHARLES MATURIN	**Melmoth the Wanderer**
JOHN RUSKIN	**Selected Writings**
WALTER SCOTT	**The Antiquary**
	Ivanhoe

TROLLOPE IN OXFORD WORLD'S CLASSICS

ANTHONY TROLLOPE

The American Senator

An Autobiography

Barchester Towers

Can You Forgive Her?

The Claverings

Cousin Henry

The Duke's Children

The Eustace Diamonds

Framley Parsonage

He Knew He Was Right

Lady Anna

Orley Farm

Phineas Finn

Phineas Redux

The Prime Minister

Rachel Ray

The Small House at Allington

The Warden

The Way We Live Now